2010 GEORGIA PEST MANAGEME
Homeowner Edition
Special Bulletin 48

Edited by
Paul Guillebeau, Extension Entomologist

Compiled by
Detsy Bridges

With contributions from the Departments of
Agricultural Engineering, Crop and Soil Sciences, Entomology, Forestry and Natural Resources
and Aquaculture and Fisheries, Horticulture, and Plant Pathology

The University of Georgia Cooperative Extension
College of Agricultural and Environmental Sciences

The thirty-first edition of the *Georgia Pest Management Handbook* gives current information on selection, application, and safe use of pest control chemicals. The Handbook has recommendations for pest control on farms, around homes, urban areas, recreational areas, and other environments in which pests may occur. Cultural, biological, physical, and other types of control are recommended where appropriate.

Additional information on control of insects, plant diseases, and weeds is available in bulletins, circulars, and leaflets published by the Cooperative Extension. Your county agent will provide copies upon request. Many publications are also available at http://www.caes.uga.edu/publications

Recommendations are based on information on the manufacturer's label and on performance data from Georgia research and Extension field tests. Because environmental conditions and methods of application by growers vary widely, suggested use does not imply that performance of the pesticide will always conform to the safety and pest control standards indicated by experimental data.

This publication is intended to be used only as a guide. Specific rates and application methods are on the pesticide label. Refer to the label when applying any pesticide. Please send improvement suggestions to bugman@uga.edu.

COPIES ARE AVAILABLE AT $15.00 EACH. Visit us on the web at http://www.ent.uga.edu/pmh. Please make check or money order payable to the UNIVERSITY OF GEORGIA and send to:

OFFICE OF COMMUNICATIONS
Cooperative Extension
117 - Hoke Smith Annex
The University of Georgia
Athens, Georgia 30602

Include your name, street address (UPS will not deliver to a Post Office Box), city, state and zip code. Credit card orders can be made by calling (706) 542-2657 or by faxing order information to (706) 542-0817.

PESTICIDE EMERGENCIES

Pau l Guillebeau, Extension Entomologist

POISON CONTROL CENTER (HUMAN OR ANIMAL)
National Poison Control Hotline (Spanish speakers available)
(800) 222-1222

SPILLS
(800) 241-411 3 (Dept. of Natural Resources)

Avoid emergencies/Prepare for emergencies.
1. Keep children away from pesticides!
2. Do not store pesticide in food or drink containers.
3. Keep gloves and other protective clothing wherever pesticides are used or stored.
4. Have water available to wash pesticides from skin or eyes.
5. Store and handle pesticides in areas where spills will be contained.
6. Assemble and maintain a spill kit wherever you handle pesticides.
7. Make sure that all employees understand how to handle pesticide emergencies.
8. Be familiar with the first ai d instructions on the pesticide label.

Symptoms of pesticide poisoning: nausea, vomiting, diarrhea, cramps, headache, dizziness, weakness, confusion, sweating, chills, chest pains, difficulty breathing, unconsciousness. If you have any of these symptoms while you are handling pesticides, suspect pesticide poisoning.

FIRST AID FOR POISONING

1. Stop the pesticide exposure as quickly as possible. **CALL 911 IF SYMPTOMS ARE SERIOUS! CALL POISON CONTROL (800-222-1222) FOR FIRST AID INFORMATION. YOU WILL NEED THE PESTICIDE LABEL.**
2. If the victim is not breathing, administer artificial respiration at once.
3. Consult the pesticide labeling if possible. Directions for first aid will be on the front panel
4. Otherwise, follow these guidelines.
   SKIN: drench skin as quickly as possible with plenty of water. Any moderately clean water can be used if not contaminated with pesticides. Remove contaminated clothing. Wash with soap if available. Dry victim and treat for shock. If skin is burned, cover with clean, loose bandage or cloth. Do not apply ointments to burned skin.
   EYE: Wash eye quickly but gently. Rinse eye with clean water for at least 15 minutes.
   INHALED: Move victim to fresh air. Warn other nearby people. Loosen clothing that restricts breathing. Administer artificial respiration if necessary.
   SWALLOWED: Rinse mouth with plenty of water. Give large amounts of water or milk (up to one quart) to drink. Consult the label before you induce vomiting. Do not give liquids or induce vomiting to anyone who is unconscious or convulsive.
5. Take the pesticide label with you to the doctor or hospital. DO NOT transport pesticides in the passenger compartment of the vehicle.

HEAT STRESS

Avoid heat stress.
1. Acclimate to hot weather or new strenuous activities slowly.
2. Drink plenty of water or sports drinks.
3. Take frequent breaks during hot weather.
4. Plan strenuous activities for the cooler part of the day.

Symptoms of heat stress: sweating, nausea, headache, confusion, loss of coordination, dry mouth, fainting. Severe heat stress (heat stroke) is VERY dangerous.

The EPA Guide to Heat Stress in Agriculture is available through your local Extension office.

1. **CALL 911 IF SYMPTOMS ARE SERIOUS!**
2. Move the victim to a cooler area immediately.

FIRST AID FOR HEAT STRESS

3. Cool the victim as quickly as possible by splashing cool water on them or immersing them in cool water. Do not immerse anyone who is unconscious, convulsive, or confused.
4. Remove all protective equipment or clothing that is keeping the victim too warm.
5. If the victim is conscious, have them drink as much cool water as possible.
6. Keep the victim quiet. Get medical ad vice.

PESTICIDE SPILLS

Assemble a spill kit.
1. Protective equipment indicated on pesticide label.
2. Absorbent material to soak up liquids (cat litter, sand, sawdust, dirt).
3. Scoop to pick up contaminated absorbent material.
4. Container for contaminated absorbent material (e.g., heavy duty plastic bag).
5. Place contaminated material in heavy duty plastic bag and place in outside trash. Dispose with regular trash.

Large spills, leaks, pesticide fires
Call Georgia DNR EPD Response Team **(800) 241-4113**

Spills on public roads or other public areas
Local sheriff or police.
Georgia State Patrol ***GSP (*477) on mobile phone**

Smaller spills
1. DO NOT HOSE DOWN SPILLS!
2. Protect yourself and others.
3. Stop the spill sources.
4. Confine the spill with a dike of earth or other materials. Protect water sources.
5. Absorb liquids with cat litter, sand, earth, etc.
6. Scoop up contaminated materials. Store securely.
7. Neutralize contaminated site with bleach, activated charcoal, hydrated lime, or removing contaminated soil.
8. Absorb any liquids used in during neutralizing.
9. Contaminated absorbent materials or soil may be land-applied according to the pesticide label.

IMPORTANT TELEPHONE NUMBERS

Paul Guillebeau, Extension Entomologist

EMERGENCY NUMBERS * *In an emergency dial 911, especially if the person is unconscious, has trouble breathing, or has convulsions.*

POISON CONTROL CENTER (HUMAN OR ANIMAL)
National Poison Control Hotline (Spanish speakers available)
(800) 222-1222

Physician _____   Ambulance _____

FIRES, SPILLS, LEAKS, ETC.

Georgia DNR Environmental Protection Division Response Team (pesticide fires, spills, leaks) **(800) 241-4113**

County Police or Sheriff _____   City Police _____

Georgia Highway Patrol Post (***GSP (*477) for mobile phones**) _____   Fire Department _____

ENDANGERMENT OF GAME OR FISH

Georgia Department of Natural Resources (Non-game endangered species) **(800) 241-4113**

U.S. Fish and Wildlife Service **(800) 344-WILD**

PHONE NUMBERS FOR PESTICIDE INFORMATION (NON-EMERGENCY)
University of Georgia Cooperative Extension Service
(voice) (706) 542-2816 or (fax) (706) 542-3872
email: bugman@uga.edu

PESTICIDE INFORMATION

National Pesticide Telecommunications Network (NPTN), Oregon State University – General information on toxicology, environmental hazard, etc. (M-F, 9:30am-7:30p m EST) **(800) 858-7378**

Pesticide Manufacturer – The telephone number should be listed on the pesticide label

CropLife America – General information about the pesticide industry (M-F, 9:00 am-5:00pm EST) **(202) 296-1585**

National Response Center – Refers caller to proper government agency for hazardous materials **(800) 424-8802** (Voice/TTY)

PESTICIDE DISPOSAL

Georgia Department of Agriculture **(800) 282-5852**
EPA Hazardous Waste Hotline (Superfund) **(800) 424-9346**

EPA SAFE DRINKING WATER HOT LINE – Interprets residue data and give EPA drinking water regulations. **(800) 426-4791**

Or call your local Health Department or Sanitarian. County _____ City _____

ENFORCEMENT OF PESTICIDE LAWS

Georgia Department of Agriculture, Entomology & Pesticides Division **(800) 282-5852**

EPA Region IV Pesticides Section **(404) 562-8956**

Safety/Training/Information – Dr. Paul Guillebeau (UGA Cooperative Extension) **(706) 542-2816, bugman@uga.edu**

WEB SITES WITH PESTICIDE INFORMATION

Ga. Integrated Pest Management	(IPM) http://ipm.ent.uga.edu
The University of Georgia Cooperative Extension Home Page	http://www.caes.uga.edu/extension
Georgia Department of Agriculture – Pesticide Division	http://agr.georgia.gov (click on Divisions and Plant Industry)
Pesticide Risks	http://extoxnet.orst.edu
Pesticides and Cancer	http://www.pestmanagement.rutgers.edu/NJinPAS/postings/EPAcancerevalchem704.pdf
U.S. Fish & Wildlife Service: Endangered Species	http://www.fws.gov
Pesticide Questions	http://npic.orst.edu
USDA National Organic Program	http://www.ams.usda.gov/nop
Georgia Organics	http://www.georgiaorganics.org
EPA Office of Pesticide Programs	http://www.epa.gov/pesticides/

FREQUENTLY ASKED QUESTIONS

How can I find my local Extension office?

Look in phone book or http://ipm.uga.edu

How are my children most likely to be injured by pesticides?

Although the media gives much attention to pesticide risk on food, children are most likely to be injured by pesticides around the home. According to an EPA survey, 50% of households with a child under five years store pesticides within the reach of children.

Many household disinfectants are pesticides that can injure children very quickly. ALWAYS store pesticides safely. NEVER store pesticides in food or drink containers.

Will pesticides hurt my pets?

Some pesticides are dangerous to pets, but the degree of risk depends on the particular pesticide and the type of animal. Fish, small animals (e.g., lizards), and arthropods (e.g., tarantula) are very sensitive to many pesticides. Remove these types of pets or securely cover their cage/tank whenever pesticides are applied. Pets may be attracted to pesticides formulated as baits. Squirrels or other rodents will eat mouse/rat baits. Dogs will eat slug baits.

The pesticide label will provide more information about the pesticide risks in the section entitled 'Hazards to Humans and Domestic Animals'. Follow these precautions very carefully. Also, keep pets away from treated areas until pesticide sprays are dry or as directed by the label. Never allow pets to play with pesticide containers.

How can I get more information about the health and environmental risks of pesticides?

Visit this web site http://ace.orst.edu/info/extoxnet/ It is an excellent source of information about pesticide risk written in language that you can understand. The EPA website is also a good source of pesticide information. www.epa.gov/pesticides

Which pesticides are the most dangerous?

Pesticides must carry one of three signal words that indicate the acute toxicity of the product.
The most dangerous pesticides carry the word DANGER. 'DANGER-POISON' indicates a pesticide that can kill in small amounts. 'DANGER' pesticides can cause irreversible eye damage or severe injury to the skin. Less dangerous pesticides will carry the signal words 'WARNING' or 'CAUTION'.

Look for the signal word before you buy the pesticide. Do not buy 'DANGER ' pesticides un less you are prepared to use them responsibly and store them securely.

Even pesticides with the signal words 'WARNING' or 'CAUTION' can be associated with chronic illnesses like cancer. Minimize your exposure to all pesticides.

I have heard that almost all pesticides cause cancer. Is that true?

Some pesticides have been linked with chronic illnesses like cancer, but most pesticides will not cause cancer. According to the American Cancer Society, there is no strong evidence that pesticide residues on food contribute to human cancer. You can find more information about pesticides and cancer at the EXTOXNET web site. http://ace.orst.edu/info/extoxnet/

To minimize your risks, use pesticides sparingly and ALWAYS follow all label directions. You can find more information about pesticide safety at our web site www.ent.uga.edu/pesticide.htm.

What are restricted use pesticides?

Pesticides fall into two broad categories: general use (or unclassified) and restricted use. Any adult may purchase general-use pesticides in many department stores, garden centers, and supermarkets. Restricted-u se pesticides (RUP) are more hazardous to humans or the environment. Only applicators that have received special training may purchase restricted-use pesticides at stores licensed to sell RUP. We advise homeowners to avoid the use of any restricted-use pesticide.

I want to control pests around my home with fewer pesticides. Where can I go for information?

IPM or 'Integrated Pest Management' is a way to control pests wit h a combination of tactics. Pesticides may be a part of an IPM program, but using other techniques can reduce the need for pesticides.

If you have roaches in the kitchen, for example, a weekly application of insecticide could control the roaches. However, your family would also be exposed to the pesticide each week. Through an IPM approach , you would reduce the roach's food source through better sanitation; you would remove sources of water (e.g. a leaky pipe); and you would try to seal cracks where roaches like to hide. You may still have to use pesticides occasionally, but an IPM program can greatly reduce the amount of pesticide needed to control the roaches.

Check with your local county Extension office. They can provide a wealth of information. You may also be interested in the Master Gardener program available through your local Extension office.

The University of Georgia has a tremendous amount of information about all kinds of plants and pest problems around the home. You can easily find them by using the plant name and 'UGA' in a search engine. For example, to find information about azalea, use the terms "azalea uga" as search terms.

In many cases, it is possible to reduce the amount of pesticide needed to control pests around the home using IPM. Our web site will help you get started. http://ipm.ent.uga.edu

How can I dispose of unwanted pesticide?

Avoid leftover pesticide. Only buy the amount of pesticide that you will use within a few weeks. Measure pesticides carefully to avoid mixing more than you need. If you have leftover pesticide mix, apply it to a site listed on the pesticide label. NEVER pour pesticide down the drain.

Rinse empty pesticide containers three times, and pour the rinse water into your sprayer for application to a site listed on the pesticide label. Discard the properly rinsed container with your household trash. DO NOT place any pesticide container with recyclable materials.

If you have pesticide that you do not want, ask your loc al Extension office for advice. They can tell how to dispose of the pesticide safely and legally.

What does 'organic' mean on a food label?

If it includes the USDA seal, it means the product is made with at least 9 5% organic ingredients. Visit this web site for information www.ams.usda.gov/nop

Can I still use chlorpyriphos and diazinon products around my home?

Yes, but the products will no longer be available in stores. FOLLOW the label directions.

How can I use pesticides safely?

Use IPM to reduce the amounts of pesticides you use (http://ipm.ent.uga.edu) ALWAYS follow the label directions even if this handbook or someone else gives you different information.

6

CONTRIBUTING AUTHORS

ENTOMOLOGY
John All
Keith Delaplane
Elmer Gray
Paul Guillebeau
Nancy Hinkle
Dan Horton
Will Hudson
Dean Kemp
Ray Noblet
Ron Oetting
Alton Sparks
Dan Suiter

PLANT PATHOLOGY
David Langston
Elizabeth Little
Jean Williams-Woodward

CROP AND SOIL SCIENCES
Stanley Culpepper
Andrew MacRae
Patrick McCullough
Wayne Mitchem
Tim Murphy
Eric Prostko
Walter Reeves

AGRICULTURAL ENGINEERING
Paul Sumner

**FOREST RESOURCES AND
AQUACULTURE & FISHERIES**
Mike Mengak

HORTICULTURE
Mark Czarnota

CONTENTS

PESTICIDE EMERGENCIES 2

IMPORTANT TELEPHONE NUMBERS 4

FREQUENTLY ASKED QUESTIONS 5

CONTRIBUTING AUTHORS 7

ABBREVIATIONS AND EQUIVALENTS 10

SUBMITTING SPECIMENS FOR IDENTIFICATION COLLECTION, PREPARATION AND SHIPMENT 11

HORTICULTURAL CROPS 12

    HOME VEGETABLE INSECT CONTROL 12

    HOME VEGETABLE DISEASE CONTROL 21

    WEED CONTROL IN HOME VEGETABLE GARDENS 31

    FOLIAR CALCIUM SPRAYS 33

    FOLIAR BORON SPRAYS 36

HOME ORCHARD PEST MANAGEMENT GUIDE PREFACE 37

    HOME ORCHARD INSECT PEST MANAGEMENT GUIDE 38

    HOME ORCHARD APPLE DISEASE SPRAY GUIDE 41

    HOME ORCHARD BLUEBERRY DISEASE SPRAY GUIDE 43

    HOME ORCHARD BRAMBLE SPRAY GUIDE 44

    HOME ORCHARD BUNCH GRAPE DISEASE SPRAY GUIDE 46

    HOME ORCHARD MUSCADINE GRAPE DISEASE SPRAY GUIDE 47

    HOME ORCHARD PEACH, NECTARINE AND PLUM DISEASE SPRAY GUIDE 48

    HOME ORCHARD PEAR DISEASE SPRAY GUIDE 50

    HOMEOWNER STRAWBERRY DISEASE CONTROL 51

    HOME FRUIT INSECTICIDE EFFECTIVENESS CHART 52

    WEED RESPONSE TO HERBICIDES USED IN FRUITS AND NUTS 55

    HOMEOWNER OUTDOOR INSECT CONTROL 61

FLOWERS 64

    HOMEOWNER OUTDOOR WEED CONTROL 64

    HOMEOWNER INDOOR INSECT CONTROL 65

WOODY ORNAMENTALS 66

    WOODY ORNAMENTALS (INCLUDES SHRUBS AND GROUND COVERS) 66

    HOME INSECT CONTROL 66

    WOODY ORNAMENTALS WEED CONTROL FOR HOMEOWNERS 68

    ORNAMENTALS – WEED RESPONSE TO HERBICIDES 70

    HOMEOWNER ORNAMENTAL AND TREE DISEASE CONTROL 73

HOMEOWNER FUNGICIDE GUIDE 85

ORGANIC STRATEGIES FOR THE GARDEN AND HOME LANDSCAPE 89

TURF 94

    HOME TURF INSECT CONTROL 94

    HOMEOWNER TURF DISEASE CONTROL 95

    TURFGRASS WEED CONTROL FOR HOMEOWNERS 99

    TURFGRASS HERBICIDES COMMONLY FOUND IN RETAIL LAWN AND GARDEN STORES/CENTERS 103

    TURFGRASS WEED RESPONSE TO HERBICIDES – HOMEOWNER PRODUCTS 105

ANIMALS 107

    PETS (Companion Animals) EXTERNAL PARASITE CONTROL 107

    FLEA CONTROL PRODUCTS 109

    HONEY BEE DISEASE AND PEST CONTROL 110

HOUSEHOLD AND STORED PRODUCTS 113

    HOUSEHOLD AND STRUCTURAL INSECT CONTROL 113

    HOUSEHOLD PESTICIDE DILUTION TABLE 122

HUMANS 123

    PUBLIC HEALTH INSECT CONTROL OUTDOORS AND PARASITES OF MAN 123

AQUATIC ENVIRONMENTS 133

    FISHERY CHEMICALS — (PARASITES, PISCICIDES AND OTHER TREATMENTS) 133

    AQUATIC WEED CONTROL 134

    RESPONSE OF COMMON AQUATIC WEEDS TO HERBICIDES 137

    AQUATIC WEED CONTROL USE RESTRICTIONS 138

    CALCULATING PESTICIDE CONCENTRATIONS IN AQUATIC SITUATIONS 140

VERTEBRATE PEST CONTROL 141

    MAMMALS 141

    REPELLENTS FOR DEER, RABBITS AND OTHER MAMMALS 143

    REPTILES AND AMPHIBIANS 144

PESTICIDE SAFETY AND OTHER PESTICIDE INFORMATION 145

    USE PESTICIDES SAFELY 145

    PROTECT HONEY BEES FROM PESTICIDES 147

    COMMON PESTICIDE PRODUCTS AVAILABLE FOR HOMEOWNERS 149

    NAMES, CLASSIFICATION AND TOXICITY OF PESTICIDES 163

    PESTICIDE RATE AND DOSAGE CALCULATIONS 164

    AIRBLAST SPRAYER CALIBRATION FOR ORCHARD AND VINEYARD 167

    CALIBRATION METHOD FOR HYDRAULIC BOOM AND BAND SPRAYERS, AND OTHER LIQUID APPLICATORS 168

    CALIBRATION METHOD FOR BOOMLESS BROADCAST SPRAYERS 170

    CALIBRATION METHOD FOR GRANULAR APPLICATIONS 171

    CALIBRATION OF BACKPACK SPRAYERS 1000 FT^2 METHOD 173

    CALIBRATING TURFGRASS SPRAYERS (GALLONS PER 1000 SQ FT) 174

    HAND SPRAYER CALIBRATION FOR ORNAMENTAL AND TURF 175

    ATTENTION! PESTICIDE PRECAUTIONS 176

INDEX 177

ABBREVIATIONS AND EQUIVALENTS

FORMULATIONS[1]

a.i. = active ingredient	EC = emulsifiable concentrate	S = sprayable powder
AC = aqueous concentrate	EL = emulsifiable liquid	SC = spray concentrate
AS = aqueous suspension	F = flowable	SP = soluble powder
DF = dry flowable	FC = flowable concentrate	W = wettable powder
DG = dispersible granules	G = granules	WDL = water dispersible liquid
B = bait	L = liquid	WM = water miscible
D = dust	LC = liquid concentrate	WP = wettable powder
E = emulsifiable	M = microencapsulated	

[1] Numbers preceding abbreviations for liquid formulations equal pounds of active ingredient per gallon (e.g., 4EC = 4 lbs./gal. emulsifiable concentrate); numbers preceding abbreviations for solid formulations equal percent active ingredient by weight (e.g., 50WP = 50 percent wettable powder).

METHOD OR TIME OF APPLICATION

CR = cracking stage	PEI = preemergence incorporated	PRE = preemergence
LV = low volume	PO = postemergence	PT = post transplant
NS = nonselective	POT = postemergence over-the-top	RCS = recirculating sprayer
PDS = postemergence directed spray	PP = preplant	ULV = ultra low volume[2]
PE = preemergence on surface	PPI = preplant soil incorporated	WICK = rope wick applicator

[2] Ultra low volume refers to a total spray volume of one/half gallon or less per acre.

MEASURES AND EQUIVALENTS

tsp.	=	teaspoonful			1 teaspoonful	=	4.9 milliliters
Tbs.	=	tablespoonful	1 Tbs.	=	3 teaspoonfuls	=	14.8 milliliters
fl. oz.	=	fluid ounce	1 fl. oz.	=	2 tablespoonfuls	=	29.6 milliliters
c.	=	cupful	1 c.	=	8 fluid ounces	=	236.6 milliliters
pt.	=	pint(s) (1 .04 lb. of water)	1 pt.	=	2 cupfuls	=	473.2 milliliters
pt./100	=	pint(s) per 100 gallons	1 pt./100	=	1 teaspoonful per gallon		
qt.	=	quart(s) (2.09 lbs. of water)	1 qt.	=	2 pints	=	946.4 milliliters
gal.	=	gallon(s) (8.35 lbs. of water)	1 gal.	=	4 quarts	=	2.7854 liters
oz.	=	ounce			1 ounce	=	28.35 grams
lb.	=	pound	1 lb.	=	16 ounces	=	453.59 grams
in.	=	inch	1 in.	=	1000 mils	=	2.54 centimeters (25,400 microns)
ft.	=	feet	1 ft.	=	12 inches	=	30.48 centimeters
yd.	=	yard	1 yd.	=	3 feet	=	91.44 centimeters
mi.	=	mile	1 mi.	=	5280 feet	=	1609 meters (16.09 kilometers)
sq. in.	=	square inch			1 square inch	=	6.45 square centimeters
sq. ft.	=	square feet	1 sq. ft.	=	144 square inches	=	929.03 square centimeters
A.	=	acre	1 A.	=	43560 square feet	=	0.4047 hectare
cu. in.	=	cubic inch			1 cubic inch	=	16.387 cubic centimeters
cu. ft.	=	cubic feet	1 cu. ft.	=	1728 cubic inches	=	0.0283 cubic meter
cu. yd.	=	cubic yard	1 cu. yd.	=	27 cubic feet	=	0.7646 cubic meter
p.p.m.	=	parts per million	1 p.p.m.	=	1000 p.p. billion	=	1 milligram/Kilogram[3]
p.s.i.	=	pounds per square inch			1 p.s.i.	=	70.3 grams per cubic centimeter

[3] 1 milligram/Kilogram or 1 p.p.m. is equal to 1 milligram/Liter of water.

SUBMITTING SPECIMENS FOR IDENTIFICATION
COLLECTION, PREPARATION AND SHIPMENT
INSECTS, PLANT DISEASES, VIRUS DIAGNOSIS, NEMATODES, WEEDS, FISH, VERTEBRATES

Proper identification of pest problems is the foundation of any control program. The UGA Cooperative Extension Service will help you identify pest problems at little or no cost to you. Contact your local Extension office. In most cases, your local agent can diagnose the problem and advise you about proper control. If the local office can not identify the pest, they will contact the appropriate specialist at the University of Georgia. The telephone number of your local Extension office is listed below. You may also check the web for updated or changed phone numbers http://www.caes.uga.edu/extension/statewide.cfm

Appling County, 912-367-8130
Atkinson County, 912-422-3277
Bacon County, 912-632-5601
Baker County, 229-734-3015
Baldwin County, 478-445-4394
Banks County, 706-677-6230
Barrow County, 770-307-3029
Bartow County, 770-387-5142
Ben Hill County, 229-426-5175
Berrien County, 229-686-5431
Bibb County, 478-751-6338
Bleckley County, 478-934-3220
Brantley County, 912-462-5724
Brooks County, 229-263-4103
Bryan County, 912-653-2231
Bulloch County, 912-871-6130
Burke County, 706-554-2119
Butts County, 770-775-8209
Calhoun County, 229-849-2685
Camden County, 912-576-3219
Candler County, 912-685-2408
Carroll County, 770-836-8546
Catoosa County, 706-935-4211
Charlton County, 912-496-2040
Chatham County, 912-652-7981
Chattooga County, 706-857-0744
Cherokee County, 770-479-0421
Clarke County, 706-613-3640
Clay County, 229-768-2247
Clayton County, 770-473-3945
Clinch County, 912-487-2169
Cobb County, 770-528-4070
Coffee County, 912-384-1402
Colquitt County, 229-616-7455
Columbia County, 706-868-3413
Cook County, 912-896-7456
Coweta County, 770-254-2620
Crawford County, 478-836-3121
Crisp County, 229-276-2612
Dade County, 706-657-4116
Dawson County, 706-265-2442
Decatur County, 229-248-3033
DeKalb County, 404-298-4080
Dodge County, 478-374-8137
Dooly County, 229-268-4171
Dougherty County, 229-436-7216
Douglas County, 770-920-7224
Early County, 229-723-3072
Echols County, 229-559-5562
Effingham County, 912-754-2134
Elbert County, 706-283-2037
Emanuel County, 478-237-1226
Evans County, 912-739-1292

Fannin County, 706-632-3061
Fayette County, 770-460-5730, ext. 5412
Floyd County, 706-295-6210
Forsyth County, 770-887-2418
Franklin County, 706-384-2843
Fulton County, 404-730-7000
Gilmer County, 706-635-4426
Glascock County, 706-598-2811
Glynn County, 912-554-7577
Gordon County, 706-629-8685
Grady County, 229-377-1312
Greene County, 706-453-2083
Gwinnett County, 678-377-4010
Habersham County, 706-754-2318
Hall County, 770-531-6988
Hancock County, 706-444-7573
Haralson County, 770-646-2026
Harris County, 706-628-4824
Hart County, 706-376-3134
Heard County, 706-675-3513
Henry County, 770-228-8421
Houston County, 478-987-2028
Irwin County, 229-468-7409
Jackson County, 706-367-6344
Jasper County, 706-468-6479
Jeff Davis County, 912-375-6648
Jefferson County, 478-625-3046
Jenkins County, 478-982-4408
Johnson County, 478-864-3373
Jones County, 478-986-3958
Lamar County, 770-358-5163
Lanier County, 229-482-3895
Laurens County, 478-272-2277
Lee County, 229-759-6025
Liberty County, 912-876-2133
Lincoln County, 706-359-3233
Long County, 912-545-9549
Lowndes County, 229-333-5185
Lumpkin County, 706-864-2275
Macon County, 478-472-7588
Madison County, 706-795-2281
Marion County, 229-649-2625
McDuffie County, 706-595-1815
McIntosh County, 912-437-6651
Meriwether County, 706-672-4235
Miller County, 229-758-4106
Mitchell County, 229-336-2066
Monroe County, 478-994-7014
Montgomery County, 912-583-2240
Morgan County, 706-342-2214
Murray County, 706-695-3031
Muscogee County, 706-653-4200
Newton County, 770-784-2010

Oconee County, 706-769-3946
Oglethorpe County, 706-743-8341
Paulding County, 770-443-7616
Peach County, 478-825-6466
Pickens County, 706-253-8840
Pierce County, 912-449-2034
Pike County, 770-567-2010
Polk County, 770-749-2142
Pulaski County, 478-783-1171
Putnam County, 706-485-4151
Quitman County, 229-334-4303
Rabun County, 706-782-3113
Randolph County, 229-732-2311
Richmond County, 706-821-2350
Rockdale County, 770-785-5952
Schley County, 229-937-2601
Screven County, 912-564-2064
Seminole County, 229-524-2326
Spalding County, 770-467-4225
Stephens County, 706-886-4046
Stewart County, 229-838-4908
Sumter County, 229-924-4476
Talbot County, 706-665-3230
Tattnall County, 912-557-6724
Taylor County, 478-862-5496
Telfair County, 229-868-6489
Terrell County, 229-995-2165
Thomas County, 229-225-4130
Tift County, 229-391-7980
Toombs County, 912-526-3101
Towns County, 706-896-2024
Treutlen County, 912-529-3766
Troup County, 706-883-1675
Turner County, 229-567-3448
Twiggs County, 478-945-3391
Union County, 706-439-6030
Upson County, 706-647-8989
Walker County, 706-638-2548
Walton County, 770-267-1324
Ware County, 912-287-2456
Warren County, 706-465-2136
Washington County, 478-552-2011
Wayne County, 912-427-5965
Webster County, 229-828-2325
Wheeler County, 912-568-7138
White County, 706-865-2832
Whitfield County, 706-278-8207
Wilcox County, 912-365-2323
Wilkes County, 706-678-2332
Wilkinson County, 478-946-2367
Worth County, 229-776-8216

HORTICULTURAL CROPS
HOME VEGETABLE INSECT CONTROL

Alton N. Sparks, Jr., Extension Entomologist

NOTE: Insecticide registrations can change rapidly and can vary with the specific product or formualtion of the product used (e.g. not all products containing malathion are labeled for use on the same crops; not all formulations of Sevin have the same use patterns). Always carefully read and follow the label instructions for the specific product being applied. If using transplants, make sure plants are free of pests before purchasing.

VEGETABLE	INSECT	INSECTICIDE AND FORMULATION	AMOUNT OF FORMULATION PER GALLON OF SPRAY	PHI (DAYS)	REMARKS AND PRECAUTIONS
All crops	Multiple pests	pyrethrins pyrethrins+PBO	RTU	0	Provides rapid knock down and suppression of most pests directly contacted. Little or no residual activity.
	Soil pests	bifenthrin 0.115% granular	1 lb. per 500 sq. ft.		Apply prior to planting and work into top 4-6 inches of soil. (May also be applied to bifenthrin labeled crops with PHI same as foliar application s).
	Slugs and Snails	metaldehyde	See label		Do not contact plants with material.
		iron phosphate	See label		Do not contact plants with material.
	Fire Ants	Esteem Ant Bait is registered for use in man y vegetable crops (see label). Spinosad products may be used as a mound drench in crops where foliar applications are allowed (see label). Other ant bait s may be used around the garden, which for small gardens is frequently ad equate.			
	Leafminers	No general use insecticides provide control of leafminer larvae inside leaves. Spinosad products may provide some suppression on registered crops. Leafminer problems are frequently caused by overuse of insecticides. Hand-pick mined leaves.			
Asparagus	asparagus beetle, cutworms	carbaryl (Sevin) 22.5%	1.5-3 oz.	1	Also available as a ready-to-use product.
		permethrin 2.5% 0.25% dust	1.5 oz. Dust plants lightly	1 1	
		spinosad 0.5%	2 oz.	60	Post-harvest treatment only.
Beans, Peas	aphids	bifenthrin 0.3%	1.5 oz.	3	Also available as a ready-to-use product.
		esfenvalerate 0.425%	2 Tbs.	green-3 dry-21	Also available as a ready-to-use product.
		gamma-cyhalothrin 0.25%	1 Tbs	7	
		malathion 50%	1.5-2 tsp.	bean-1 peas-3	
		insecticidal soap	follow label directions	0	No residual activity. Thorough coverage is essential.
	bean beetles (Mexican bean beetle, bean leaf beetle), caterpillars (corn earworm), cowpea curculio, stink bugs	bifenthrin 0.3%	1.5 oz.	3	Also available as a ready-to-use product.
		carbaryl 22.5% 5% dust 10% dust	0.75-1.5 oz. 0.5-1 lb. 0.25-0.5 lb.	fresh-3 dry-21	Also available as a ready-to-use product. Not for stink bugs or caterpillars.
		esfenvalerate 0.425%	2 Tbs.	green-3 dry-21	Also available as a ready-to-use product.
		gamma-cyhalothrin 0.25%	1 Tbs	7	
		spinosad 0.5%	2 oz.	3	For caterpillar pests only. Will also suppress thrips and leafminers.
	NOTE: For cowpea curculio make 3 applications at 5 day intervals starting when pods are ½ inch long.				

VEGETABLE	INSECT	INSECTICIDE AND FORMULATION	AMOUNT OF FORMULATION PER GALLON OF SPRAY	PHI (DAYS)	REMARKS AND PRECAUTIONS
Beans, Peas (cont.)	spider mites	malathion 50%	1 Tbs.	beans-1 peas-3	Marginal control of this pest.
		sulfur 90%	2 Tbs.	0	Do not use if > 95 degrees. Do not use within 3 weeks of oil spray.
		insecticidal soap	follow label directions	0	No residual activity. Thorough coverage is essential.
		NOTE: Bifenthrin applied at high rates may provide suppression of mites.			
	whitefly	bifenthrin 0.3%	1.5 oz.	3	Also available as a ready-to-use product.
		insecticidal soap	follow label directions	0	No residual activity. Thorough coverage is essential.
		pyrethrins+PBO	RTU	0	No residual activity.
Beets	flea beetles	carbaryl 22.5% 5% dust 10% dust	0.75-1.5 oz. 0.25-0.5 lb. 0.125-0.25 lbs.	Root-7 tops-14	Also available as a ready-to-use product.
		malathion 50%	1 Tbs.	7	
Broccoli, Brussels Sprouts, Cabbage, Cauliflower	aphid	acetamiprid 0.006%	RTU	7	
		bifenthrin 0.3%	1.5 oz.	7	Also available as a ready-to-use product.
		esfenvalerate 0.425%	2 Tbs.	3	Not for use on Brussels Sprouts. Also available as a ready-to-use product.
		gamma-cyhalothrin 0.25%	1 Tbs	1	Also available as a ready-to-use product.
		lambda-cyhalothrin 0.5%	1 Tbs.	1	Also available as a ready-to-use product.
		malathion 50%	1.5-2 tsp.	brocolli-3 others-7	
		permethrin 2.5% 0.25% dust	1 oz. Dust plants lightly	1	
		insecticidal soap	follow label directions	0	No residual activity. Thorough coverage is essential.
	caterpillars on foliage, cutworms	Bacillus thuringiensis (Dipel, Thuricide and other formulations)	Follow label directions.	0	Not for cutworms. Treat as soon as damage is found and repeat as needed. Susceptible larvae will stop feeding soon after eating treated foliage but may not die for several days.
		bifenthrin 0.3%	1.5 oz.	7	Also available as a ready-to-use product.
		esfenvalerate 0.425%	2 Tbs.	3	Not for use on Brussels Sprouts. Also available as a ready-to-use product.
		gamma-cyhalothrin 0.25%	1 Tbs	1	Also available as a ready-to-use product.
		lambda-cyhalothrin 0.5%	1 Tbs.	1	Also available as a ready-to-use product.
		permethrin 2.5% 0.25% dust	1 oz. Dust plants lightly	1	Not registered for cutworms.
		spinosad 0.5%	2 oz.	1	Not registered for cutworms.

VEGETABLE	INSECT	INSECTICIDE AND FORMULATION	AMOUNT OF FORMULATION PER GALLON OF SPRAY	PHI (DAYS)	REMARKS AND PRECAUTIONS
Broccoli, Brussels Sprouts, Cabbage, Cauliflower (cont.)	flea beetles, stink bugs, harlequin bug	bifenthrin 0.3%	1.5 oz.	7	Also available as a ready-to-use product.
		carbaryl 22.5% 5% dust 10% dust	0.75-1.5 oz. 0.25-0.5 lb. 0.125-0.25 lb.	3	Also available as a ready-to-use product.
		esfenvalerate 0.425%	2 Tbs.	3	Not for use on Brussels Sprouts. Also available as a ready-to-use product.
		gamma-cyhalothrin 0.25%	1 Tbs		Also available as a ready-to-use product.
		lambda-cyhalothrin 0.5%	1 Tbs.	1	Also available as a ready-to-use product.
		permethrin 2.5% 0.25% dust	1 oz. Dust plants lightly	1	
Cantaloupe, Cucumber, Pumpkin, Squash, Watermelon Apply sprays late in the day to reduce kill of pollinating insects.	aphid	bifenthrin 0.3%	1.5 oz.	3	Also available as a ready-to-use product.
		esfenvalerate 0.425%	2 Tbs.	3	Also available as a ready-to-use product.
		malathion 50%	2 tsp.	Pumpkin-3 Others-1	Use and registration varies with specific product. Do not apply unless leaves are dry.
		permethrin 0.25% dust	Dust plants lightly	0	
		insecticidal soap	follow label directions	0	No residual activity. Thorough coverage is essential.
	cucumber beetle adults, squash bug, pickleworm, melonworm, rindworms	bifenthrin 0.3%	1.5 oz.	3	Also available as a ready-to-use product.
		carbaryl 22.5% 5% dust 10% dust	1.5 oz. 0.5 lb. 0.25 lb.	3	Also available as a ready-to-use product.
		esfenvalerate 0.425%	2 Tbs.	3	Also available as a ready-to-use product.
		permethrin 0.25% dust	Dust plants lightly	0	
		spinosad 0.5%	2 oz.	cucumber-1 others-3	For caterpillar control only.
	NOTE: Late planted crops are heavily attacked by pickleworm and melonworm. Begin treatments at first bloom and repeat weekly as needed.				
	Squash vine borer	bifenthrin 0.3%	1.5 oz.	3	Also available as a ready-to-use product. Direct sprays at base of plants.
		esfenvalerate 0.425%	2 Tbs.	3	Also available as a ready-to-use product. Direct sprays at base of plant.
	Spider mites	insecticidal soap	follow label directions	0	No residual activity. Thorough coverage is essential.
		malathion 50%	2 tsp.	Pumpkin-3 Others-1	Use and registration varies with specific product. Marginal control of this pest. Do not apply unless leaves are dry.
	NOTE: Bifenthrin applied at high rates may provide suppression of mites.				

VEGETABLE	INSECT	INSECTICIDE AND FORMULATION	AMOUNT OF FORMULATION PER GALLON OF SPRAY	PHI (DAYS)	REMARKS AND PRECAUTIONS
Cantaloupe, Cucumber, Pumpkin, Squash, Watermelon (cont.)	whitefly	bifenthrin 0.3%	1.5 oz.	3	Also available as a ready-to-use product.
		insecticidal soap	follow label directions	0	No residual activity. Thorough coverage is essential.
		pyrethrins+PBO	RTU	0	No residual activity.
Collards	aphid	acetamiprid 0.006%	RTU	7	
		esfenvalerate 0.425%	2 Tbs.	7	Also available as a ready-to-use product.
		malathion 50%	2 tsp.	7	Use and registration varies with specific product.
		insecticidal soap	follow label directions	0	No residual activity. Thorough coverage is essential.
	caterpillars on foliage	Bacillus thuringiensis (Dipel, Thuricide and other formulations)	Follow label directions.	0	Treat as soon as damage is found and repeat as needed. Susceptible larvae will stop feeding soon after eating treated foliage but may not die for several days.
		carbaryl 22.5% 5% dust 10% dust	1.5-3 ozs. 0.5-1 lb. 0.25-0.5 lb.	14	Also available as a ready-to-use product.
		esfenvalerate 0.425%	2 Tbs.	7	Also available as a ready-to-use product.
		spinosad 0.5%	2 oz.	1	
	flea beetles, harlequin bug, stink bugs	carbaryl 22.5% 5% dust 10% dust	0.75-1.5 ozs. 0.25-0.5 lb. 0.125-0.25 lb.	14	Also available as a ready-to-use product.
		esfenvalerate 0.425%	2 Tbs.	7	Also available as a ready-to-use product.
Corn, Sweet	corn earworm, fall armyworm, European corn borer flea beetle, cucumber beetle, stink bug	bifenthrin 0.3%	1.5 oz.	1	Also available as a ready-to-use product.
		carbaryl 22.5% 5% dust 10% dust	1.5-3 oz. 0.75-1.0 lb. 0.4-0.5 lb.	2	Not for stink bug control. Also available as a ready-to-use product.
		cyfluthrin 0.75%	1 Tbs.	0	Also available as a ready-to-use product.
		esfenvalerate 0.425%	2 Tbs.	1	Also available as a ready-to-use product.
		gamma-cyhalothrin 0.25%	1 Tbs	21	Also available as a ready-to-use product.
		lambda-cyhalothrin 0.5%	1 Tbs.	21	Also available as a ready-to-use product.
		permethrin 2.5% 0.25% dust	1.5 oz. Dust plants lightly	1	
		spinosad 0.5%	2 oz.	1	For control of caterpillar pests only.
		NOTE: For caterpillar pests of ears, begin treatment when silks appear. Repeat at 2 day interval with sprays directed at ears.			

VEGETABLE	INSECT	INSECTICIDE AND FORMULATION	AMOUNT OF FORMULATION PER GALLON OF SPRAY	PHI (DAYS)	REMARKS AND PRECAUTIONS
Eggplant	aphid	acetamiprid 0.006%	RTU	7	
		bifenthrin 0.3%	1.5 oz.	7	Also available as a ready-to-use product.
		esfenvalerate 0.425%	2 Tbs.	7	Also available as a ready-to-use product.
		gamma-cyhalothrin 0.25%	1 Tbs	5	
		malathion 50%	2 tsp.	3	Use and registration varies with specific product.
		insecticidal soap	follow label directions	0	No residual activity. Thorough coverage is essential.
	Caterpillars on foliage Colorado potato beetle flea beetle	bifenthrin 0.3%	1.5 oz.	7	Also available as a ready-to-use product.
		carbaryl 22.5%	1.5-3 oz.	3	Also available as a ready-to-use product.
		esfenvalerate 0.425%	2 Tbs.	7	Also available as a ready-to-use product.
		gamma-cyhalothrin 0.25%	1 Tbs	5	
		permethrin 2.5% 0.25% dust	3 oz. Dust plants lightly	3	
		spinosad 0.5%	2 oz.	1	Not for use against flea beetles..
	lacebug	bifenthrin 0.3%	1.5 oz.	7	Also available as a ready-to-use product.
		carbaryl 22.5%	1.5-3 oz.	3	Also available as a ready-to-use product.
		gamma-cyhalothrin 0.25%	1 Tbs	5	Also available as a ready-to-use product.
	spider mite	insecticidal soap	follow label directions	0	No residual activity. Thorough coverage is essential.
		malathion 50%	2 tsp.	3	Use and registration varies with specific product. Marginal control of this pest.
		NOTE: Bifenthrin applied at high rates may provide suppression of mites.			
	whitefly	acetamiprid 0.006%	RTU	7	
		bifenthrin 0.3%	1.5 oz.	7	Also available as a ready-to-use product.
		insecticidal soap	follow label directions	0	No residual activity. Thorough coverage is essential.
		pyrethrins+PBO	RTU	0	No residual activity.
Lettuce, Spinach	aphid	acetamiprid 0.006%	RTU	7	
		bifenthrin 0.3%	1.5 oz.	7	For use on head lettuce only. Also available as a ready-to-use product.
		gamma-cyhalothrin 0.25%	1 Tbs	1	For use on lettuce only. Also available as a ready-to-use product.
		lambda-cyhalothrin 0.5%	1 Tbs.	1	For use on lettuce only. Also available as a ready-to-use product.
		malathion 50%	1.5-2 tsp.	head - 7 leaf - 14 spinach - 7	Use and registration varies with specific product.
		insecticidal soap	follow label directions	0	No residual activity. Thorough coverage is essential.

VEGETABLE	INSECT	INSECTICIDE AND FORMULATION	AMOUNT OF FORMULATION PER GALLON OF SPRAY	PHI (DAYS)	REMARKS AND PRECAUTIONS
Lettuce, Spinach	caterpillars on foliage, flea beetles, harlequin bug, and stink bug	*Bacillus thuringiensis* (Dipel, Thuricide and other formulations)	Follow label directions.	0	For control of caterpillar pests only. Treat as soon as damage is found and repeat as needed. Susceptible larvae will stop feeding soon after eating treated foliage but may not die for several days.
		bifenthrin 0.3%	1.5 oz.	7	For use on head lettuce only. Also available as a ready-to-use product.
		carbaryl 22.5% 5% dust 10% dust	1.5 - 3 oz. 0.5 - 1 lb. 0.25 - 0.5 lb.	14	Also available as a ready-to-use product.
		gamma-cyhalothrin 0.25%	1 Tbs.	1	For use on lettuce only. Also available as a ready-to-use product.
		lambda-cyhalothrin 0.5%	1 Tbs.	1	For use on lettuce only. Also available as a ready-to-use product.
		permethrin 2.5% 0.25% dust	2 oz. Dust plants lightly		
		spinosad 0.5%	2 oz.	1	For control of caterpillar pests only.
Mustard greens	aphid	insecticidal soap	follow label directions	0	No residual activity. Thorough coverage is essential.
		acetamiprid 0.006%	RTU	7	
		malathion 50%	2 tsp.	7	Use and registration varies with specific product.
	caterpillars on foliage	*Bacillus thuringiensis* (Dipel, Thuricide and other formulations)	Follow label directions.	0	Treat as soon as damage is found and repeat as needed. Susceptible larvae will stop feeding soon after eating treated foliage but may not die for several days.
		carbaryl 22.5% 5% dust 10% dust	1.5 - 3 oz. 0.5 - 1.0 lb. 0.25 - 0.5	14	Also available as a ready-to-use product.
		spinosad 0.5%	2 oz.	1	
	flea beetles	carbaryl 22.5% 5% dust 10% dust	0.75 - 1.5 oz. 0.25 - 0.5 lb. 0.125 - 0.25 lb.	14	Also available as a ready-to-use product.
Okra	aphid	insecticidal soap	follow label directions	0	No residual activity. Thorough coverage is essential.
		malathion 50%	2 tsp.	1	Use and registration varies with specific product.
	caterpillar pests	spinosad 0.5%	2 oz.	1	

VEGETABLE	INSECT	INSECTICIDE AND FORMULATION	AMOUNT OF FORMULATION PER GALLON OF SPRAY	PHI (DAYS)	REMARKS AND PRECAUTIONS
Onions	thrips	gamma-cyhalothrin 0.25%	1 Tbs	14	Also available as a ready-to-use product.
		lambda-cyhalothrin 0.5%	1 Tbs.	14	Also available as a ready-to-use product.
		malathion 50%	2 tsp.	3	Use and registration varies with specific product.
Peppers	aphid	acetamiprid 0.006%	RTU	7	
		bifenthrin 0.3%	1.5 oz.	7	Also available as a ready-to-use product.
		esfenvalerate 0.425%	2 Tbs.	7	Also available as a ready-to-use product.
		gamma-cyhalothrin 0.25%	1 Tbs	5	
		malathion 50%	2 tsp.	3	Use and registration varies with specific product.
		insecticidal soap	follow label directions	0	No residual activity. Thorough coverage is essential.
	caterpillar pests, flea beetle	bifenthrin 0.3%	1.5 oz.	7	Also available as a ready-to-use product.
		carbaryl 22.5% 5% dust 10% dust	1.5 - 3 oz. 0.5 - 1 lb. 0.25 - 0.5 lb.	3	Also available as a ready-to-use product.
		cyfluthrin 0.75%	1 Tbs.	7	Also available as a ready-to-use product.
		esfenvalerate 0.425% ·	2 Tbs.	7	Also available as a ready-to-use product.
		gamma-cyhalothrin 0.25%	1 Tbs	5	
		permethrin 2.5% 0.25% dust	2 oz. Dust plants lightly	3	
		spinosad 0.5%	2 oz.	1	For control of caterpillar pests only.
	spider mites	insecticidal soap	follow label directions	0	No residual activity. Thorough coverage is essential.
		malathion 50%	2 tsp.	3	Use and registration varies with specific product. Marginal control of this pest.
	NOTE: Bifenthrin applied at high rates may provide suppression of mites.				
Potatoes, Irish	aphid	esfenvalerate 0.425%	2 Tbs.	7	Also available as a ready-to-use product.
		malathion 50%	1.5-2 tsp.	0	
		permethrin 2.5% 0.25% dust	1.5 oz. Dust plants lightly	14	
		insecticidal soap	follow label directions	0	No residual activity Thorough coverage is essential.

VEGETABLE	INSECT	INSECTICIDE AND FORMULATION	AMOUNT OF FORMULATION PER GALLON OF SPRAY	PHI (DAYS)	REMARKS AND PRECAUTIONS
Potatoes, Irish (cont.)	Colorado potato beetle, flea beetles, potato tuberworm	carbaryl 22.5% 5% dust 10% dust	1.5 - 3 oz. 0.25 - 0.5 lb. 0.125 - 0.25 lb.	7	Not for control of potato tuberworm. Also available as a ready-to-use product.
		esfenvalerate 0.425%	2 Tbs.	7	Also available as a ready-to-use product.
		permethrin 2.5% 0.25% dust	1.5 oz. Dust plants lightly	14	
		spinosad 0.5%	2 oz.	7	
		NOTE: For potato tuberworm, treat when foliage or tuber damage is noticed. Store tubers promptly after digging to avoid tuberworm infestation in storage.			
Potatoes, sweet	Flea beetles, cucumber beetles	carbaryl 22.5%	1.5 - 3 oz.	7	Also available as a ready-to-use product.
		malathion 50%	4 tsp.	3	
	Caterpillars on foliage	*Bacillus thuringiensis* (Dipel, Thuricide and other formulations)	Follow label directions.	0	Treat as soon as damage is found and repeat as needed. Susceptible larvae will stop feeding soon after eating treated foliage but may not die for several days.
		carbaryl 22.5%	1.5 - 3 oz.	7	Also available as a ready-to-use product.
		spinosad 0.5%	2 oz.	7	
	sweet potato weevil	carbaryl 22.5%	1.5 - 3 oz.	7	Also labeled as pre-plant dip (follow label). Also available as a ready-to-use product.
Radishes	aphid	esfenvalerate 0.425%	2 Tbs.	7	Also available as a ready-to-use product.
		malathion 50%	1.5 - 2 tsp.	7	
		insecticidal soap	follow label directions	0	No residual activity. Thorough coverage is essential.
	flea beetle	carbaryl 22.5% 5% dust 10% dust	0.75 - 1.5 oz. 0.25 - 0.5 lb. 0.125 - 0.25 lb.	7	Also available as a ready-to-use product.
		cyfluthrin 0.75%	1 Tbs.	0	Also available as a ready-to-use product.
		esfenvalerate 0.425%	2 Tbs.	7	Also available as a ready-to-use product.
Tomato	aphid	acetamiprid 0.006%	RTU	7	
		bifenthrin 0.3%	1.5 oz.	1	Also available as a ready-to-use product.
		cyfluthrin 0.75%	1 Tbs.	0	Also available as a ready-to-use product.
		esfenvalerate 0.425%	2 Tbs.	1	Also available as a ready-to-use product.
		gamma-cyhalothrin 0.25%	1 Tbs	5	Also available as a ready-to-use product.
		lambda-cyhalothrin 0.5%	1 Tbs.	5	Also available as a ready-to-use product.
		malathion 50%	1.5 - 2 tsp.	1-7	PHI varies with specific product.
		insecticidal soap	follow label directions	0	No residual activity. Thorough coverage is essential.

VEGETABLE	INSECT	INSECTICIDE AND FORMULATION	AMOUNT OF FORMULATION PER GALLON OF SPRAY	PHI (DAYS)	REMARKS AND PRECAUTIONS
Tomato (cont.)	flea beetles, Colorado potato beetle, fruitworm, hornworm, tomato pinworm	bifenthrin 0.3%	1.5 oz.	1	Also available as a ready-to-use product.
		carbaryl 22.5% 5% dust 10% dust	1.5 - 3 oz. 0.5 - 1 lb. 0.25 - 0.5 lb	3	Primarily for control of beetles. Also available as a ready-to-use product.
		cyfluthrin 0.75%	1 Tbs.	0	Also available as a ready-to-use product.
		esfenvalerate 0.425%	2 Tbs.	1	Also available as a ready-to-use product.
		gamma-cyhalothrin 0.25%	1 Tbs	5	Also available as a ready-to-use product.
		lambda-cyhalothrin 0.5%	1 Tbs.	5	Also available as a ready-to-use product.
		permethrin 2.5% 0.25% dust	1.5 oz. Dust plants lightly	0	Not registered for cutworms.
		spinosad 0.5%	2 oz.	1	Not registered for flea beetles or cutworms.
	spider mites	sulfur 90%	2 Tbs.	0	Do not use if > 95 degrees. Do not use within 3 weeks of oil spray.
		insecticidal soap	follow label directions	0	No residual activity Thorough coverage is essential.
	NOTE: Bifenthrin applied at high rates may provide suppression of mites.				
	stink bug, leaffooted bug	bifenthrin 0.3%	1.5 oz.	1	Weekly treatments may be needed for late season control.
		cyfluthrin 0.75%	1 Tbs.	0	Also available as a ready-to-use product.
		esfenvalerate 0.425%	2 Tbs.	1	Also available as a ready-to-use product.
		gamma-cyhalothrin 0.25%	1 Tbs	5	Also available as a ready-to-use product.
		lambda-cyhalothrin 0.5%	1 Tbs.	5	Also available as a ready-to-use product.
	NOTE: Weekly treatments may be needed for late season control.				
	whitefly	acetamiprid 0.006%	RTU	7	
		bifenthrin 0.3%	1.5 oz.	1	Also available as a ready-to-use product.
		insecticidal soap	follow label directions	0	No residual activity. Thorough coverage is essential.
		pyrethrins+PBO	RTU	0	No residual activity.
Turnips	aphid	insecticidal soap	follow label directions	0	No residual activity. Thorough coverage is essential.
		malathion 50%	2 tsp.	7	Use and registration varies with specific product.
	caterpillars on foliage	carbaryl 5% dust 10% dust	0.5 - 1 lb. 0.25 - 0.5	Tops - 14 Root - 7	Also available as a ready-to-use product.
		Bacillus thuringiensis (Dipel, Thuricide and other formulations)	Follow label directions.	0	Treat as soon as damage is found and repeat as needed. Susceptible larvae will stop feeding soon after eating treated foliage but may not die for several days.
	flea beetles, harlequin bug	carbaryl 5% dust 10% dust	0.25 - 0.5 lb. 1.25 - 2.5 lb.	Tops - 14 Root - 7	Also available as a ready-to-use product.

HOME VEGETABLE DISEASE CONTROL

Elizabeth Little, Extension Homeowner IPM Specialist

**Please note: This is not an all-inclusive list of products available to homeowners. It is a list of commonly used products available at local retail locations. This guide can be used to find additional products by referencing the active ingredient and searching for products containing that active ingredient at your local store. Remember to ALWAYS read the label carefully and follow ALL directions, restrictions, and precautions listed in the manufacturer's label!

COMMODITY DISEASE	BRAND/TRADE NAME	ACTIVE INGREDIENT	RATE	MINIMUM DAYS TO HARVEST	METHOD, SCHEDULE REMARKS
ASPARAGUS					
Cercospora Leaf spot	Bonide Mancozeb Flowable	Mancozeb	2 tbsp./gal.	120	
Crown Rot and Root Rot	Dragon Mancozeb Disease Control	Mancozeb	6 tsp./gal.		
Bacterial Blight	Bonide Copper Spray or Dust	Copper	2 ½ - 5 ozs./gal.	NTL	See label
	Dragon Copper Fungicide		4 tsp./gal.	NTL	
	Hi-Yield Copper Fungicide		2 - 4 tsp./gal.	NTL	
Powdery Mildew	Sulfur - spray or dust (Several brands until available)	See label	NTL		Apply at first appearance and continue on 7- 10 day intervals disease is no longer present.
Rust	Ortho Garden Disease Control	Chlorothalonil	1.0 Tbs./gal.	7	See Label.
	Sulfur (spray or dust)	Sulfur	NTL		Begin application during early bloom stage. (With Top Cop: 4 applications are usually sufficient).
	Dragon Mancozeb Disease Control	Mancozeb	3 tsp./gal	180	Apply these products only after harvest.
	Bonide Mancozeb Flowable	Mancozeb	4 tsp./gal	180	4 applications are usually sufficient
BEANS (Lima and Snap)					
Anthracnose	GardenTech Daconil Fungicide	Chlorothalonil	2.25 lbs./acre	7	9 lbs. Maximum Seasonal Application rate
Bacterial Blight	Bonide Liquid Copper fungicide	Copper Soap	0.5-2 oz/gal	NTL	For protective sprays, begin application 2 weeks before disease normally appears.
Botrytis (Gray mold)	GardenTech Daconil Fungicide Ortho Garden Disease Control	Chlorothalonil	2.25 lbs.acre	7	9 lbs. Maximum Seasonal Application rate
	Topsin M 70WP	Thiophanate-methyl	1-2 lbs./acre	See label.	Make first application when 10-3 0% of plants have at least one open bloom.
Powdery mildew	Safer Garden Fungicide Bonide Sulfur Plant Fungicide Hi-Yield Dusting Wettable Sulfur	Sulfur (Several products)	4 tbsp /gal water 1.5 to 3 tbsp /gal. water see label	Up to day before harvest.	Spray at first sign of disease. Begin when first true leaves form or at first sign of disease.
Root rot and seedling disease (Rhizoctonia)	Terraclor 75%WP	PCNB	see label	Apply only at planting time.	Apply as directed at planting time.

COMMODITY DISEASE	BRAND/TRADE NAME	ACTIVE INGREDIENT	RATE	MINIMUM DAYS TO HARVEST	METHOD, SCHEDULE REMARKS
BEANS (Lima and Snap) (continued)					
Rust	Sulfur Dragon Mancozeb Disease Control Ortho Garden Disease Control	Sulfur Mancozeb Chlorothalonil	2 qts/ac. see label see label		Begin during early bloom or when disease first threatens.
White mold (Sclerotinia)	Terraclor 75%WP	PCNB	see label		Apply only at planting time.
Root Knot (Nematode)	Hi-Yield Nem-A-Cide Nematode Control	Chitin	See label		A single application is sufficient for nematode. For best results, a soil analysis for nematode typing and counts of adults should be done before and after each crop season.
BEETS					
Downy Mildew, Leaf spots, and Blights	Copper Sulfate Bonide Liquid Copper Fungicide Dragon Copper Fungicide	Sulfur Copper Copper	2.0 -3.0 lbs. 1 tsp./gal. 1 ½ tsp./gal.	NTL NTL	Begin when disease appears and repeat every. 7-10 days. Begin when disease appears and repeat every. 7-10 days. Begin application when disease first appears and then every 7-14 days.
Seed-rot & Damping off	Hi-Yield Captan Fungicide 50% WP	Captan	½ tsp./1 Dry seed		Not for use at or immediately before planting. Mix thoroughly in a paper bag or glass jar.
BROCCOLI, CABBAGE, BRUSSELS SPROUTS					
Wire Stem	Terraclor 75WP	PCNB	15 -20 lbs./100 gals./water		Apply ½ pint of solution around each plant at transplanting.
Alternaria Leaf spot & Downy mildew	Dragon Copper Fungicide Ortho Garden Disease Control (Daconil 2787) Bonide Copper Spray or Dust Bonide Liquid Copper Fungicide Basic Copper Sulfate Hi-Yield Daconil	Copper Chlorothalonil Copper Copper Chlorothalonil	1 tsp./gal. 1 ½ tsp./gal. 2 ¼ - 3 ¼ tsp./gal. 4 - 6 tsp./gal. 1.0 - 3.0 lbs. 3 tbs./5 -15 gals. /water	NTL 0 NTL NTL NTL	Apply to 500 ft² of garden area. Apply after transplant, emergence of seeded crop, or when conditions favor disease development.
Powdery mildew	Sulfate Hi-Yield Copper Fungicide See label, several brands available	Sulfur Copper	 2 -3 tsp./gal.	NTL NTL	
CABBAGE					
Alternaria Leaf spot	Ortho Garden Disease Control (Daconil 2787)	Chlorothalonil	1 ½ tsp./gal.	0	See Label.
Club Root	Terraclor 75%WP + hydrated lime	PCNB	2 lbs./100 gals. 1,500 lbs.		Broadcast and disc lime in soil 0 to 3 days before planting.
Damping-Off (plant bed)	Terraclor 75%WP	PCNB	½ lbs. (actual)		Sterilize seedbed soil. Drench seedbed after planting. If plants are purchased, be sure they are disease-free.

COMMODITY DISEASE	BRAND/TRADE NAME	ACTIVE INGREDIENT	RATE	MINIMUM DAYS TO HARVEST	METHOD, SCHEDULE REMARKS
CABBAGE (continued)					
Seed-rot & Damping Off	Hi-Yield Captan Fungicide 50% WP	Captan	½ tsp./1 lb. Dry seed		Not for use at or immediately before planting. Mix thoroughly in a paper bag or glass jar.
Downy Mildew	Ortho Garden Disease Control (Daconil 2787)	Chlorothalonil	1 ½ tsp./gal	0	Apply every 14 days.
	Bonide Liquid Copper	Copper	1 1/3 - 2 tsp./gal.	None	
CANTALOUPE					
Alternaria Leafspot	Ortho Garden Disease Control (Daconil 2787)	Chlorothalonil	2.0 tsp./gal.	0	See Label. Apply every 7 -10 days as needed.
	Bonide Copper Sulfate	Copper	2 ¼ tsp.	NTL up to day of harvest	
	Bonide Liquid Copper Fungicide	Mancozeb	4 tsp./gal	5	
	Dragon Mancozeb Disease Control		3 - 4 ¼ tsp./gal.	5	
	Bonide Mancozeb Plant Fungicide	Copper	2 - 3 tbs./gal.	up to day of harvest	
	Dragon Copper Fungicide				
Anthracnose	Ortho Garden Disease Control (Daconil 2787)	Chlorothalonil	2.0 tsp./gal.	0	Use western-grown seed. Apply fungicides when true leave fully expand. Continue every 7 - 14 days until harvest.
	Basic Copper Sulfate		1.0 - 3.0 lbs.	NTL	Apply every 7 - 10 days as needed.
	Dragon Mancozeb Disease Control	Mancozeb	3.0 - 4.75 tsp./gal.	5	
	Bonide Mancozeb Plant Fungicide		2.0 - 3.0 tsp./gal.	5	
	Bonide Copper Spray or Dust	Copper	2.25 - 5.75 oz../gal.	NTL	
Downy mildew	Ortho Disease Control (Daconil 2787)	Chlorothalonil	2.0 tsp./gal.	0	See Label
	Bonide Copper Sulfate	Copper	2.0 lbs.	NTL	
	Dragon Mancozeb Disease Control	Mancozeb	3.0 - 4.75 tsp./gal.	5	
	Bonide Mancozeb Plant Fungicide		2.0 - 3.0 tsp./gal.	5	
	Bonide Copper Spray or Dust	Copper	2.25 - 5.75 oz./gal.	NTL	
Gummy Stem Blight	Ortho Garden Disease Control (Daconil 2787)	Chlorothalonil	2.0 tsp./gal.	NTL	Use western-grown seed. Apply fungicides when true leave fully expand. Continue every 7 - 14 days until harvest.
	Basic Copper Sulfate	Cooper		NTL	
	Dragon Mancozeb Disease Control	Mancozeb	3.0 - 4.75 tsp./gal.	5	Apply every 7 - 10 days as needed.
	Bonide Mancozeb Plant Fungicide		2.0 - 3.0 tsp./gal.	5	
	Bonide Copper Spray or Dust	Copper	2.25 - 5.75 oz../gal.	NTL	
Powdery Mildew	Basic Copper Sulfate	Copper	2.0 lbs.	NTL	
	Bonide Liquid Copper Fungicide		4 - 6 tsp./gal	up to day of harvest.	
	Dragon Copper Fungicide		4 - 6 tsp./gal	up to day of harvest	
	Bonide Copper Spray or Dust		2 ¼ - 5 ¾ ozs./gal	NTL	
	Ortho Garden Disease Control (Daconil 2787)	Chlorothalonil	1 tbs./gal.	0	
Seed-rot & Damping Off	Hi-Yield Captan Fungicide 50% WP	Captan	½ tsp./1 lb. Dry seed		Not for use at or immediately before planting. Mix thoroughly in a paper bag or glass jar.

COMMODITY DISEASE	BRAND/TRADE NAME	ACTIVE INGREDIENT	RATE	MINIMUM DAYS TO HARVEST	METHOD, SCHEDULE REMARKS
CARROTS					
Alternaria Blight	Ortho Garden Disease Control (Daconil 2787)	Chlorothalonil	2.0 tsp./gal.	7	Apply every 7-14 days as needed.
	Bonide Copper Fungicide (Bordeaux)	Copper-lime	4-6 tsp./gal.	up to day of harvest	
Cercospora Leaf Blight	Hi-Yield Copper Fungicide	Copper	2-3 tsp./gal	NTL	
	Dragon Copper Fungicide		4-6 tsp./gal.	up to day of harvest	
	Ortho Garden Disease Control (Daconil 2787)	Chlorothalonil	1 tbs./gal.	see label	
	Bonide Copper Spray or Dust	Copper	0.5-2 oz/gal	see label	
COLLARDS					
Alternaria Leafspot & Downy Mildew	Sulfur products	Sulfur	1 - 2 qts.	NTL	
	Safer Garden fungicide		2 qts	NTL	
CORN (SWEET)					
Leaf Blights and Rust	Ortho Garden Disease Control (Daconil 2787)	Chlorothalonil	2 tsp./gal.	7	See Label.
	Dragon Mancozeb Disease Control	Mancozeb	1½ tbsp./gal.	7	
	Bonide Mancozeb Plant Fungicide				
Seed-rot & Damping Off	Hi-Yield Captan Fungicide 50%WP	Captan	½ tsp./1 lb. Dry seed		Not for use at or immediately before planting. Mi x thoroughly in a paper bag or glass jar.
CUCUMBER					
Angular Leafspot	Hi-Yield Copper Fungicide	Copper Hydroxide	2 tsp./gal.	NTL	
	Bonide Copper Spray or Dust	Copper	2¼-5¾ ozs./gal.	NTL	
	Dragon Copper Fungicide		4-6 tbs./gal.	NTL	
	Ortho Garden Disease Control (Daconil 2787)	Chlorothalonil	1 tbs./gal.	NTL	
	Dragon Mancozeb Disease Control	Mancozeb	3 - 4¾ tsp./gal.	NTL	
	Bonide Mancozeb	Mancozeb	4-5 tsp/gal	5	
Anthracnose	Ortho Disease Control (Daconil 2787)	Chlorothalonil	2 tsp./gal.	NTL	
	Basic Copper Sulfate	Copper Sulfate	2¼-5¾ ozs./gal.	NTL	Apply every 7-10 days as needed.
	Bonide Copper Spray or Dust	Bordeaux	4.5-11.5 tsp/gal	0	
	Dragon Mancozeb Disease Control	Mancozeb	See label	5	
Alternaria Leafspot	Ortho Disease Control (Daconil 2787)	Chlorothalonil	2¼ - 2¾ tsp.	NTL	
	Basic Copper Sulfate	Copper Sulfate	4 tsp./gal.	NTL up to day of harvest	Apply every 7-10 days as needed.
	Bonide Liquid Copper Fungicide		2¼-5¾ ozs./gal.	NTL	
	Bonide Copper Spray or Dust		4-6 tsp/gal	up to day of harvest	
	Dragon Copper Fungicide				

COMMODITY DISEASE	BRAND/TRADE NAME	ACTIVE INGREDIENT	RATE	MINIMUM DAYS TO HARVEST	METHOD, SCHEDULE REMARKS
CUCUMBER (cont inued)					
Corynespora Leafspot	Ortho Disease Control (Daconil 2787)	Chlorothalonil	2.0 tsp./gal.	NTL	
	Bonide Copper Spray or Dust	Copper	2¼-5¾ ozs./gal.	up to day of harvest	
Downy Mildew	Ortho Disease Control (Daconil 2787)	Chlorothalonil	2 tsp./gal.	NTL	Apply when disease threatens and every 7-10 days.
	Basic Copper Sulfate	Copper Sulfate	NTL		Apply every 7-10 days as needed.
	Hi-Yield Copper Fungicide	Copper	2 tsp./gal.	up to day of harvest	
	Bonide Copper Spray or Dust		2¼-5¾ ozs./gal.	up to day of harvest	
	Bonide Liquid Copper Fungicide		4 tsp./gal.	0	
	Dragon Copper Fungicide		4-6 tsp./gal.		
	Dragon Mancozeb Disease Control	Mancozeb	3-4¾ tsp./gal.	5	
Fruit & Belly Rot	Ortho Disease Control (Daconil 2787) (Supression only)	Chlorothalonil	1 tbs./gal.	See Label.	
Gummy Stem Blight	Ortho Disease Control (Daconil 2787)	Chlorothalonil	2.0 tsp./gal.	NTL	Use western-grown seed. Apply fungicides when true leaves fully expand. Continue every 7-14 days until harvest.
	Basic Copper Sulfate	Copper Sulfate		NTL	Apply every 7 - 10 days as needed.
	Dragon Mancozeb Disease Control	Mancozeb	3.0 - 4.75 tsp./gal.	5	
	Bonide Mancozeb Plant Fungicide		2.0 - 3.0 tsp./gal.	5	
	Bonide Copper Spray or Dust	Copper	2.25 - 5.75 oz./gal.	NTL	
Powdery Mildew	Basic Copper Sulfate	Copper Sulfate		NTL	Apply every 7-10 days as needed.
	Bonide Liquid Copper Fungicide	Copper	4 - 6 tsp./gal.	up to day of harvest	
	Dragon Copper Fungicide		4 - 6 tsp./gal.	up to day of harvest	
	Bonide Copper Spray or Dust		2¼-5¾ ozs./gal.	NTL	
	Ortho Disease Control (Daconil 2787)	Chlorothalonil	1 tbs./gal.	0	
Scab	Ortho Garden Disease Control (Daconil 2787)	Chlorothalonil		NTL NTL	
	Basic Copper Sulfate	Copper Sulfate		NTL	Apply every 7-10 days as needed.
	Bonide Copper Spray or Dust	Copper	2¼-5¾ ozs./gal.	up to day of harvest	
	Dragon Copper Fungicide		4-6 tsp./gal.	0	
	Dragon Mancozeb Disease Control	Mancozeb	3-4¾ tsp./gal.	5	
EGGPLANT					
Damping-Off (plant bed)	Captan 50WP	Captan	4 ½ Tbs.		Begin when all seeds have germinated and repeat at 10-day intervals.
Phomopsis, Alternaria, Anthracnose, Fruit Rots & Leaf Blights	Sulfur products	Sulfur	NTL		
	Hi-Yield Copper Fungicide	Copper	2 tsp./gal.	NTL	Apply at first sign of disease.
GARLIC	(See Onion)				

COMMODITY DISEASE	BRAND/TRADE NAME	ACTIVE INGREDIENT	RATE	MINIMUM DAYS TO HARVEST	METHOD, SCHEDULE REMARKS
IRISH POTATO					
Black Scurf	Terraclor 10 G	PCNB	See label.		Apply according to label directions.
	Terraclor 75 WP	PCNB			
Early Blight and Late Blight	Ortho Garden Disease Control (Daconil 2787)	Chlorothalonil	1 Tbs./gal.	NTL	See Label.
	Bonide Copper Spray or Dust	Copper	2¼ - 6 ozs./gal.		
	Dragon Copper Fungicide		4-6 tsp./gal		
	Dragon Mancozeb Disease Control	Mancozeb	2-3 tsp./gal.		
	Bonide Mancozeb Plant Fungicide		1-2 tbsp./ gal.		
KALE					
Powdery Mildew	Sulfur	Sulfur	See Label	0	Spray when disease threatens; 7-10 day intervals.
Alternaria Leafspot Downy Mildew	Sulfur products	Sulfur	See Label	0	
LETTUCE					
Downy Mildew	Hi-Yield Copper Fungicide	Copper	1 tsp./gal.	NTL	
OKRA					
Pod Blight	No foliar fungicides available				Blight is associated with poor pollination— provide good air circulation.
Verticillium Wilt					Rotate crops that are not susceptible to the Wilt.
Root-knot Nematode	Hi-Yield Nem-A-Cide	Chitin	See label.		One application is usually the only one necessary.
ONION (DRY)					
Purple Blotch Bacterial Leaf Blight Botrytis Leaf Blight Downy Mildew	Ortho Garden Disease Control (Daconil 2787)	Chlorothalonil	1.0 Tbs./gal.		
	Dragon Mancozeb Disease Control	Mancozeb	4¾ tsp./gal.		
	Bonide Mancozeb Plant Fungicide		4 tbsp./gal.		
ONION (GREEN AND GREEN BUNCHING) – GARLIC, LEEK, SHALLOT, ONION GROWN FOR SEED					
Botrytis Leaf Blight Downy Mildew Neck Rot Purple Blotch	Ortho Garden Disease Control (Daconil 2787)	Chlorothalonil	1.0 Tbs./gal.	14	See Label.
	Hi-Yield Copper Fungicide	Copper	2 tsp./gal.	NTL	
	Bonide Liquid Copper Fungicide		4 tsp./gal.	up to day of harvest	
	Dragon Copper Fungicide		4-6 tsp./gal.	up to day of harvest	
	Dragon Mancozeb Disease Control	Mancozeb	2 tsp./gal.	7	
	Bonide Mancozeb Plant Fungicide		3 tbsp./gal.	7	

COMMODITY DISEASE	BRAND/TRADE NAME	ACTIVE INGREDIENT	RATE	MINIMUM DAYS TO HARVEST	METHOD, SCHEDULE REMARKS
PEAS (ENGLISH)					
Powdery Mildew	Sulfur (spray or dust)	Sulfur	See label	NTL	Start application at first sign of disease and repeat every 7-10 days. Do not apply when temperature is above 90 degrees or when plants are wet.
Seed-rot & Damping Off	Hi-Yield Captan Fungicide 50%WP	Captan	½ tsp./1 lb. Dry seed	NTL	Not for use at or immediately before planting. Mix thoroughly in a paper bag or glass jar.
BLACK-EYED PEAS (SOUTHERN)					
Scab Anthracnose Mildew Rust	Sulfur	Sulfur	See Label	NTL	Begin during early bloom or when disease first threatens.
Cercospora Leafspot Powdery Mildew Rust	Sulfur products	See Label		NTL	Spray early bloom; repeat at 7 to 10 day intervals. See Label
PEPPER					
Cercospora, Anthracnose, Phytophthora blight Fruit Rots, Bacterial Spot	Sulfur	Sulfur	1.0 - 2.0 qts.	NTL	
	Copper	Copper	2.0 - 3.0 qts.	NTL	
	Hi-Yield Copper Fungicide	Copper Hydroxide	2 2/3 - 4 tsp /gal.	NTL	
	Bonide Liquid Copper Fungicide	Copper	4 - 6 tsp./gal.	NTL	
	Dragon Copper Fungicide		4 - 6 tsp./gal.		up to day of harvest
Blossom End Rot	CAB	Calcium	2.0 Tbs.	NTL	Apply at bloom. Make two to three applications at weekly intervals.
Southern Blight	Terraclor or PCNBP 75W	PCNB	3.0 - 5.0 Tbs		Use ½ pint per plant when transplanting. Rotate with corn or other grasses. Deep plow to cover debris.
PUMPKIN					
Downy Mildew Verticillium Wilt	Ortho Garden Disease Control (Daconil 2787)	Chlorothaloni	2.0 tsp./gal.	0	See Label Apply every 7 - 10 days as needed.
	Basic Copper Sulfate	copper sulfate		NTL	
	Dragon Mancozeb Disease Control	Mancozeb	3.0 - 4.75 tsp./gal.	5	
	Bonide Mancozeb Plant Fungicide		2.0 - 3.0 tsp./gal.	5	
	Bonide Copper Spray or Dust	Copper	2.25 - 5.75 oz./gal.	NTL	
Anthracnose	Ortho Garden Disease Control (Daconil 2787)	Chlorothalonil	1/3 Tbs.	5	Apply every 7 - 10 days as needed
	Basic Copper Sulfate	Copper Sulfate		NTL	
	Dragon Mancozeb Disease Control	Mancozeb	3.0 - 4.75 tsp./gal.	5	
	Bonide Mancozeb Plant Fungicide		2.0 - 3.0 tsp./gal.	5	
	Bonide Copper Spray or Dust	Copper	2.25 - 5.75 oz./gal.	NTL	

COMMODITY DISEASE	BRAND/TRADE NAME	ACTIVE INGREDIENT	RATE	MINIMUM DAYS TO HARVEST	METHOD, SCHEDULE REMARKS
PUMPKIN (continued)					
Gummy Stem Blight	Ortho Garden Disease Control (Daconil 2787)	Chlorothalonil	1/3 Tbs.		See Label. Apply every 7 - 10 days as needed.
	Basic Copper Sulfate	Copper Sulfate	3.0 - 4.75 tsp./gal.	NTL	
	Dragon Mancozeb Disease Control	Mancozeb	2.0 - 3.0 tsp./gal.	5	
	Bonide Mancozeb Plant Fungicide			5	
	Bonide Copper Spray or Dust	Copper	2.25 - 5.75 oz./gal.	NTL	
Powdery Mildew	Basic Copper Sulfate	Copper Sulfate		NTL	Apply every 7-10 days as needed. Do not apply when temperatures exceed 95°F.
	Bonide Liquid Copper Fungicide	Copper	4.0 tsp./gal.	up to day of harvest	
	Dragon Copper Fungicide		2.25 - 5.75 oz./gal.	up to day of harvest	
	Bonide Copper Spray or Dust		2.0 - 4.0 tsp./gal.	NTL	
	Ortho Garden Disease Control (Daconil 2787)	Chlorothalonil	2.0 tsp./gal	0	
Alternaria Leafspot	Ortho Garden Disease Control (Daconil 2787)	Chlorothalonil	2.0 tsp./gal.	0	See Label. Apply every 7-10 days as needed.
	Basic Copper Sulfate	Copper Sulfate		NTL	
	Bonide Liquid Copper Fungicide	Copper	2 ¼ tsp.	up to day of harvest	
	Dragon Mancozeb Disease Control	Mancozeb	4 tsp./gal.	5	
	Bonide Mancozeb Plant Fungicide		3 - 4¾ tsp./gal.	5	
	Dragon Copper Fungicide	Copper	2 - 3 tbsp./gal.	up to day of harvest	
Viruses	No chemical control available.				Reflective mulches, resistant varieties, plant earlier in season, watch for insect vectors (such as aphids).
RADISH					
Alternaria Leafspot	Top Cop with Sulfur	Sulfur			Begin application as soon as disease threatens and repeat at 7-10 day intervals. Use 3 day interval in plant beds. See label.
	Top Cop Tri Basic	Copper			
SPINACH					
Anthracnose & Cercospora Leafspot	Copper Sulfate	Copper Sulfate	1.0 Tbs.	NTL	Begin at first sign of disease and repeat every 7 days.
Downy Mildew & White Rust	Sulfur	Sulfur			
	Copper	Copper	1 ½ Tbs.	NTL	
	Copper Sulfate	Copper Sulfate			
	Hi-Yield Copper Fungicide	Copper Hydroxide	2-4 tsp./gal.	NTL	See Label.
Seed-rot & Damping Off	Hi-Yield Captan Fungicide 50%WP	Captan	1.25 tsp.		Not for use at or immediately before planting. Mix thoroughly in a paper bag or glass jar.

COMMODITY DISEASE	BRAND/TRADE NAME	ACTIVE INGREDIENT	RATE	MINIMUM DAYS TO HARVEST	METHOD, SCHEDULE REMARKS
SQUASH					
Angular Leafspot	Copper Bonide Copper Spray or Dust Basic Copper Sulfate	Copper	See label	NTL	Apply every 7-10 days as needed.
Anthracnose, Downy Mildew, Cercospora, Scab	Ortho Garden Disease Control (Daconil 2787) Basic Copper Sulfate Dragon Mancozeb Disease Control Bonide Mancozeb Plant Fungicide Bonide Copper Spray or Dust	Chlorothalonil Copper Sulfate Mancozeb Copper	2.0 tsp./gal. 3.0 - 4.75 tsp./gal. 2.0 - 3.0 tsp./gal. 2.25 - 5.75 oz./gal.	0 NTL 5 5 NTL	See Label.
Powdery Mildew	Basic Copper Sulfate Bonide Liquid Copper Fungicide Dragon Copper Fungicide Bonide Copper Spray or Dust Ortho Garden Disease Control (Daconil 2787)	Copper Sulfate Copper Chlorothalonil	4.0 tsp./gal. 2.25 - 5.75 oz./gal. 2.0 - 4.0 tsp./gal. 2.0 tsp./gal	NTL up to day of harvest up to day of harvest NTL 0	Apply every 7-10 days as needed.
Seed-rot & Damping Off	Hi-Yield Captan Fungicide 50%WP	Captan	½ tsp./1 lb. Dry seed		Not for use at or immediately before planting. Mix thoroughly in a paper bag or glass jar.
Viruses	No chemical control				Plant earlier in the season to avoid high insect populations. Row covers provide early-season protection. Select resistant varieties.
TOMATO					
Anthracnose Early Blight Gray Leaf Spot Gray Leaf Mold Late Blight Septoria Leaf Spot	Ortho Garden Disease Control (Daconil 2787) Bonide Copper Spray or Dust Dragon Copper Fungicide Dragon Mancozeb Disease Control Bonide Mancozeb Plant Fungicide	Chlorothalonil Copper Mancozeb	1 Tbs./gal. 2¼ - 6 ozs./gal. 4-6 tsp./gal 2-3 tsp./gal. 1-2 tbsp./ gal.	NTL	See Label.
Bacterial Spot Bacterial Speck	Basic Copper Sulfate Hi-Yield Copper Fungicide Bonide Liquid Copper Fungicide Bonide Copper Spray or Dust Dragon Copper Fungicide	Copper	3-5 tsp./gal. 4-6 tsp./gal. 2¼-6 ozs./gal. 4-6 tsp./gal.	NTL up to day of harvest NTL up to day of harvest	
Botrytis (Gray Mold)	Ortho Garden Disease Control (Daconil 2787)	Chlorothalonil	1.0 Tbs./gal.	0	See Label.
TURNIPS					
Cercospora Cercosporella Anthracnose Powdery Mildew	Copper Sulfur	Copper Sulfur	See label	NTL NTL	Do not make more than 3 applications per growing season.

COMMODITY DISEASE	BRAND/TRADE NAME	ACTIVE INGREDIENT	RATE	MINIMUM DAYS TO HARVEST	METHOD, SCHEDULE REMARKS
TURNIPS, MUSTARD, & COLLARDS					
Alternaria Leafspot Downy Mildew	Copper Sulfur	Copper Sulfur	see label	NTL NTL	
Powdery Mildew	Wettable Sulfur 95%	Sulfur	2.0 Tbs.	NTL	Begin at first sign of disease. Apply every 7-10 days.
WATERMELON					
Anthracnose	Ortho Garden Disease Control (Daconil 2787)	Chlorothalonil	2.0 tsp./gal	5	Apply every 7 - 10 days as needed.
	Basic Copper Sulfate	Copper Sulfate		NTL	
	Dragon Mancozeb Disease Control	Mancozeb	3.0 - 4.75 tsp./gal.	5	
	Bonide Mancozeb Plant Fungicide		2.0 - 3.0 tsp./gal.	5	
	Bonide Copper Spray or Dust	Copper	2.25 - 5.75 oz./gal.	NTL	
Bacterial Fruit Blotch	Basic Copper Sulfate	Copper Sulfate		NTL	Studies have shown that ½ rate of copper materials applied weekly is as effective as applying the full rate on a 14 day schedule.
	Hi-Yield Copper Fungicide	Copper	2-4 tsp./gal.	NTL	
	Dragon Mancozeb Disease Control	Mancozeb	3-4¾ tsp./gal.	NTL	
	Dragon Copper Fungicide	Copper	4-6 tsp./gal.	NTL	
Downy Mildew	Ortho Garden Disease Control (Daconil 2787)	Chlorothalonil	2.0 tsp./gal.	0	See Label.
	Basic Copper Sulfate	Copper Sulfate		NTL	
	Dragon Mancozeb Disease Control	Mancozeb	3.0 - 4.75 tsp./gal.	5	
	Bonide Mancozeb Plant Fungicide		2.0 - 3.0 tsp./gal.	5	
	Bonide Copper Spray or Dust	Copper	2.25 - 5.75 oz./gal.	NTL	
Fusarium Wilt	No chemical control.				Plant resistant varieties. Long rotations should be used (do not plant more than once every 5 years).
Gummy Stem Blight	Ortho Garden Disease Control (Daconil 2787)	Chlorothalonil		NTL	Apply every 7 - 10 days as needed.
	Basic Copper Sulfate	Copper Sulfate			
	Dragon Mancozeb Disease Control	Mancozeb	3.0 - 4.75 tsp./gal.	5	
	Bonide Mancozeb Plant Fungicide		2.0 - 3.0 tsp./gal.	5	
	Bonide Copper Spray or Dust	Copper	2.25 - 5.75 oz./gal.	NTL	
Powdery Mildew	Bonide Liquid Copper Fungicide	Copper	4 - 6 tsp./gal.	NTL	
	Dragon Copper Fungicide		4 - 6 tsp./gal.	up to day of harvest	
	Bonide Copper Spray or Dust		2¼-5¾ ozs./gal.	NTL	
	Ortho Garden Disease Control (Daconil 2787)	Chlorothalonil	1 tbs./gal.	0	

Always check label for proper rates.
NTL = No time limit

WEED CONTROL IN HOME VEGETABLE GARDENS

A. Stanley Culpepper, Extension Agronomist – Weed Science
Lynn Sosnoskie – Weed Science

APPLICATION/ TIMING	HERBICIDE	CROPS	REMARKS AND PRECAUTIONS
Preplant or Preemergence	glyphosate (Roundup, many others)	Beans, Beet greens, Garden Beets, Broccoli, Brussels sprouts, Cabbage, Carrot, Cauliflower, Celery, Collards, Endive, Garlic, Kale, Leek, Lettuce, Mustard greens, Okra, Onion, Peas, Potato, Spinach, Sweet potato, Tomato, Turnip, Yams	Controls most annual weeds and suppresses or controls many perennial weeds. **Apply at least 3 days prior to the emergence of direct seeded vegetables or at least 3 days prior to transplanting vegetables.** Most weeds can be controlled by applying 0.75 to 2.0% glyphosate-solution using a hand held sprayer and spraying to wet; see label for exact rates for specific weed problems and application methods. For nutsedge and bermudagrass, sequential applications at 1.5 to 2.0 % glyphosate solution will likely be necessary.
		Cantaloupe, Cucumber, Eggplant, Gourds, Melons (all), Muskmelon, Pepper, Pumpkin, Squash (summer, winter), Tomato, Watermelon	Allow at least 3 days after application before planting these crops.
		All vegetables listed above	If growing vegetables on plastic or in high plant residues, care must be taken to remove the glyphosate from the plastic or plant residue prior to transplanting. Glyphosate can be removed by a single 0.5 inch application of water by irrigation or rainfall.
Preplant incorporated, preemergence, or postemergence	trifluralin, (many brands including Weed Preventer, Preen 'n Green Granules, Weed and Grass Preventer) See label for specific product used.	**From Seed:** Broccoli, Brussels Sprouts, Cabbage, Carrots, Cauliflower, Celery, Collard, Green Peas, Kale, Lima Beans, Mustard Greens, Okra, Snap Beans, Southern Pea, and Turnip Greens	**DOES NOT CONTROL EMERGED WEEDS.** **From Seed:** For residual control of annual grasses and small seeded broadleaf weeds. Apply to prepared soil and incorporate 2 inches deep before planting. Be careful with use rate especially on broccoli, cabbage, cauliflower, turnip greens, mustard greens, collard and kale.
		Before Transplanting: Broccoli, Brussels Sprouts, Cabbage, Cauliflower, Celery, Eggplant, Onions, Pepper and Tomato	**Before Transplanting:** For residual control of annual grasses and small seeded broadleaf weeds. Apply to prepared soil and incorporate 2 inches deep before planting.
		Post Emergent: Cantaloupe, Cucumber and Watermelon	**Post Emergent:** Provides residual control of annual grasses and small seeded broadleaf weeds. Apply after plants have developed at least 5 leaves. Apply between plants taking care to limit spray drift on plants.
		After planting: Potato	**After planting but before emergence:** Use care not to damage seed pieces in cultivating nor to allow treated soil to contact emerged plant foliage.
		All vegetables listed above	In all cases, cultivate into the soil after application using care not to damage emerged crops.

APPLICATION/ TIMING	HERBICIDE	CROPS	REMARKS AND PRECAUTIONS
Preplant incorporated, preemergence, or postemergence (cont.)	DCPA (Dacthal) W-75 (Dacthal) 6°F		**DOES NOT CONTROL EMERGED WEEDS** Apply uniformly to soil as a spray at time of planting for residual control of grasses and small seeded broadleaf weeds.
		At seeding: Mustard greens, Turnip	
		At seeding or transplanting: Broccoli, Brussels Sprouts, Cauliflower, Cabbage, Collards, Kale, Garlic, Onions, Sweet potato	Apply uniformly to the soil as a spray for residual control of grasses and small seeded broadleaf weeds. Can be sprayed directly over transplants without injury.
		When plants have 4 to 5 true leaves: Seeded melons: (Cantaloupe, Honeydew, Watermelon)	Apply only when plants have 4 to 5 true leaves, are well established, and growing conditions are favorable. Will not control emerged weeds.
		4-6 weeks after transplanting or direct seeding plants at 4-6 inches tall: Tomato and Eggplant	Can be applied overtop of transplants for residual control of annual grasses and small seeded broadleaf weeds.
Postemergence	sethoxydim (Poast) 1.53 EC	Broccoli, Cabbage, Carrots, Cantaloupe, Cauliflower, Celery, Collard, Cucumber, Eggplant, Garlic, Green pea, Kale, Leek, Lettuce, Lima bean, Mustard, Okra, Onion, Pepper, Potato (Irish and sweet), Pumpkin, Spinach, Squash, Snap bean, Southern pea, Tomato, Watermelon	Does not control broadleaf weeds or sedges. Apply postemergence over-the-top for control of emerged annual and perennial grasses at 1 pt per acre or approximately 0.75 Tbs/gal/1000 sq. ft . Use a crop oil concentrate (adjuvant) at a rate of 1 qt. per acre or approximately 1.5 Tbs./gal./1000 sq. ft. Do not apply within 14 days of harvesting cantaloupe. cucumber, okra, pumpkin, squash, or watermelon. Do not apply within 15 days of harvesting lettuce, spinach, succulent beans, or succulent peas. Do not apply within 30 days of harvesting broccoli, cabbage, carrots, cauliflower, celery, collard, eggplant, garlic, kale, lettuce, mustard, potato, or onion. Do not apply within 20 days of harvesting eggplant, pepper, or tomato.
	bentazon (Basagran) 4 SL	English pea, Green pea, Kidney bean, Lima bean, Navy bean, Pinto bean, Snap bean, Southern pea	For postemergence control of yellow nutsedge and some broadleaf weeds. Does not control grasses. Apply when weeds are small and actively growing. Adjust rate according to weed size as suggested on label. Do not apply before the third trifoliate leaf is fully expanded. Add adjuvant according to label.
	glyphosate (Roundup WeatherMax) 5.5 SL	*Brassica:* broccoli, cabbage, collard, kale, mustard *Bulb crops:* garlic, leak, onion *Cucurbits:* cucumber, melons, pumpkin, squash *Leafy vegetables:* celery, lettuce, spinach *Fruiting vegetables:* eggplant, pepper *Legumes:* lima bean, snap bean, southern pea, English pea, garden pea *Root and Tuber:* beet, carrot, parsley, radish, rutabaga, sweet potato *Other:* globe artichoke, okra, sugar beet	Apply as a hooded spray in row middles or as a wiper application in row middles. **DO NOT ALLOW HERBICIDE MIXTURE TO CONTACT ANY PART OF THE CROP INCLUDING THE ROOTS!** For crops that vine, applications must be made to row middles prior to vine development. Application must be made at least 14 days before harvest. May be applied as a POST-harvest application. Apply at least 30 days prior to planting any non-labeled crop. See label for use on additional crops.

FOLIAR CALCIUM SPRAYS

George Boyhan, Professor and Extension Vegetable Specialist

CROP	MATERIAL	AMOUNT OF FORMULATION	REMARKS
Asparagus	Stoller Calcium 5X	1-2 qt/A	Apply when crowns begin to grow. Repeat after each cutting.
	Sorba-Spray CaB	1-4 qt/A	Apply when flowers are in bud stage. Repeat every 2-3 weeks. Also contains 5% nitrogen and 1.5% Boron.
Beans	Stoller Calcium 5X	1-2 pt/A	Apply at 4-5 inch stage, at early bloom and at early pod set.
	Stoller Calcium 5S	16 oz/A	Apply before flower bud formation or use half rate every 7-10 days beginning at third trifoliate.
	Sorba-Spray CaB	1-2 qt/A	First application at bud to early bloom. Repeat in 2-3 weeks. Also contains 5% nitrogen and 1.5% Boron.
Broccoli	Ele-Max Clear Cal 12.1%	2 qt/A	Apply in 20 gallons water at head development. Repeat two to three times at 10-14 day intervals. Also contains 21% Cl.
	Stoller Calcium 5X	1-2 pt/A	Apply at 4-5 leaves and every 10-14 days.
	Stoller Calcium 5S	12 oz/A	Apply at 4-5 leaf stage and then every 7-14 days.
	Sorba-Spray CaB	1-4 qt/A	Make 1-3 applications at intervals of 2-3 weeks beginning when plants are 3-4 weeks old. Also contains 5% nitrogen and 1.5% Boron.
Cabbage	Ele-Max Clear Cal 12.1%	2 qt/A	Apply in 20 gallons water at head development. Repeat two to three times at 10-14 day intervals. Also contains 21% Cl.
	Stoller Calcium 5X	1-2 pt/A	Apply at 4-5 leaves and every 10-14 days.
	Stoller Calcium 5S	12 oz/A	Apply at 4-5 leaf stage and then every 7-14 days.
	Sorba-Spray CaB	1-4 qt/A	Make 1-3 applications at intervals of 2-3 weeks beginning when plants are 3-4 weeks old. Also contains 5% nitrogen and 1.5% Boron.
Cantaloupe	Ele-Max Clear Cal 12.1%	2 qt/A	Make two to three applications in 20 gallons of water beginning at first fruit set at seven day intervals. Also contains 21% Cl.
	Sorba-Spray CaB	1-2 qt/A	Make two or more applications at 2-3 week intervals starting just prior to bloom. Also contains 5% nitrogen and 1.5% Boron.
	Stoller CabY	1-2 qt/A	To correct physiological disorders begin 2-3 weeks after full bloom and continue at two week intervals. Also contains Boron.
Carrots	Ele-Max Clear Cal 12.1%	2 qt/A	Apply in 20 gallons water when crop is 4-6 inches tall. Repeat two to three times at 10-14 day intervals. Also contains 21% Cl.
	Stoller Calcium 5X	1 qt/A	Apply at enlarged root initiation and 2-3 weeks later.
	Sorba-Spray CaB	1-4 qt/A	Apply when plants are 3-4 weeks old. Repeat every 3-4 weeks. Also contains 5% nitrogen and 1.5% Boron.
Corn	Stoller Calcium 5S	16 oz/A	Apply at 2-6 leaf stage and half rate at 7-21 day intervals until end of tasseling.
	Stoller Calcium 5X	1 qt/A	Apply at 4-6 leaf stage.
	Sorba-Spray CaB	1-4 qt/A	As needed for nutrient stress. Also contains 5% nitrogen and 1.5% Boron.
Cucumbers	Ele-Max Clear Cal 12.1%	2 qt/A	Make two to three applications in 20 gallons of water beginning at first fruit set at seven day intervals. Also contains 21% Cl.
	Stoller Calcium 5X	1-2 pt/A	Apply at 4-8 inch stage, at early bloom and at start of fruiting.
	Stoller Calcium 5S	8 oz/A	Apply at flower bud initiation and then at 7-10 day intervals.

CROP	MATERIAL	AMOUNT OF FORMULATION	REMARKS
Eggplant	Stoller Calcium 5X	1-2 qt/A	Apply just prior to first bloom then 10 and 20 days later.
Leafy vegetables	Sorba-Spray CaB	1-4 qt/A	Make 1-3 applications at intervals of 2-3 weeks beginning when plants are 3-4 weeks old. Also contains 5% nitrogen and 1.5% Boron.
	Stoller Calcium 5S	12 oz/A	Apply at 4-5 leaf stage and then every 7-14 days.
Melons	Ele-Max Clear Cal 12.1%	2 qt/A	Make two to three applications in 20 gallons of water beginning at first fruit set at seven day intervals. Also contains 21% Cl.
	Stoller Calcium 5X	1-2 pt/A	Apply at 4-8 inch stage, at early bloom and at start of fruiting.
	Stoller Calcium 5S	8 oz/A	Apply at flower bud initiation and then at 7-10 day intervals.
	Sorba-Spray CaB	1-2 qt/A	Make two or more applications at 2-3 week intervals starting just prior to bloom. Also contains 5% nitrogen and 1.5% Boron.
	Stoller CabY	1-2 qt/A	To correct physiological disorders begin 2-3 weeks after full bloom and continue at two week intervals. Also contains Boron.
Onions	Ele-Max Calcium FL 4%	1-2 qt/A	Apply at 6-leaf stage and 10-14 days later in 3-20 gallons of water.
	Ele-Max Clear Cal 12.1%	2-4 qt/A	Apply in 20 gallons per acre at bulb swelling and repeat at 7-14 days intervals as needed. Also contains 21% Cl.
	Stoller Calcium 5S	12 oz/A	Apply two weeks after emergence and at 10-14 day intervals.
	Sorba-Spray CaB	1-4 qt/A	As needed for nutritional stress. Also contains 5% nitrogen and 1.5% Boron.
Peas	Ele-Max Calcium FL 4%	2 qt/A	Apply at 4-6 inch stage and 10-14 days later in 3-20 gallons of water.
	Stoller Calcium 5X	1-2 pt/A	Apply at 4-5 inch stage, at early bloom and at early pod set.
	Sorba-Spray CaB	1-2 qt/A	First application at bud to early bloom. Repeat in 2-3 weeks. Also contains 5% nitrogen and 1.5% Boron.
Peppers	Ele-Max Calcium FL 4% Ele-Max	2 qt/A	One to four applications from flowering up to one month before harvest in 50 gallons of water. Allow 7 days between applications.
	Clear Cal 12.1%	2 qt/A	Apply one to four applications in 50 gallons water beginning at flowering. Also contains 21% Cl.
	Stoller Calcium 5X	1-2 qt/A	Apply just prior to first bloom then 10 and 20 days later.
	Stoller Calcium 5S	8 oz/A	Begin at transplant then at 7-14 day intervals.
	Sorba-Spray CaB	1-4 qt/A	Make 1-3 applications at intervals of 3-4 weeks starting prior to bloom. Also contains 5% nitrogen and 1.5% Boron.
Potatoes	Ele-Max Calcium FL 4% Ele-Max	2 qt/A	Two to three applications commencing at tuber initiation in 20 gallons of water. Allow 10-14 days between applications.
	Clear Cal 12.1%	2-4 qt/A	Two to three applications commencing at tuber initiation in 20 gallons of water. Allow 10-14 days between applications. Also contains 21 % Cl.
	Stoller Calcium 5X	1 qt/A	Apply at first tuber set and then 2-3 weeks later.
	Stoller Calcium 5S	1 qt/A	Apply at tuber initiation and use half rate at 8-10 leaf stage and every 10-14 days.
	Sorba-Spray CaB	1-4 qt/A	Apply when plants are 4-12 inches high and repeat three weeks later. Also contains 5% nitrogen and 1.5% Boron.

CROP	MATERIAL	AMOUNT OF FORMULATION	REMARKS
Squash	Ele-Max Clear Cal 12.1%	2 qt/A	Make two to three applications in 20 gallons of water beginning at first fruit set at seven day intervals. Also contains 21% Cl.
	Stoller Calcium 5X	1-2 pt/A	Apply at 4-8 inch stage, at early bloom and at start of fruiting.
	Stoller Calcium 5S	8 oz/A	Apply at flower bud initiation and then at 7-10 day intervals.
	Sorba-Spray CaB	1-2 qt/A	Make two or more applications at 2-3 week intervals starting just prior to bloom. Also contains 5% nitrogen and 1.5% Boron.
Sweet Potatoes	Sorba-Spray CaB	1-4 qt/A	Apply when plants are 3-4 weeks old. Repeat every 3-4 weeks. Also contains 5% nitrogen and 1.5% Boron.
Tomatoes	Ele-Max Calcium FL 4%	2 qt/A	One to four applications from flowering up to one month before harvest in 50 gallons of water. Allow 7 days between applications.
	Ele-Max Clear Cal 12.1%	2 qt/A	Apply one to four applications in 50 gallons water beginning at flowering. Allow 7 days between applications. Also contains 21% Cl.
	Stoller Calcium 5X	1 qt/A	Apply at transplanting and 2-3 weeks after first bloom.
	Stoller Calcium 5S	8 oz/A	Apply at flower bud initiation and at 7-10 day intervals.
	Sorba-Spray CaB	1-4 qt/A	Make 1-3 applications at intervals of 3-4 weeks starting prior to bloom. For blossom end rot apply 2qt/A every 7-10 days. Also contains 5% nitrogen and 1.5% Boron.
	Stoller CabY	1-2 qt/A	To correct physiological disorders begin 2-3 weeks after full bloom and continue at two week intervals. Also contains Boron.
	Tracite Calcium 6%	1-2 qt/A	Apply every two weeks after first bloom.
Vegetables	Dyna Gold Calcium 8.25% (Solanceous, Brassica and Cucurbits)	1-2 qt/A	Apply in enough water for thorough coverage at regular intervals.
	Dyna Gold CB Mix 6.0% (flowering crops)	1-1½ qt/A	Apply in enough water for thorough coverage. Make 2 to 3 applications. Also contains 2% boron.
	Foli-Gro Link Calcium 6%	1-2 pt/A	Apply at appropriate crop stage in 20 gallons of water.
	Foli-Gro Calcium 6%	1-2 pt/A	Apply each week in normal spray program in 20 gallons of water.
	Metalosate Calcium 6%	1-2 pt/A	Apply during periods of rapid growth. May repeat two times.
	Pro Natural Calcium 5%	2-32 oz/A	Apply during periods of rapid growth. May repeat two times.
	Tracite Calcium 6%	1-2 pt/A	Apply in normal spray program at the low rate once per week. Increase to maximum rate during times when deficiency usually occurs.
Watermelons	Ele-Max Clear Cal 12.1%	2 qt/A	Make two to three applications in 20 gallons of water beginning at first fruit set at seven day intervals. Also contains 21% Cl.
	Stoller Calcium 5X	1-2 pt/A	Apply at 4-8 inch stage, at early bloom and at start of fruiting.
	Stoller Calcium 5S	8 oz/A	Apply at flower bud initiation and then at 7-14 day intervals.
	Sorba-Spray CaB	1-2 qt/A	Make two or more applications at 2-3 week intervals starting just prior to bloom. Also contains 5% nitrogen and 1.5% Boron.
	Stoller CabY	1-2 qt/A	To correct physiological disorders begin 2-3 weeks after full bloom and continue at two week intervals. Also contains Boron.

FOLIAR BORON SPRAYS

George Boyhan, Professor and Extension Vegetable Specialist

CROP	MATERIAL	AMOUNT OF FORMULATION	REMARKS
Asparagus	Tracite Liquid Boron 10%	1-2 qt/A	As needed for nutrient stress at two week intervals.
Beans and Peas	Foli-Gro Boron 10	½-1 pt/A	Apply pre-bloom and repeat in 14-21 days.
	Tracite Liquid Boron 10%	1-2 qt/A	As needed for nutrient stress at two week intervals.
Broccoli, Cabbage, Cauliflower	Tracite Liquid Boron 10%	2-4 qt/A	As needed for nutrient stress at two week intervals.
Carrots	Tracite Liquid Boron 10%	1-2 qt/A	As needed for nutrient stress at two week intervals.
Cucumbers	Tracite Liquid Boron 10%	1-2 qt/A	As needed for nutrient stress at two week intervals.
Melons	Foli-Gro Boron 10	1-3 pt/A	Apply pre-bloom and repeat in 14-21 days.
Onions	Tracite Liquid Boron 10%	1-2 qt/A	As needed for nutrient stress at two week intervals.
	Foli-Gro Boron 10	1-2 qt/A	Apply three weeks after establishment and then three weeks later.
Potatoes	Tracite Liquid Boron 10%	1-2 qt/A	As needed for nutrient stress at two week intervals.
Peppers	Tracite Liquid Boron 10%	1-2 qt/A	As needed for nutrient stress at two week intervals.
Tomatoes	Tracite Liquid Boron 10%	1-2 qt/A	As needed for nutrient stress at two week intervals.
Vegetables	Metalosate Boron 5%	8-16 oz/A	Apply during periods of rapid growth or nutrient stress. May be repeated 2-3 times during the season.

Note: Never apply more than two pounds of elemental Boron to any crop during the season.

HOME ORCHARD PEST MANAGEMENT GUIDE PREFACE

Elizabeth Little, Extension Homeowner IPM Specialist

Home Orchard Pest Management Guides suggest cultural and chemical control practices that offer a reasonable degree of protection from important fruit diseases and insect pests. Home orchardists should note that producing quality edible fruit is challenging, and that commercial quality, blemish-free fruit is often an unrealistic expectation. During the growing season, weekly monitoring of the crop and pests which may be present is important. Insecticides work best when pest levels are low. Timely application of controls helps minimize damage to fruit. In order to be effective, fungicides need to be applied before appearance of symptoms and/ or just prior to and during weather conditions favorable for disease development. In most cases these are cool to mild periods with moderate to high amounts of rainfall. Pruning and removal of diseased and/or dead twigs and branches, raking and removal of leaves and debris, periodically mowing around vines, trees or bushes, and disposing of rotten and/or diseased fruit greatly improves disease and insect control. Collectively these practices are referred to as sanitation. Sanitation, in combination with choosing disease resistant cultivars and the use of chemicals as needed, is usually necessary for acceptable control of fruit diseases and insects. A few fruits can be grown successfully with good sanitation alone.

Pre-mixed home fruit or orchard spray products containing pesticides for both disease and insect control are commonly available. Home orchard pesticides are often less effective than their commercial counterparts. Using the highest label rate, and spraying more often when the weather is wet, will generally improve disease and insect control. For the sake of brevity not all brand names of pesticides are listed. Many may be found by their generic names in the Homeowner Fungicide Guide.

Always consult the label when purchasing or using pesticides. Be sure the label states the material(s) are labeled for use on your crop, whether it be apple, peach, pear, etc. Carefully follow all precautionary statements. They serve to protect you, the environment and those who consume your crop. Label restrictions are legally binding. General considerations for home orchard pesticide applicators are as follows:

- Wear goggles or other eye protection to shield yourself from spray drift;

- Wear long sleeves, long trousers and shoes;

- Remove and launder clothing worn while applying pesticides, launder these clothes separately from family laundry before reusing them;

- Always check for and follow the pre-harvest interval(s) listed on the pesticide container(s), and use the longest one, often they are listed in days or hours in (parenthesis);

- Many pesticides, especially insecticides, are toxic to honey bees as well as other pollinators, do not spray during bloom unless the product label specifically recommends bloom sprays, and do not apply insecticides if bees are foraging on orchard weeds;

- Assume pesticides to be toxic to fish and other non-target organisms, do not apply to water or where run off can occur;

- Store pesticides in the original container only.

HOME ORCHARD INSECT PEST MANAGEMENT GUIDE

Dan Horton, John All, and Dean Kemp, Entomology

Home orchardists face the same insect and mite pests as their commercial counterparts. Unfortunately, home orchard pest pressures are often as high, or higher, than is experienced in commercial orchards. Edge effect, a biological phenomenon wherein the abundance of organisms, in this case pests, is higher where two different habitat types meet. Edge effect is often evident in commercial orchards, where many pest species are much more common on the outside rows. In home orchards, all the trees, bushes or vines fall within the "border rows," so pest pressure is often quite high.

Pesticide options for managing home orchard pests are modest. While there are many different trade named products on the market, there are relatively few active ingredients. The effectiveness of, and the range of pests controlled by, any trade name product is determined by its active ingredient(s) and amount of active ingredient(s) applied.

Product labels, which should be present on all pesticide containers, indicate what crops that particular trade name product may be used on. Home garden pesticide labels vary, but they will indicate where that particular product may be used. Generic crop groupings, such as trees, shrubs, lawns, vegetables or fruit, are often seen. Federal law clearly restricts use of any pesticides to the crops, or sites, listed on the package's label. Home garden pesticides for use on fruits must specifically list fruits, or cite individual fruits such as apples, pears or peaches. These federal restrictions are based on rigorous food, applicator and environmental safety considerations, and they are legally binding.

Active ingredients vary in their effectiveness, depending on the pest. When comparing products containing the same active ingredients, product effectiveness is heavily influenced by how much active ingredient is applied. Dose, the amount of product applied, is determined by two factors, the amount applied (tablespoons, fluid ounces or ounces), and by the active ingredient's concentration. The amount of product applied is limited by the product label. Higher dosages normally provide better control. Remember, by following the product label you are assured of using safe amounts. Sometimes products containing the same active ingredients will have varying amounts of active ingredient. To get the best control, it is important to check the label carefully, and buy the product which has the highest concentration of the active ingredient you select.

Fruit Insect & Mite Pest Overview

Fruit-attacking Insect Pests:
- Scale Insects
- Catfacing Insects
- Fruit-feeding caterpillars
- Fruit-feeding beetles

Tree, Bush & Vine–Attacking Insect Pests:
- Scale
- Borers (caterpillars such as grape root borer, dogwood borer, peachtree borer, lesser peachtree borer)
  Flatheaded borers of apple, pear, blueberries
- Roundheaded borers of blackberry & raspberry
- European red mite & Two spotted spider mite

HOME ORCHARD APPLE DISEASE SPRAY GUIDE

Elizabeth Little, Extension IPM Homeowner Specialist

TIME OF APPLICATION	TO CONTROL	MATERIAL	AMT/GAL	REENTRY INTERVAL	PREHARVEST INTERVAL	REMARKS
Dormant	Black rot, bitter rot and white (Bot) rot survive the winter on dead wood in the tree and on the ground. Spores disseminated to apple buds in December, January, and February may infect at silver tip. Carefully prune to remove all dead wood from the tree. Disinfect pruners with 10% bleach or rubbing alcohol after each cut. Complete sanitation by removing dead wood from the ground. To control bitter rot, it is also necessary to remove all dried fruit (last year's crop) from trees and the ground. After you have done this for 2 years, you may not need the pre-pink, pink, bloom and petal fall captan sprays. Consult your county Extension agent for advice on deleting these preventive sprays if your fruit has very little disease and your sanitation is good. Scab, Brooks spot, Alternaria leaf blotch, and Necrotic leafblotch of `Goldens' overwinter on dead leaves on the ground. Raking and composting or destroying these leaves will control or greatly aid in control of these diseases. Do this as soon after leaf fall as possible.					
Silver tip (when swollen buds first break and develop a silver color)	Black rot	Captan 50WP Thiophanate methyl	3 1/3 Tbs. See label	4 days	day of harvest	Black rot infection occurs around this time. A very important spray for this disease. Good sanitation is also important for control.
Delayed Dormant	Leaf Spot	Lime Sulfur Spray (Hi-Yield)	9.5-13 oz.			Use on Delicious Apples may result in injury. No time limitation.
	Scab	Lime Sulfur Spray (Hi-Yield)	2-2.5 oz.	see label		Use on Delicious Apples may result in injury. No time limitation.
		Bordeaux	8-9 tbsp	see label		
		Sulfur (Ferti-lome)	1 tbsp	see label		Plant resistant varieties for best control.
		Thiophanate methyl	see label	see label		
		Captan	2 tbsp	see label		
Between Silver tip and Green tip	Fire blight	copper hydroxide (Hi-Yield Copper; others)	2 2/3 - 5 1/3 tsp	1 day	pre-green tip only	Kills bacteria which ooze from over wintering cankers. Crop injury may occur if applied later than ½ inch green tip. Important spray after a bad fire blight year.
		Streptomycin sulfate (Fertilome)	1 tbsp (makes 2.5 gal)			Make application as a full cover spray.
Prepink (when center buds first show pink)	Black rot Brooks spot scab	Captan 50WP Thiophanate methyl	2 Tbs. See label	4 days	day of harvest	
	Cedar apple rust	Immunox	½ oz.	1 day	14 days	Only use Immunox when cedar apple rust is an annual problem.
	Scab Powdery Mildew	Lime Sulfur Spray (Hi-Yield), Copper Sulfate, Wettable Sulfur, Triadimefon - powdery mildew only	2-2.5 oz. 3.2 oz. see label 1 tbsp.	1 day see label 1 day see label		Use on Delicious Apples may result in injury. No time limitation.
Pink	black rot Brooks spot scab	captan 50 WP, Thiophanate methyl	2 Tbs.	4 days	day of harvest	Fire blight develops on tender shoots and blooms when temperatures are between 65 and 80°F and it is humid and/or raining. If these conditions occur or are forecast, apply streptomycin **within 24 hours before rain.** Re-spray before the next rain if bee activity has occurred.
	cedar apple rust	Immunox	½ oz.	1 day	14 days	
	fire blight	streptomycin (Fertilome Fire Blight Spray)	1 tbsp (makes 2.5 gal)	12 hrs	50 days	Use on Delicious Apples may result in injury. No time limitation.
	Scab Powdery Mildew	Lime Sulfur Spray (Hi-Yield), Copper Sulfate, Wettable sulfur, Triadimefon - powdery mildew	2-2.5 oz. 3.2 oz. See labels			

TIME OF APPLICATION	TO CONTROL	MATERIAL	AMT/GAL	REENTRY INTERVAL	PREHARVEST INTERVAL	REMARKS
Bloom	black rot scab	captan 50WP, Thiophanate methyl	2 Tbs. See label	4 days	day of harvest	Conditions conducive to fire blight are listed above. Always spray streptomycin under these conditions. Spray within 24 hours before rain. Re-spray before the next rain if bee activity has occurred or every 3-4 days during the bloom period.
	Fire blight	streptomycin (bactericide-Fertilome Fire blight Spray)	1 tbsp (makes 2.5 gal)	12 hrs	50 days	
	cedar apple rust	Immunox	½ oz.	1 day	14 days	Prune out all fire blight affected twigs 12 inches below the disease-killed tissue. Dip pruners in 10% chlorine bleach or rubbing alcohol and wipe between cuts. Oil pruners after use.
			see label	1 day	7 days	
						Do not use Immunox more than ten times per season.
			NO INSECTICIDE DURING BLOOM			
Petal fall (when most petals are off) through Covers 1, 2, and 3 (3 sprays after petal fall); spray every 7-10 days	black rot scab	captan 50WP Thiophanate methyl	2 Tbs. See label	4 days	day of harvest	Spray more frequently, when weather is wet.
	cedar apple rust	Immunox	½ oz.	1 day	14 days	Only use Immunox when cedar apple rust is an annual problem. Several available home orchard sprays may be used for control of both diseases and insect pests.
Summer cover sprays (every 14 days until 6 weeks before harvest)	bitter rot sooty blotch fly speck	Captan 50WP Thiophanate methyl	2 Tbs. See label	4 days	day of harvest	Spray promptly at first sign of bitter rot. This disease spreads rapidly if left unchecked. Several available home orchard sprays may be used for control of both disease and insect pests.
Six weeks, 4 weeks and 2 weeks before harvest	bitter rot white rot sooty blotch fly speck	Captan 50WP or sulfur	2 Tbs. / see label	4 days / 1 day	day of harvest / day of harvest	Important disease control sprays, particularly for bitter rot and white rot. Do not use sulfur when temperatures are expected above 90 degrees. Some varieties such MacIntosh, Red Delicious, Staymen, Baldwin, King, Golden Delicious and Jonathan are sensitive to sulfur.

HOME ORCHARD BLUEBERRY DISEASE SPRAY GUIDE

Elizabeth Little, Extension Homeowner IPM Specialist

TIME OF APPLICATION	TO CONTROL	MATERIAL	AMT/GAL	REENTRY INTERVAL	PREHARVEST INTERVAL	REMARKS
Dormant	Phomopsis twig blight	Lime sulfur (Hi-Yield Lime Sulfur Spray)	see label			Apply when bud begins to swell. Avoid excessive nitrogen fertilization. Avoid any drought stress - irrigate plants adequately. Most effective when applied before buds break dormancy.
Before bud break						

Sanitation, in the form of removing dead berries and debris under the bushes during the winter will reduce disease pressure from Botrytis blight and mummy berry. Compost or destroy debris. Replace with new mulch. Do not place mulch right up against the trunk of the plant. With good sanitation, and little or no history of Botrytis blight and mummy berry, there should be no need for green tip and pre-bloom sprays. If these diseases have been damaging in the past, spray every 7-10 days thru bloom.

| Green tip, from the first green tissue after bud break to first bloom, spray every 7-10 days | Botrytis blight | Captan 50WP | 2.5 Tbs. | 4 days | day of harvest | |

The fungi causing Botrytis blight and mummy berry overwinter in dead berries and debris under the bushes. Remove dead berries, debris, and mulch during the winter and compost or destroy it. Replace with new mulch. Do not place mulch right up against the trunk of the plant. With good sanitation and little or no history of Botrytis blight and mummy berry, there should be no need for green tip and pre-bloom sprays. If these diseases have been damaging in the past, spray every 7-10 days thru bloom.

| 10-20% bloom and full bloom | Botrytis blight, Mummy berry, Anthracnose, & various Leaf spots | Captan 50WP | 2.5 Tbs. | 4 days | day of harvest | DO NOT APPLY INSECTICIDES DURING BLOOM Botrytis causes flower and twig blight. Good air circulation around fruit clusters will help prevent Anthracnose. For leaf spots, apply post bloom to August/Sept at 7 to 10 day intervals. SANITATION is key for mgmt of these diseases (esp. mummy berry). |

HOME ORCHARD BRAMBLE SPRAY GUIDE

Elizabeth Little, Extension Homeowner IPM Specialist

Blackberries can often be grown successfully without pesticides, if you practice good sanitation, and have no wild blackberries nearby. Several important fungal and insect pests of blackberry canes overwinter on old canes that were infected the previous season. Cut and remove old canes to the ground after harvest. Do not cut with a rotary mower as pieces will become too small to remove. Cut old fruiting canes from fall-fruiting raspberry cultivars such as 'Heritage' in early spring before new shoots begin to develop. This method produces a single fall crop. Strawberry weevil is not a problem on fall bearing raspberry cultivars such as 'Heritage'. A week to 10 days after cutting, plants should to be fertilized and irrigated to force new growth for next year's crop. Plants infected with orange rust, which can be detected from green tip to early cane growth must be promptly dug up and removed or destroyed. Copper fungicides are toxic to humans and other life forms. Phytotoxicity is a problem with both copper and sulfur products. In addition, copper is a heavy metal which can accumulate in the soil. Copper and sulfur have limited effectiveness and non-chemical methods of disease management should be used before turning to the use of fungicides.

TIME OF APPLICATION	TO CONTROL	MATERIAL	AMT/GAL	REENTRY INTERVAL	PREHARVEST INTERVAL		REMARKS
Delayed dormant (Blackberries only)	Leaf and cane spot	copper hydroxide (Hi-Yield Copper Fungicide)	5 1/3 tsp	1-2 days (see label)	None listed		Apply as delayed dormant spray after training in the spring (Make fall application after harvest.
	Anthracnose	liquid lime sulfur (Polysul, Lilly Miller Dormant Spray, or Bonide Lime Spray)	see label (6 to 12 gal/100gal water)	48 hrs	Dormant/ delayed dormant only		Apply lime-sulfur at delayed dormant, but prior to 3/4-inch shoot stage to avoid leaf burn.
Green tip	Anthracnose, Leaf and cane spot	copper (Dragon Copper Fungicide, Bonide Liquid Copper)	see label	Until dry	None listed		See remarks above this guide. Avoid overhead watering Labeled copper products available under several different brand names.

Orange rust attacks all brambles except for red raspberries. The fungus infects in a systemic fashion, once plants are infected they remain so for life. Infected plants are stunted and produce very little fruit. They can be identified in the early spring. Shortly after leafing out, the lower surface of infected leaves develops orange pustules that gives the disease its name. The timely removal of infected plants is most important to control this disease. Inspect plants in early spring and try to identify the pustules before the orange spores are produced. Once spores are released, they cause new infections that may not show up until the following spring. Dig up, remove and dispose of or destroy these plants. Nearby wild brambles should also be destroyed.

TIME OF APPLICATION	TO CONTROL	MATERIAL	AMT/GAL	REENTRY INTERVAL	PREHARVEST INTERVAL		REMARKS
When buds appear and new canes are 8-12" high	Anthracnose, Leaf and cane spot	copper (Dragon Copper Fungicide, Bonide Liquid Copper) or	see label	Until dry	None listed		
		Liquid lime sulfur (Hi-Yield Lime Sulfur Spray)	4 tsp		None listed		Apply before blossoms have opened.
Pre-bloom	Anthracnose, Leaf and cane spot	copper (Dragon Copper Fungicide, Bonide Liquid Copper)	see label	Until dry	None listed		Repeat at 10-14 day intervals as necessary
Bloom	Botrytis Flower Blight						Apply copper at the start of flowering and continue every 7 to 10 days until harvest.
	Powdery Mildew	copper (Bonide Liq. Copper)	0.5 to 2.0 fl. oz	see label	None listed		
	Botrytis Fruit Rot						DO NOT SPRAY INSECTICIDE DURING BLOOM.

TIME OF APPLICATION	TO CONTROL	MATERIAL	AMT/GAL	REENTRY INTERVAL	PREHARVEST INTERVAL	REMARKS
Rosette or double blossom (Cercosporella rubi) occurs on both blackberries and raspberries, but is most damaging to blackberries. Symptoms are unusual and markedly change the appearance of the plant. In the spring, infected buds from the previous year produce numerous leafy sprouts. This proliferation of shoots is referred to as a witch's broom. Several of these witch's brooms may occur on one cane. As flower buds open, petals are pinkish in color, wrinkled and twisted. Berries do not develop from infected blossoms, uninfected parts of the same plant produce smaller, poorer quality fruit. Sanitation to prevent this disease is similar to that of orange rust. Wild brambles should be removed from the immediate area. They can serve as sources of inoculum. Remove and destroy old fruited canes after harvest. Infected blossom clusters should be removed before they open. Where this disease is especially severe on trailing blackberries, cut off plants at the ground after fruiting. This extreme practice only works well where the growing season is long. For other brambles, cut all canes back to 12 inches immediately after harvest. Fertilize and irrigate plants to force new growth before winter.						
After old canes have been removed	Anthracnose, leaf and cane spot	copper (Dragon Copper Fungicide, Bonide Liquid Copper)	see label	Until dry	none listed	See introductory section. Labeled copper products available under several different brand names.
	Orange rust	*				Avoid overhead watering.

*Carbamate WDG is no longer registered by the U.S. Environmental Protection Agency for blackberries or raspberries. There are no other labeled chemicals available to control orange rust. If any become available, we will notify your county agent.

HOME ORCHARD BUNCH GRAPE DISEASE SPRAY GUIDE

Elizabeth Little, Extension Homeowner IPM Specialist
Dan L. Horton, Extension Entomologist

TIME OF APPLICATION	TO CONTROL	MATERIALS	AMT/GAL	REENTRY INTERVAL	PREHARVEST INTERVAL	REMARKS
Dormant season sanitation helps reduce disease pressure. Fungal rot organism of grapes overwinter on old vines and dried fruit on the vines and ground. Vines should be pruned back to the main stem each winter, leaving only 1 vine of the previous year's growth for each wire. Fruit and leaves on the ground should be raked and composted or destroyed.						
Dormant - mid-winter	Anthracnose	liquid lime sulfur	see label	see label	see label	Do not apply lime sulfur and superior oil within 30 days of each other. Objective of lime sulfur spray at this time is to reduce fungal inoculum on canes.
	Powdery Mildew	Hi-Yield Improved Lime Sulfur Spray	2.5-6.5 fl. oz.			
Pre-bloom beginning with 1-2 inches green, apply every 7 days until bloom	Black rot Powdery mildew, downy mildew, anthracnose	mancozeb or Immunox	see label 2 oz.	1 day 1 day	see label 14 days	Use mancozeb if downy mildew is a problem Use Immunox if anthracnose is a problem. Do not make more than 6 applications of Immunox (@ 2 oz./gal) per season.
Bloom - 10% bloom and full bloom	Black rot, Powdery mildew	Captan 50WP or mancozeb or Immunox	2 Tbs see label 2 oz.	4 days 1 day 1 day	day of harvest see label 14 days	DO NOT APPLY INSECTICIDE DURING BLOOM. Do not apply mancozeb within 66 days of harvest.
DO NOT APPLY INSECTICIDES OF ANY KIND DURING BLOOM, OR INJURY TO BEES AND OTHER POLLINATORS MAY OCCUR.						
Cap fall and 1st Cover (10 days after cap fall)	Black rot, powdery mildew	Captan 50WP or Immunox	2 Tbs 2 oz.	4 days 1 day	day of harvest 14 days	
	downy mildew	as needed copper hydroxide (Hi-Yield Copper Fungicide and others)	see label	1 day	see label	Foliage injury may occur on copper sensitive varieties such as Concord, Delaware, Niagara and Rosettes. Test for sensitivity.
Summer cover sprays every 14 days until 14 days before harvest	black rot powdery mildew	Captan 50WP or Immunox	2 Tbs 2 oz.	4 days 1 day	day of harvest 14 days	Do not make more than 6 applications of Immunox (@ 2 oz./gal) per season.
Preharvest (7 days before harvest)	Black rot	Captan 50WP	2 Tbs	4 days	day of harvest	

HOME ORCHARD MUSCADINE GRAPE DISEASE SPRAY GUIDE

Elizabeth Little, Extension Homeowner IPM Specialist

Muscadine grapes may yield satisfactorily without the aid of pesticides. It is advisable to watch and treat as-needed for angular leaf spot and for insect pests. Angular leaf spot is most damaging in July or early August. Uncontrolled angular leaf spot often can result in almost complete defoliation which terminates further fruit development. When wet weather favors disease cover sprays from bloom to harvest will sometimes be needed to prevent severe losses from ripe rot, Macrophoma rot and bitter rot. Dormant season sanitation will reduce disease pressure. Most diseases overwinter on dead leaves and fruit on the vine and the ground. Removing this material usually will benefit or give sufficient disease control.

TIME OF APPLICATION	TO CONTROL	CHEMICAL	AMT/GAL	REENTRY INTERVAL	PREHARVEST INTERVAL	REMARKS
DORMANT						
Dormant season sanitation helps reduce disease pressure. Fungal rot organism of grapes overwinter on old vines and dried fruit on the vines and ground. Vines should be pruned back to the main stem each winter, leaving only 1 vine of the previous year's growth for each wire. Fruit and leaves on the ground should be raked and composted or destroyed.						
PRE-BLOOM						
Every 14 days from Bud Break until Bloom	Black Rot Bitter Rot Angular leaf spot Powdery mildew	mancozeb or	2 Tbs	1 day	4 days	BLACK ROT susceptible varieties should be sprayed with fungicide every 14 days from the start of new growth until after bloom. This disease develops on the fruit during and just after bloom. Where ripe rot is a problem, use Captan 50WP.
		captan 50WP or	3 Tbs	4 days	day of harvest	
		Immunox (myclobutanil) or	2 oz	1 day	14 days	
		ferbam or	see label	see label	7 days	Do not make more than 6 applications of Immunox (@ 2 oz./gal) per season.
		Copper Hydroxide (Hi-Yield)	1 3/4 tsp	until dry	not listed	**DO NOT SPRAY INSECTICIDE DURING BLOOM.**
Bloom	Black Rot Bitter Rot Angular leaf spot Powdery mildew	mancozeb or	2 Tbs	1 day	4 days	BLACK ROT susceptible varieties should be sprayed with fungicide every 14 days from the start of new growth until after bloom. This disease develops on the fruit during and just after bloom. Where ripe rot is a problem, use Captan 50WP.
		captan 50WP or	3 Tbs	4 days	day of harvest	
		Immunox (myclobutanil) or	2 oz	1 day	14 days	
		ferbam	see label	see label	7 days	Do not make more than 6 applications of Immunox (@ 2 oz./gal) per season.
DO NOT APPLY INSECTICIDES OF ANY SORT DURING BLOOM OR INJURY TO BEES AND OTHER POLLINATORS MAY OCCUR.						
COVER SPRAYS						
Cap fall, First Cover and every 14 days from second cover until 6 to 8 weeks before harvest	Black rot, ripe rot Macrophoma rot	Captan 50WP or	3 tbs	4 days	0 days	Captan may cause mild phytotoxicity to fruit if applied when conditions are cool and wet.
		Immunox	2 oz	1 day	14 days	
PREHARVEST SPRAYS						
Every 10 to 14 days during the last 6-8 weeks before harvest (Start July 1 on the Coastal Plain and July 10-14 in Middle Georgia)	Bitter Rot Macrophoma Rot Ripe Rot Angular Leaf spot	Captan 50WP or	3 Tbs	4 days	day of harvest	Captan may be applied up to day of harvest.
		fruit tree spray	see label	see label	see label	Most home fruit sprays require a 14 day preharvest interval for grapes. Check the individual product label.

HOME ORCHARD PEACH, NECTARINE AND PLUM DISEASE SPRAY GUIDE

Elizabeth Little, Extension Homeowner IPM Specialist

TIME OF APPLICATION	TO CONTROL	MATERIAL	AMT/GAL	REENTRY INTERVAL	PREHARVEST INTERVAL	REMARKS
Dormant sprays - Leaf drop until early bud swell	Bacterial spot, Leaf curl	copper hydroxide (Hi-Yield Copper Fungicide, Polysul Summer and Dormant Spray)	2 2/3 tsp	Until dry	21 days	Bacterial spot - chemical control is difficult - dormant sprays - are somewhat effective against fall infections. Apply copper hydroxide fungicide when leaves just begin to shed. Do not apply copper hydroxide with oil. Leaf curl - once symptoms become visible, control is impossible.
	Leaf curl Shot hole Scab	Ortho Garden Disease Control (Daconil 2787) or Bordeaux mixture or Lime Sulfur Spray (Hi-Yield &others) or Copper Hydroxide (Hi-Yield & others)	see label 3/4 Tbs 12.5 - 15 gal 2 2/3 - 5 1/3 tsp	see label 2 days see label Until dry	Do not apply after petal fall Dormant spray only Dormant spray only Apply at leaf fall	Preventative leaf curl sprays at this time are for cooler areas of the state where leaf curl occurs (primarily upper piedmont and mountains). **Liquid lime sulfur can be combined with one of the oil sprays listed below. Ortho Daconil 2787 and copper hydroxide cannot.** If leaf curl has been severe, a fungicide application should also be made after leaf drop in the fall. **Do not apply oil or oil plus fungicide after buds break.**
	Bacterial spot	copper hydroxide (Hi-Yield & others)	2 2/3 tsp	2 days	21 days	Cooper rate reductions are tied to crop development, rates must be reduced as the season progresses. Note rates at various stages.
Pink to 5% bloom	Brown Rot Shot Hole Scab Jacket rot	copper hydroxide (Hi-Yield & others) or Lime Sulfur or Captan	2 2/3 - 4 tsp 4 tsp 2 tsp	until dry see label	see label see label	Full cover spray at pink bud. apply 3 to 5 times weekly before harvest repeat at 7 to 10 day intervals as needed to maintain cover
Bloom	Blossom blight (early season phase of brown rot - blossoms turn brown and die) Scab	Ortho Daconil 2787 or captan 50WP or liquid lime sulfur (Hi-Yield) or Immunox	3/4 tsp 2 Tbs see label 1/2 oz	2 days 4 days see label 1 day	Do not apply after shuck split day of harvest Do not apply after petal fall day of harvest	This a very important spray for suppression of pre-harvest brown rot. Make this preventative application every year. Do not make more than 6 applications of Immunox (@ 2 oz./gal) per season.

DO NOT USE INSECTICIDE DURING BLOOM.

TIME OF APPLICATION	TO CONTROL	MATERIAL	AMT/GAL	REENTRY INTERVAL	PREHARVEST INTERVAL	REMARKS
Petal fall (when most of the petals have fallen) through Cover Sprays 1, 2 and 3 apply every 7 to 10 days	Bacterial spot	copper hydroxide (Hi-Yield Cooper Fungicide)	see label	2 days	21 days	Use caution if coppers are used post-bloom. The recommended rate reductions lessen, but do not eliminate phytotoxicity.
	Brown rot Scab	Ortho Daconil 2787	3/4 tsp	2 days	shuck split only	Avoid use of sulfur when temperatures are above 90/F.
		or captan 50WP	2 Tbs	4 days	day of harvest	
		or sulfur	see label	1 day	day of harvest	
		or Immunox	½ oz	1 day	day of harvest	
Summer cover sprays (every 14-21 days until mid-June)	Scab Brown rot	Captan 50WP	2 Tbs	4 days	day of harvest	Do not use Ortho Home Orchard Spray **within 21 days of harvest.**
		or sulfur	see label	1 day	day of harvest	
		or Immunox	½ oz	1 day	day of harvest	
	Powdery Mildew	Lime Sulfur Spray (Hi-Yield)	0.5 fl. oz.			
Pre-harvest Disease Spray - 2 weeks and 1 week before harvest for each variety	Brown rot	Captan 50WP	2 Tbs	4 days	day of harvest	Avoid use of sulfur when temperatures are above 90/F.
		or sulfur	see label	1 day	day of harvest	
		or Lime Sulfur Spray (Hi-Yield)	4 tsps.			Apply 3 to 5 times at weekly intervals before harvest.

HOME ORCHARD PEAR DISEASE SPRAY GUIDE

Elizabeth Little, Extension Homeowner IPM Specialist

TIME OF APPLICATION	TO CONTROL	MATERIAL	AMT/GAL	REENTRY INTERVAL	PREHARVEST INTERVAL	REMARKS
Dormant - before buds begin to swell	fire blight	Bordeaux mixture	8 Tbs. copper sulfate plus 8 Tbs. hydrated lime	see label	dormant spray only	**DO NOT APPLY AFTER GREEN IS SHOWING.** Several leaf spot fungi overwinter on cankers on diseased or dead twigs and on leaves on the ground. Pruning and removing diseased wood and raking, composting or destroying these leaves each fall will aid in disease control.
Green cluster bud	Scab	or if needed Ortho Home Orchard Spray or Hi-Yield Improved Lime Sulfur Spray	5 Tbs 4-6 tsp	12 hrs	7 days	If **scab has been a problem use Ortho Home Orchard Spray** (same as white bud) instead of malathion. Scab spores are at their highest number just after this spray.
White bud (Popcorn)	fire blight	streptomycin sulfate or copper hydroxide (Hi-Yield Copper Fungicide and others)	100 parts per million - see table below see label	12 hrs 1 day	30 days see label	Apply streptomycin just before the earliest blooms open, and every 3-4 days thru petal fall for fireblight. Fire blight starts only when the trees are blooming, temperatures are between 65 and 80°F, and it is very humid or raining. If these conditions occur, streptomycin needs to be applied within 24 hours before the rain. Do not re-apply until there has been a period of bee activity and another rain occurs. Prune out all fire blight affected twigs 12 inches below the disease-killed tissue. Dip pruners in 10% chlorine bleach or rubbing alcohol between cuts. Oil pruners after use.
Bloom - every 5 days	Fire blight	streptomycin sulfate (Fertilome Fire blight) or copper hydroxide (Hi-Yield Copper Fungicide and others)	100 parts per million - see table below. see label	12 hrs 1 day	30 days see label	DO NOT APPLY INSECTICIDE **DURING BLOOM.** Apply streptomycin every 5-7 days when weather is favorable for fire blight (see above).
Petal fall - when most of the petals are off and again 10-14 days after petal fall	Scab fungal leaf spots	Ortho Home Orchard Spray	5 Tbs.	12 hrs	7 days	Avoid use of sulfur when temperatures are above 90/F. D'Anjou pears are sensitive to sulfur.
When first leaves have completely unfolded	Scab bitter rot fungal leaf spots	Ortho Home Orchard Spray	5 Tbs.	12 hrs	7 days	Ortho Home Orchard Spray contains captan (a fungicide) and malathion and methoxychlor (insecticides).
Preharvest 28 days and 14 days pre-harvest	Scab Bitter rot	Ortho Home Orchard Spray	5 Tbs	12 hrs	7 days	

ANTIBIOTIC FORMULATIONS FOR A 100 PPM SOLUTION

MATERIAL	TSP./GAL.	OZS./100 GALS.
Agrimycin 17, 21.3% streptomycin sulfate	3/4 tsp.	8 ozs.
Agristrep, 21.2% streptomycin sulfate	3/4 tsp.	8 ozs.
Ortho Streptomycin, 21% streptomycin sulfate	3/4 tsp.	8 ozs.

HOMEOWNER STRAWBERRY DISEASE CONTROL

Elizabeth Little, Extension Homeowner IPM Specialist

TIME OF APPLICATION	TO CONTROL	MATERIAL	AMT/GAL	REENTRY INTERVAL	PREHARVEST INTERVAL	REMARKS
Dormant season sanitation will reduce disease pressure most years. Strawberry leaf spots and Botrytis blight overwinter on old leaves and debris on the bed. Clipping old leaves, raking, and composting or destroying greatly aids in disease control.						
New growth, begin as soon as new growth starts, and every 10-14 days until just before bloom.	Leaf spots Anthracnose Botrytis blight (Gray mold)	Captan 50WP	2 Tbs	1 day	day of harvest	During periods of frequent rainfall, sprays at 7-10 day intervals may be necessary. Do not use more than 48 lbs of Captan per acre per crop.
10% bloom	Leaf spots, Botrytis blight and other fruit rots	Captan 50WP	2 Tbs	1 day	day of harvest	DO NOT APPLY INSECTICIDES DURING BLOOM. Critical time for Botrytis (Gray mold) control begins here.
Full bloom	Leaf spots, Botrytis blight and other fruit rots	Captan 50WP	2 Tbs	1 day	day of harvest	DO NOT APPLY INSECTICIDES DURING BLOOM.
Every 10-14 days from bloom until harvest.	Leaf spots, Botrytis blight and other fruit rots	Captan 50WP	2 Tbs	1 day	day of harvest	Under severe gray mold conditions, apply immediately after each picking through harvest. During periods of frequent rainfall, sprays at 7-10 day intervals or less may be necessary.

HOME FRUIT INSECTICIDE EFFECTIVENESS CHART

Dan Horton, John All, and Dean Kemp, Entomology

This list is not comprehensive. It offers pest-specific performance ratings which have been derived from in-orchard trials and observations in commercial fruit.

Insecticidal Active Ingredient	Product Name	Bugs/Mite Ratings ? = unknown, 0 = no control, 1 = poor, 2 = fair, 3 = good, 4 = excellent							
		Internal Fruit-Feeding Caterpillars (codling moth/ oriental fruit moth, etc.)	Internal Fruit-Feeding Beetles (plum curculio/ strawberry weevil, etc.))	Plant bug/ Stink bug	Leaf feeding Cater-pillars	Leaf feeding Beetles	Mites	Scales	Borers
PYRETHROIDS									
esfenvalerate	Ortho Bug-B-Gon MAX Garden & Landscape Insect Killer	4	3	3	4	3	0	0	3
esfenvalerate	Ortho Bug-B-Gon Multi-Purpose Insect Killer Ready-To-Use	4	3	3	4	3	0	0	3
gamma- cy-halothrin	Spectracide Triazicide Once & Done! Insect Killer 2 Conc. For Lawn	3	3	3	4	3	0	0	3
bifenthrin	Ortho Bug-B-Gon MAX Lawn & Garden Insect Killer 1	4	3	3	4	3	2	0	4
permethrin	Bayer Advanced Complete Insect Dust for Gardens	3	2	3	4	3	0	0	3
permethrin	Bonide Borer-Miner Killer	3	2	3	4	3	0	0	3
permethrin	Bonide Eight Vegetable, Fruit & Flower	3	2	3	4	3	0	0	3
permethrin	Green Light Borer Killer	3	2	3	4	3	0	0	3
permethrin	Green Light Conquest Insecticide Concentrate	3	2	3	4	3	0	0	3
permethrin	Ortho Ant-B-Gon Dust	3	2	3	4	3	0	0	3
permethrin	Ortho Bug-B-Gon MAX Garden Insect Dust	3	2	3	4	3	0	0	3
permethrin	Ortho Bug-B-Gon Multi-Purpose Garden Dust 1	3	2	3	4	3	0	0	3
permethrin	Spectracide Bug Stop for Gardens	3	2	3	4	3	0	0	3
permethrin	Total Kill Lawn & Garden Insect Killer Concentrate	3	2	3	4	3	0	0	3
ORGANOPHOSPHATES									
malathion	Spectracide Malathion Insect Spray	2	2	2	2	3	2	2	1

| Insecticidal Active Ingredient | Product Name | Bugs/Mite Ratings ? = unknown, 0 = no control, 1 = poor, 2 = fair, 3 = good, 4 = excellent | | | | | | | |
		Internal Fruit-Feeding Caterpillars (codling moth/ oriental fruit moth, etc.)	Internal Fruit-Feeding Beetles (plum curculio/ strawberry weevil, etc.))	Plant bug/ Stink bug	Leaf feeding Cater-pillars	Leaf feeding Beetles	Mites	Scales	Borers
ORGANOPHOSPHATES (continued)									
captan + **malathion** + **carbaryl**	Bonide Fruit Tree Spray	3	3	2	3	3	1	1	1
captan + **malathion** + **carbaryl**	Bonide Insecticide-Miticide Fungicide	3	3	2	3	3	1	1	1
Carbamates									
carbaryl	Bayer Advanced Complete Insect Killer for Gardens R-T-U	2	2	2	2	3	1	1	1
carbaryl	GardenTech Sevin Bug Killer	2	2	2	2	3	1	1	1
carbaryl	GardenTech Sevin-5 Dust	2	2	2	2	3	1	1	1
captan + **malathion** + **carbaryl**	Bonide Fruit Tree Spray	3	3	2	3	3	1	1	1
captan + **malathion** + **carbaryl**	Bonide Insecticide-Miticide Fungicide	3	3	2	3	3	1	1	1
OILS									
horticultural oil	Ortho Volck Oil Spray	0	0	1	1	1	2	4	0
refined horticultural oil	SunSpray Ultra-Fine Pest Oil	0	0	1	1	1	2	2	0
SOAPS									
insecticidal soap + pyrethrin	Safer Tomato & Vegetable Insect Killer II	1	1	1	1	1	1	1	0
potassium salts of fatty acids	Safer Insect Killing Soap	1	1	1	1	1	1	1	0
NATURAL PRODUCT DERIVATIVES									
chemical from chrysanthemum flowers	Pyrethrin products	0	0	2	3	2	0	0	0
diatomaceous earth	Safer Ant & Crawling Insect Killer	0	0	2	2	2	1	1	0
diatomaceous earth	Diatomaceous earth	0	0	2	2	2	1	1	0
kaolin clay	Gardens Alive Surround at Home Crop Protectant	2	2	2	2	2	0	1	0
leaf extracts from the neem tree	Azadirachtin	0	0	1	2	0	0	1	0
neem + pyrethrin	Green Light Rose Defense II	0	0	2	1	2	0	1	0
neem oil	Green Light Rose Defense	0	0	1	2	2	0	1	0

HOME FRUIT INSECTICIDE EFFECTIVENESS CHART

Insecticidal Active Ingredient	Product Name	Bugs/Mite Ratings ? = unknown, 0 = no control, 1 = poor, 2 = fair, 3 = good, 4 = excellent							
		Internal Fruit-Feeding Caterpillars (codling moth/ oriental fruit moth, etc.)	Internal Fruit-Feeding Beetles (plum curculio/ strawberry weevil, etc.))	Plant bug/ Stink bug	Leaf feeding Cater-pillars	Leaf feeding Beetles	Mites	Scales	Borers
NATURAL PRODUCT DERIVATIVES (continued)									
oil extracted from neem tree nuts	Neem	0	0	1	2	2	0	1	0
pyrethrin	Schultz Houseplant & Garden Insect Spray	0	0	2	1	1	0	1	0
pyrethrins + canola oil	Garden Safe House Plant & Garden Insect Spray	0	0	2	1	1	0	1	0
pyrethrins + piperonyl butoxide	Spectracide Garden Insect Killer R-T-U	0	0	2	1	1	0	1	0
pyrethrins + piperonyl butoxide + hydrophdoic extract of neem oil	Green Light Fruit Tree Spray	0	0	2	1	1	0	1	0
sesame oil	Organocide Organic Insecticide & Fungicide	0	0	0	?	1	1	1	0
spinosad	Ferti-Lome 'Come and Get It' Fire Ant Killer	2	0	0	4	0	0	0	0
spinosad	Ferti-Lome Borer, Bagworm, Leafminer & Tent Caterpillar Spray	2	0	0	4	0	0	0	0
spinosad	Gardens Alive Bulls Eye Bioinsecticide	2	0	0	4	0	0	0	0
BIOLOGICALS									
Bacillus thuringiensis subspecies *kurstaki*	Green Light BT Worm Killer	2	0	0	4	0	0	0	0
Steinernema rio-brave nematodes	Biovector (available online from Becker Underwood)		Effective on in ground life stages of plum curculio if soil is kept moist						
Steinernema carpocapsae nematodes	available online as: Millennium (Becker Underwood) NemaAttack (Arbico Organics) Capsanem (Koppert Biological Systems) SE Insectaries, Perry, GA 478-988-9412								effective on in-ground stages of peach tree borer if soil is kept moist

FLOWERS
HOMEOWNER OUTDOOR INSECT CONTROL

Ronald D. Oetting and Will Hudson, Extension Entomologists

PEST	INSECTICIDE AND FORMULATION*	AMOUNT FORMULATION PER GALLON SPRAY	REMARKS AND PRECAUTIONS
Aphids	acephate		Follow label directions.
	bifenthrin		Follow label directions.
	cyfluthrin		Follow label directions.
	disulfoton		Follow label directions
	pyrethroids	Ready to use and concentrate	Follow label directions.
	imidacloprid		Follow label directions.
	insecticidal soap	1-2%	Thorough coverage necessary. Spray must contact pest to be effective. Repeat spray 3 times at 5-7 day intervals.
	horticultural oils	1-2%	Follow label directions.
	pyrethrum		Follow label directions.
	resmethrin		Follow label directions.
Beetles (foliage feeding such as Japanese beetle, Elm leaf beetle)	carbaryl (Sevin) 50WP	2 Tbs.	Apply to foliage when injury first noted.
	disulfoton		Follow label directions
Caterpillars such as Armyworms, Cutworms and Loopers	acephate		Follow label directions.
	bifenthrin		Follow label directions.
	Bacillus thuringiensis (Dipel, Thuricide)		Follow manufacturer's suggestions.
	bifenthrin	ready to use	Follow label directions.
	carbaryl (Sevin) 50WP	2 Tbs.	
	cyfluthrin		Follow label directions.
	pyrethroids	ready to use and concentrate	Follow label directions.
Mealybugs	acephate		Follow label directions.
	bifenthrin		Follow label directions.
	bifenthrin 0.012%	ready to use	Follow label directions.
	cyfluthrin		Follow label directions.
	imidacloprid		Follow label directions.
	insecticidal soap	1-2%	Thorough coverage necessary. Spray must contact pest to be effective. Repeat spray 3 times at 5-7 day intervals.
	horticultural oil	1-2%	Coverage important, spray must contact pest.
	pyrethroids	ready to use and concentrate	Follow label directions.
Plant bugs Leafhopper	acephate		Follow label directions.
	carbaryl (Sevin) 50 WP	2 Tbs.	Apply to foliage as needed.
	cyfluthrin		Follow label directions.

PEST	INSECTICIDE AND FORMULATION*	AMOUNT FORMULATION PER GALLON SPRAY	REMARKS AND PRECAUTIONS
Plant bugs Leafhopper (cont.)	pyrethroids	ready to use and concentrate	Follow label directions.
	insecticidal soap	1-2%	Thorough coverage necessary. Spray must contact pest to be effective. Repeat spray 3 times at 5-7 day intervals.
Scale Insects	acephate .		Follow label directions.
	bifenthrin		Follow label directions.
	cyfluthrin		Follow label directions.
	pyrethroids	ready to use and concentrate	Follow label directions.
	horticultural oils	1-2%	Follow label directions.
	imidacloprid		Follow label directions.
	insecticidal soap	1-2%	
	malathion		Follow label directions.
Slugs and Snails	iron phosphate		Follow label directions.
	Methaldehyde		Attention should be given to moist areas or water leaks. Do not use in home gardens.
	Mesurol 2B	1 lb./100 sq. ft.	Follow label directions.
Sowbugs and Pillbugs	carbaryl (Sevin) 50WP 5D	2 Tbs. Follow label	Clean up breeding and hiding places, i.e., treat any mulched area of ornamental shrubbery.
Spider mites	bifenthrin 0.012%	ready to use	Follow label directions.
	disulfoton		Follow label directions.
	horticultural oil	1-2%	
	insecticidal soap	1-2%	Coverage is important, spray must contact pest to be effective.
Stalk borer	carbaryl (Sevin) 50 WP 5D	2 Tbs. Follow label	Treat as often as needed beginning when first damage noted. Do not allow ragweeds to grow near flower beds.
Thrips	acephate		Follow label directions.
	cyfluthrin		Follow label directions.
	disulfoton		Follow label directions.
	imidacloprid		Follow label directions.
	insecticidal soap	1-2%	Thorough coverage necessary, spray must contact pest to be effective. Repeat spray 3 times at 5-7 day intervals.
Whitefly	acephate		Follow label directions.
	bifenthrin		Follow label directions.
	bifenthrin 0.012%	ready to use	Follow label directions.
	cyfluthrin		Follow label directions.
	disulfoton		Follow label directions.
	malathion		Follow label directions.
	pyrethroids	ready to use and concentrate	Follow label directions.

PEST	INSECTICIDE AND FORMULATION*	AMOUNT FORMULATION PER GALLON SPRAY	REMARKS AND PRECAUTIONS
Whitefly (cont)	horticultural oils	1-2%	
	imidacloprid		Follow label directions.
	insecticidal soap	1-2%	

*Numerous products containing insecticide are available to homeowners. Products containing the same insecticide may vary in the concentration of the active ingredient. Always consult the product label for information on rate of application. The following table provides the common name, brand name and lists manufacturers that package insecticides in a product(s) for homeowner use.

COMMON NAME	BRAND NAME AND COMMONLY AVAILABLE PRODUCTS
acephate	Orthene
Bacillus thuringiensis (Bt)	Biotrol, Dipel, Thuricide, Sok-Bt; found in various Green Light, Ortho, Ford's, Rigo and Safer products
bifenthrin	Ortho products
carbaryl	Sevin; found in various KGro, Green Light, Ford's, Rigo and Dexol products
cyfluthrin	Bayer Advanced Rose and Flower Insect Killer
disulfoton	Bayer Advanced
horticultural oil	SunSpray Ultrafine, Saf-T-Side, Superior Oil, Golden Natural Spray Oil, Volck Oil; found in Green Light products, neem oil, organic insect control and others
imidacloprid	Bayer Advanced Garden 2-in-1 Plant Spikes
insecticidal soap	M-Pede and Safer's Soap
iron phosphate	Bayer Advanced Snail & Slug Bait
malathion	Ortho
pyrethrins	Pyrethrin; found in various Ortho, KGro, Green Light, Dexol, Rigo, Black Flag, Garden Safe
pyrethroids	esfenvalerate, lambda-cyhalothrin, permethrin, and others
pyrethrum	Pyrethrum; found in several Safer products
resmethrin	Resmethrin; found in Ortho, Dexol, Hot Shot and Rid-a-Bug products

FLOWERS
HOMEOWNER OUTDOOR WEED CONTROL

Mark A. Czarnota, Extension Horticulturist – Weed Science

USE STAGE AND HERBICIDE	FORMULATION	AMOUNT OF FORMULATION/ GAL. PER 1000 SQ. FT.	REMARKS AND PRECAUTIONS
HERBACEOUS FLOWERS			
PREEMERGENCE [1,2,3,4]			
benefin + oryzalin (Amaze 2G)	2.0% granular	4.6 - 6.9 lb.	Can be applied over-the-top of several established bedding plants (see label). Provides broad spectrum control of many broad leaf and annual grass weeds.
oryzalin (Surflan 4AS)	4.0 lb/gal	1.5 - 3.0 fl oz	Controls annual grasses and some broadleaf weeds. Can be applied over-the-top to certain established flowers. One-half inch of rainfall or irrigation water immediately after application will aid in weed control. Do not use on Coleus or Begonia species.
trifluralin (Preen 1.47G)	1.47% granular	6.25 lbs.[1]	Apply to established flowers to control annual grasses and some broadleaf weeds from seed. Optimum weed control is obtained when rainfall or irrigation occurs within a few hours of application. DO NOT apply to seedbeds or to non-rooted plants. Preen is also available on a dry fertilizer carrier.
POSTEMERGENCE			
clethodim (Envoy Plus)	0.97 lb/gal	0.3 - 0.7 fl oz	Apply to actively-growing grasses, which are not drought stressed. Make sure to add a crop oil concentrate at 1% V/V to the spray solution. Refer to label for recommended list of ornamentals. Envoy will not control broadleaf weeds or nutsedges.
fluazifop-p (Grass-B-Gon and others)	See label.	See label.	Apply to actively-growing grasses, which are not drought stressed. Refer to label to determine if the addition of a surfactant is necessary. Refer to label for recommended list of ornamentals. Fluazifop will not control broadleaf weeds or nutsedges.
sethoxydim (Segment)	1.0 lb/gal	0.8 - 1.4 fl oz	Apply to actively growing grasses, which are not drought stressed. DO NOT add a crop oil concentrate or surfactant to Vantage (the formulation contains an adjuvant). Vantage will not control broadleaf weeds or nutsedge(s).
AREAS ADJACENT TO ORNAMENTAL FLOWERS (POSTEMERGENCE)			
glufosinate (Finale 1.0L)	1.0 lb/gal	2.2-4.4 fl oz	Apply glufosinate to control emerged weeds. <u>DO NOT</u> allow spray mist to contact ornamental foliage or severe injury will occur. Glufosinate is poor on well established perennial weeds with extensive underground storage structures (Florida betony, bermudagrass, nutsedge, etc.)
glyphosate Various trade names and formulation available	See label.	See label.	Apply glyphosate to control most emerged weeds. <u>DO NOT</u> allow spray mist to contact ornamental foliage or severe injury will occur. Avoid applications to drought stressed weeds.
halosulfuron (Sedgehammer 75DF)	75DF	0.9 grams (spray weeds to runoff)	Apply as a post-directed application to control yellow and purple nutsedge in established woody ornamentals. Apply with 1/3 fluid ounce of nonionic surfactant. DO NOT allow the spray to contact foliage of desirable woody ornamentals. Wait three months after transplanting before application. On areas scheduled to be planted in woody ornamentals wait 4 weeks between application and transplanting.

[1] All preemergent herbicides require a rain or irrigation event in order for herbicide activation to occur (approximately 0.5 to 1.0 inch of water). If no rain event occurs and no supplemental watering is provided after a preemergent herbicide application, weed control can be extremely poor or totally fail.

[2] Most preemergent herbicides will only control germinating weed seed. Generally, they will not control weeds after they have become established (1st or 2nd true leaf), and most preemergent herbicides will not control weeds coming from vegetative structures (i.e. yellow and purple nutsedge).

[3] As long as the treated area remains undisturbed, most pre-emergent herbicides will provide weed control for 2 to 4 months in most growing mediums.

[4] Do not apply preemergence herbicides to seeded beds or to non-rooted plants in greenhouses.

FLOWERS
HOMEOWNER INDOOR INSECT CONTROL

Ronald D. Oetting, Extension Entomologist

Note: Many formulations of insecticides for use in the home are combinations of active ingredients. The following list of pesticides is given as a guide to determine which pests an active ingredient is effective in controlling. Many pyrethroids, and other compounds, are now off label and there may be several brand names for different chemicals. Only the active ingredient of insecticides is listed. Other compounds, especially oils, contain a mixture of oils and these are listed under the general category of oils. The trade names below are only examples of several different formulations available and are not given as recommendations. Check the label on the insecticide container to determine what plants can be treated and the active ingredients present in the product. When possible, place plants outdoors or in an area not likely to come in contact with people, pets, or food while making insecticide application. If plants cannot be moved outside for treatment follow label precautions for indoor treatment.

INSECTICIDE AND FORMULATION*		RATE	COMMENT
bifenthrin	Ortho Houseplant and Garden Insect Killer	as directed	mealybugs, mites, whitefly, aphids.
cyfluthrin	Bayer Advanced Home Pest Control	as directed	gnats, centipedes, earwigs, scorpions. Follow label directions.
dienchlor	Pentac (aerosol)	as directed	spider mites.
imidacloprid + fertilizer	Bayer Advanced Garden 2- in-1 Plant Spikes	as directed	aphids, mealybugs, whitefly.
insecticidal soap	M-Pede	1-2%	aphids, mealybugs, scale, thrips, mites, whitefly. Coverage is important, spray must contact pest to be effective.
horticultural oil	Plant Spray Oil (aerosol) Sunspray Ultrafine, Saf-T-Side	1-2%	scale, whitefly and mites. Coverage is important, spray must contact pest to be effective.
pyrethrum	Pyrethrum (aerosol)	as directed	aphids, mealybugs, thrips, whitefly.
resmethrin	Resmethrin (aerosol)	as directed	aphids and whitefly.
Tralomethrin		as directed	mites

*Numerous products containing insecticide are available to homeowners. Products containing the same insecticide may vary in the concentration of the active ingredient. Always consult the product label for information on rate of application. The following table provides the common name, brand name and lists manufacturers that package insecticides in a product(s) for homeowner use.

COMMON NAME	BRAND NAME AND COMMONLY AVAILABLE PRODUCTS
bifenthrin	Ortho products
cyfluthrin	Bayer Advanced Home Pest Control
dienchlor	Pentac; found in various Dexol products
horticultural oil	SunSpray Ultrafine, Saf-T-Side, Superior Oil, Golden Natural Spray Oil, Volck Oil; found in Green Light products and others
imidacloprid + fertilizer	Bayer Advanced Garden 2-in-1 Plant Spikes
insecticidal soap	M-Pede and Safer's Soap
pyrethrum	Pyrethrum; found in several Safer products, Garden Safe
pyrethroids	Ready to use and concentrate — Follow label directions
resmethrin	Resmethrin; found in Ortho, Dexol, Hot Shot and Rid-a-Bug products

WOODY ORNAMENTALS

WOODY ORNAMENTALS (INCLUDES SHRUBS AND GROUND COVERS) HOME INSECT CONTROL

Will Hudson, Extension Entomologist

INSECTS	INSECTICIDE & FORMULATION*	AMOUNT/GALLON OF WATER	REMARKS AND PRECAUTIONS
Aphids	Insecticidal soap pyrethrins pyrethrum horticultural oils imidacloprid 1.47% (Bayer Advanced) acephate (Orthrene, etc.) 75S	1-2 oz. 2 tsp.	Per label directions. Per label directions. Per label directions. Per label directions. See note below.
Azalea leaf miner	acephate (Orthene TTO) imidacloprid 1.47% (Bayer Advanced)	1 tsp.	Per label directions.
Bagworm	malathion 57EC Bacillus thuringiensis (Biotrol WP, Thuricide, Sok-Bt) Various pyrethroids	2 tsp.	In winter, hand-pick and burn if only a few bagworms are present. Per label directions. See note below.
Borers (various kinds)	permethrin imidacloprid (Bayer Advanced)	per label	Apply to trunk and lower limbs in Spring as per label directions. Imidacloprid is effective against flat-headed borers and some clear-winged moths only.
Boxwood leaf miner	acephate (Orthene, etc.) 75S imidacloprid 1.47% (Bayer Advanced)	2 tsp.	Per label directions.
Caterpillars (Misc. leaf feeders)	carbaryl (Sevin) 50 WP Bacillus thuringiensis (Biotrol WP, Thuricide, Sok-Bt) Various pyrethroids	2 Tbs.	Treat as needed. Per label directions. See note below.
Holly leaf miner	imidacloprid 1.47% (Bayer Advanced)		Spray in late spring to kill larvae in mines. Per label directions.
Japanese beetle (adults)	carbaryl (Sevin) 50WP imidacloprid (Bayer Advanced)	2 Tbs.	Treat as needed. Repeat applications as necessary.
Lace bugs	acephate (Orthene, etc.) imidacloprid 1.47% (Bayer Advanced)	1 tsp.	Apply in early spring when nymphs of first generation are present. Per label directions.
Scale Insects	malathion 57EC car- baryl (Sevin) 50WP Horticultural oils Insec- ticidal soap imidacloprid (Bayer Advanced)	2 tsp. 2 Tbs. 1-2 oz.	Apply in spring to control crawlers. Make applications at 2 week intervals. Per label directions. Per label directions. Per label directions.
Spider mites	Horticultural oils Insecticidal soap bifenthrin disulfoton 1.00% (Bayer Advanced)	1-2 oz.	Per label directions. Per label directions. Per label directions.

NOTE: A number of pyrethroid materials are available in a variety of homeowner formulations for use as broad-spectrum contact insecticides. Common names include bifenthrin, cyfluthrin, cypermethrin, deltamethrin, lambda-cyhalothin, permethrin and tralomethrin. Active ingredients are listed on the label.

Most of the materials listed in the Commercial Landscape Insect Control section of this handbook are not Restricted Use Pesticides, and so are available for homeowner use. They are not marketed for homeowners, in small quantities at retail garden centers, but they could provide options for some homeowners. Consult your county Cooperative Extension Agent for advice on alternatives.

INSECTS	INSECTICIDE & FORMULATION*	AMOUNT/GALLON OF WATER	REMARKS AND PRECAUTIONS
Slugs and snails	metaldehyde mesurol 2B iron phosphate (Slug-Go)		Follow label directions. Follow label directions.
Thrips	carbaryl (Sevin) 50WP malathion 57EC disulfoton 1.00% (Bayer Advanced) Various pyrethroids	2 Tbs. 2 tsp.	Apply as needed. Per label directions. See note below.
Whitefly	Insecticidal soap pyrethrins pyre- thrums bifenthrin imidacloprid 1.47% (Bayer Advanced) disulfoton 1.00% (Bayer Advanced)		Per label directions. Per label directions. Per label directions. Per label directions. Per label directions. Per label directions.

NOTE: A number of pyrethroid materials are available in a variety of homeowner formulations for use as broad-spectrum contact insecticides. Common names include bifenthrin, cyfluthrin, cypermethrin, deltamethrin, lambda-cyhalothin, permethrin and tralomethrin. Active ingredients are listed on the label.

Most of the materials listed in the Commercial Landscape Insect Control section of this handbook are not Restricted Use Pesticides, and so are available for homeowner use. They are not marketed for homeowners, in small quantities at retail garden centers, but they could provide options for some homeowners. Consult your county Cooperative Extension Agent for advice on alternatives.

*Numerous products containing insecticide are available to homeowners. Products containing the same insecticide may vary in the concentration of the active ingredient. Always consult the product label for information on rate of application. The following table provides the common name, brand name and lists manufacturers that package insecticides in a product(s) for homeowner use.

COMMON NAME	BRAND NAME AND COMMONLY AVAILABLE PRODUCTS
Bacillus thuringiensis (Bt)	Biotrol, Dipel, Thuricide, Sok-Bt; found in various Green Light, Ortho, Ford's, Rigo and Safer products
carbaryl	Sevin; found in various KGro, Green Light, Ford's, Rigo and Dexol products
disulfoton	Bayer Advanced Garden Systemic Rose and Flower Care; Bayer Advanced Garden Azalea, Camellia and Rhododendron Care
horticultural oil	SunSpray Ultrafine, Saf-T-Side, Superior Oil, Golden Natural Spray Oil, Volck Oil; found in Green Light products and others
imidacloprid	Bayer Advanced Garden Tree and Shrub; Bayer Advanced Garden 2-in-1 Plant Spikes
insecticidal soap	M-Pede and Safer's Soap
malathion	Malathion and Cythion; found in various Ortho, KGro, Ford's, Green Light and Dexol products
pyrethrins	Pyrethrin; found in various Ortho, KGro, Green Light, Dexol, Rigo, Black Flag
pyrethrum	Pyrethrum; found in several Safer products
resmethrin	Resmethrin; found in Ortho, Dexol, Hot Shot and Rid-a-Bug products

WOODY ORNAMENTALS WEED CONTROL FOR HOMEOWNERS[1]

Mark A. Czarnota, Extension Horticulturist-Weed Science

CROP AND USE STAGE	HERBICIDE FORMULATION	AMOUNT OF FORMULATION/ GAL. PER 1000 SQ. FT.	REMARKS AND PRECAUTIONS
PREEMERGENCE [2,3,4,5]	dichlobenil (Casoron 4G)	2.3 - 3.4 lb	USE ONLY ON ESTABLISHED WOODY ORNAMENTALS. Apply between November 15 and February 15. Good product for the controlling non-seed bearing plants (i.e. Bracken fern (Pteridium aquilinum)), winter annuals, and Florida betony (Stachys floridana). After application, Casoron must be watered in with ½ to 1 inch of water. DO NOT apply until 4 weeks after transplanting woody ornamentals.
	isoxaben + trifluralin (Snapshot 2.5 TG)	2.3 - 4.6 lb	Controls a wide range of annual weeds in certain woody ornamentals, trees and groundcovers. DO NOT apply to newly planted ornamentals until the soil has firmly settled and no cracks are present. Not recommended for applications to bedding plants. Groundcovers should be established and well-rooted prior to application. Apply one-half inch of irrigation water, or uniformly incorporate into the soil to a depth of 1 to 2 inches, if rainfall is not received within 3 days of application.
	oryzalin (Surflan 4 AS)	1.5 - 3.0 fl. oz	Controls annual grasses and some broadleaf weeds. Apply over-the-top to established ornamentals. One-half inch of rainfall or irrigation water immediately after application will aid in weed control. Surflan may be tank-mixed with glyphosate for control of emerged weeds. See REMARKS for glyphosate.
	trifluralin (Treflan 5 G) (Preen 1.47 G)	1.8 lb 6.25 lb	Apply prior to planting and to established plants. Optimum weed control is obtained when rainfall or irrigation occurs within a few hours of application. DO NOT apply to newly planted groundcovers. DO apply Treflan 5G to ornamentals with wet foliage. DO NOT apply to seeded beds or to non-rooted plants. Use the trifluralin product that is registered for ornamental use. Preen is also available on dry fertilizer carriers.
	benefin + oryzalin (XL 2 G) (Amaze 2 G)	4.6 - 6.9 lb 4.5 lb	Apply only to established ornamentals. One-half inch of rainfall or irrigation water immediately after application will aid in weed control.
POSTEMERGENCE[1]	glufosinate (Finale) 1 lb./gal.	2.2 - 4.4 fl. oz	Apply glufosinate to kill most emerged weeds. DO NOT allow spray mist to contact ornamental foliage or severe injury will occur. Avoid applications to drought stressed weeds. Ready-to-use, premixed formulations of Finale are also available. Finale is poor on well established perennial weeds with extensive underground storage systems (Florida betony, bermudagrass, nutsedge, etc.)
	glyphosate Various trade names and formulations available	See Label	Apply glyphosate to kill most emerged weeds. DO NOT allow spray mist to contact ornamental foliage or severe injury will occur. Avoid applications to drought stressed weeds. Glyphosate is very water soluble and can be tanked mixed with many preemergent herbicides. Refer to glyphosate label to determine compatibility with preemergent herbicides.

CROP AND USE STAGE	HERBICIDE FORMULATION	AMOUNT OF FORMULATION/ GAL. PER 1000 SQ. FT.	REMARKS AND PRECAUTIONS
AREAS ADJACENT TO ORNAMENTALS (POSTEMERGENCE)	halosulfuron (Manage 75DF) (SedgeHammer 75DF)	0.9 grams (spray weeds to runoff)	Apply as a post-directed application to control yellow and purple nutsedge in established woody ornamentals. Apply with 1/3 fluid ounce of nonionic surfactant. DO NOT allow the spray to contact foliage of desirable woody ornamentals. Wait three months after transplanting before application. On areas scheduled to be planted in woody ornamentals wait 4 weeks between application and transplanting.
	imazaquin (Image) 70 DG	0.2 - 0.26 oz	Can be applied over the top of several ornamentals (see label). Make sure to add a surfactant at 0.25% V/V. Controls several difficult weeds including sedges, wild onion, and wild garlic.
	Potassium salts of fatty acids Scythe 4.2L and various other trade names are available	See label	Apply Scythe to kill most emerged weeds. <u>DO NOT</u> allow spray mist to contact ornamental foliage or severe injury will occur. Avoid applications to drought stressed weeds. Scythe is poor on well established perennial weeds with extensive underground storage systems (Florida betony, bermudagrass, nutsedge, etc.). Also provides postemergent control of mosses, algae, liverworts and lichens inside greenhouses, on growing containers and benches.
POSTEMERGENCE GRASS CONTROL	clethodim (Envoy Plus 0.97 lb/gal)	0.3 - 0.7 fl oz	Apply to actively-growing grasses, which are not drought stressed. Make sure to add a crop oil concentrate at 1% V/V to the spray solution. Refer to label for recommended list of ornamentals. Envoy Plus will not control broadleaf weeds or nutsedge.
	fluazifop-P (Grass-B-Gon and others)	See Label	Apply postemergence to actively-growing grasses, which are not drought stressed. Refer to the label to determine if a surfactant is necessary, and for a recommended list of ornamentals. Fluazifop will not control broadleaf weeds or nutsedge.
	sethoxydim (Segment) 1.0 lb./gal.	0.8 - 1.4 fl. oz	Apply postemergence to actively growing weedy grasses, which are not drought stressed. <u>DO NOT</u> add a surfactant or crop oil concentrate to Vantage. Vantage will not control broadleaf weeds or nutsedge(s).

[1]There are many other herbicides available to the homeowner that are not restricted use. Most of these herbicides are available in larger packaging and can be harder to attain. Moreover, most of these commercial products can pose greater potential for plant injury if used improperly.

[2]All preemergent herbicides require a rain or irrigation event in order for herbicide activation to occur (approximately 0.5 to 1.0 inch of water). If no rain event occurs and no supplemental watering is provided after a preemergent herbicide application, weed control can be extremely poor or totally fail.

[3]Most preemergent herbicides will only control germinating weed seed. Generally, they will not control weeds after they have become established (1st or 2nd true leaf), and most preemergent herbicides will not control weeds coming from vegetative structures (i.e. yellow and purple nutsedge).

[4]As long as the treated area remains undisturbed, most pre-emergent herbicides will provide weed control for 2 to 4 months in most growing mediums.

[5]Do not apply preemergence herbicides to seeded beds or to non-rooted plants or in greenhouses.

ORNAMENTALS – WEED RESPONSE TO HERBICIDES

Mark A. Czarnota, Extension Horticulturist-Weed Science

	dichlobenil	dimethenamid	flumioxazin	isoxaben	norflurazon	oxadiazon	simazine	oryzalin	oxyfluorfen
Time of Application	PRE								
PERENNIAL WEEDS (control of plants)									
bahiagrass		P	P	P	P	P	P	P	P
bermudagrass		P	P	P	P	P	P	P	P
dallisgrass		P	P	P	P	P	P	P	P
nutsedge, purple	G	P	P	P	P	P	P	P	P
nutsedge, yellow	G	F	P	P	P	P	P	P	P
tall fescue		P	P	P	P	P	P	P	P
wild garlic / wild onion	G	P	P	P	P	P	P	P	P
ANNUAL GRASSES (control of plants from seed with pre herbicides, control of plant with post herbicides)									
annual bluegrass	G	G	E	P-F	E	G	G	E	G
crabgrass	G	G	E	P-F	G	G	G	E	G
goosegrass	G	G	E	P	G	E		E	G
ANNUAL SMALL SEEDED BROADLEAF WEEDS (control of plants from seed with pre herbicides, control of plant with post herbicides)									
bittercresses		E	E	G	G	G	F	G	G
common chickweed	G	E	E	E	G	G	E	G	G
deadnettle	G				G		G	G	
dodder	E								
henbit	G		E	E	F	G	E	G	G
hop clovers	G			G		G	E		
knotweed	G		E		G	G	E	G	G
lespedeza	G			F		G	E		
morningglories	F	F	G	G	F	F	G	F	G
mustards	G	G	G	F		E	E	P	
niruri / phyllanthus		E	E	E	G	G	G	G	G
spurge	G	E	E	E	G	F	E	G	G
woodsorrel	G	E	E	E	P-F	E	E	G	G
PERENNIAL BROADLEAF WEEDS (control of plants from seed with pre herbicides, control of plant with post herbicides)									
clovers	G	G	E	G		G	E	G	G
dandelion	G		E	G		G	G	G	G
dichondra			E						
docks	G		E						G
Florida betony	E				P				
mallow			E	G	G	G	G	G	G
mouseear chickweed	G		E	G		G	G	G	G
mugwort	E								
pennywort	G								
plantain			G	G		G		G	G

Key to Response Symbols: E = Excellent Control (>90%); G = Good Control (70 to 90%); F = Fair Control (50 to 70%); P = Poor Control (<50%)
If no symbol is given, weed response is unknown.

	prodiamine	trifluralin	clethodim	clopyralid	diquat	fluazifop	glufosinate
Time of Application	PRE		POSTEMERGENCE				
PERENNIAL WEEDS (control of plants)							
bahiagrass	P	P	G	P	P	G	P
bermudagrass	P	P	G-E	P	P	G-E	P
dallisgrass	P	P	P	P	P	G	P
nutsedge, purple	P	P	P	P	P	P	P
nutsedge, yellow	P	P	P	P	P	P	P
tall fescue	P	P	G	P	P	F	P
wild garlic	P	P	P	P	P	P	P
ANNUAL GRASSES (control of plants from seed with pre herbicides, control of plant with post herbicides)							
annual bluegrass	E	G	E	P	G	E	G
crabgrass	E	E	E	P	G	E	G
goosegrass	G	G	E	P	G	E	G
ANNUAL SMALL-SEEDED BROADLEAF WEEDS (control of plants from seed with pre herbicides, control of plant with post herbicides)							
bittercresses	G	G	P		G	P	G
common chickweed	G	G	P		G	P	E
deadnettle	G	G	P		G	P	G
dodder	P		P			P	
henbit	G	G	P		G	P	E
knotweed			P			P	E
lespedeza	G	G	P	E	F	P	F
morningglories	G	F	P		G	P	P
mustards	F	F	P		G	P	G
niruri / phyllanthus	G	P	P		G	P	G
spurge	G	G	P		G	P	G
woodsorrel	G	F	P		G	P	G
PERENNIAL BROADLEAF WEEDS (control of plants from seed with pre herbicides, control of plant with post herbicides)							
clovers	E	G	P	E	F	P	F
dandelion	G	G	P	G	G	P	P
dichondra			P	P		P	
docks	G	G	P	G	P	P	G
Florida betony			P	P	P	P	P
mallow	G	G	P		G	P	G
mouseear chickweed	G	G	P		G	P	G
mugwort			P	E	G	P	P
pennywort			P	G	G	P	P
plantain	G	G	P	P	G	P	F

Key to Response Symbols: E = Excellent Control (>90%); G = Good Control (70 to 90%); F = Fair Control (50 to 70%); P = Poor Control (<50%)
If no symbol is given, weed response is unknown.

	glyphosate	halosulfuron	paraquat	pelargonic acid	sethoxydim	triclopyr
Time of Application	POSTEMERGENCE					
PERENNIAL WEEDS (control of plants)						
bahiagrass	G	P	P	P	G	P
bermudagrass	G	P	P	P	G	P
dallisgrass	E	P	P	P	P	P
nutsedge, purple	G	E	P-F	P	P	P
nutsedge, yellow	G	E	P-F	P	P	P
tall fescue	E	P	P	P	G	P
wild garlic	G	G	P		P	
ANNUAL GRASSES (control of plants from seed with pre herbicides, control of plant with post herbicides)						
annual bluegrass	E	P	E	G	P-F	P
crabgrass	G	P	G	G	E	P
goosegrass	E	P	F-G	F	E	P
ANNUAL SMALL-SEEDED BROADLEAF WEEDS (control of plants from seed with pre herbicides, control of plant with post herbicides)						
bittercresses	G		E	F	P	G
common chickweed	E		E	G	P	G
deadnettle	G		E	G	P	G
dodder	E				P	
henbit	E		E	G	P	G
knotweed	E		E	G	P	G
lespedeza	E			F	P	G
morningglories	G		F-G	F	P	G
mustards	E		E	G	P	G
niruri / phyllanthus	E		E		P	G
spurge	E		E	G	P	G
woodsorrel	E		E	G	P	G
PERENNIAL BROADLEAF WEEDS (control of plants from seed with pre herbicides, control of plant with post herbicides)						
clovers	F			P-F	P	G
dandelion	E	G		P	P	G
dichondra	E				P	G
docks	E				P	G
Florida betony	G				P	G
mallow	E			F	P	G
mouseear chickweed	E			G	P	G
mugwort	E			F	P	F
pennywort	E				P	G
plantain	E				P	G

Key to Response Symbols: E = Excellent Control (>90%); G = Good Control (70 to 90%); F = Fair Control (50 to 70%); P = Poor Control (<50%)
If no symbol is given, weed response is unknown.

HOMEOWNER ORNAMENTAL AND TREE DISEASE CONTROL
General Fungicide Guidelines

Elizabeth Little, Extension Homeowner IPM Specialist

<u>Prevention</u> in the home garden and landscape is the key to reducing diseases in and around your yard. Several preventive practices can be utilized for disease control before resorting to spraying pesticides. They include: 1) selecting disease free plants from accredited nurseries and garden centers, 2) selecting resistant ornamental varieties, 3) site selection and planning allows one to grow plants that are appropriate for each individual yard, 4) proper plant care in the home garden, including fertilization, irrigation, and sanitation (removing dead and diseased plant parts that could harbor pathogens), 5) growing disease-free plants, and 6) regular scouting in the yard for potential disease problems and pests. The application of pesticides should be the last option for the homeowner. It is best to properly identify the pathogen before applying/spraying a pesticide. <u>REMEMBER TO ALWAYS READ AND FOLLOW THE LABEL CAREFULLY</u>, if you choose to apply a pesticide.

This guide has two sections: <u>PART A</u> is a list of commonly occurring plant pathogens/diseases a nd the materials that can be used to control them (includes active ingredient/common name and trade name); <u>PART B</u> is a list of commonly grown herbaceous and woody ornamental plants and trees and some of the diseases that occur on them. Fungicides labeled for use are listed by active ingredient, followed by the manufacturer/ trade name in PART A. Plant names in PART B are listed alphabetically according to the scientific name of the plant. If it is uncertain whether a fungicide can be safely used on a plant species, a small number of plants should be treated to test for phytotoxicity prior to treating the entire crop. Always refer to the fungicide label for directions.

The products listed can be found at local garden retails centers and on-line at particular locations.

**Keep in mind this is not an all-inclusive list of plants or products. County your local county agent for more information regarding plants or pesticide control products.

FOLLOW ALL LABEL DIRECTIONS CAREFULLY. PAY PARTICULAR ATTENTION TO RE-ENTRY PERIODS AND RE-USE INTERVALS.

PART A: LIST OF COMMONLY OCCURRING PLANT PATHOGENS/DISEASES AND THE MATERIALS USED TO CONTROL THEM.

DISEASE	ACTIVE INGREDIENT (COMMON NAME)	CONTACT OR SYSTEMIC	TRADE NAME
OOMYCETES			
Phytophthora root/crown rot	Fosetyl-Al	Systemic	Monterey Aliete
Pythium root/crown rot	Phosphorous Acid	Systemic	Monterey AGRI-FOS
Downy Mildew Phytophthora blight/dieback	Fosetyl-Al	Systemic	Monterey Aliete
	Phosphorous Acid	Systemic	Monterey AGRI-FOS
	Copper hydroxide	Contact	Hi-Yield Copper Fungicide Kocide 101
	Copper Salts	Contact	Monterey LIQUI-COP Bonide Liquid Copper Fungicide Dragon Copper Fungicide
	Chlorothalonil (Daconil)	Contact	Ferti-lome Broad Spectrum Liq. Fungicide Hi-Yield Daconil Garden Tech Fungicide Disease Control Bonide Fung-Onil Multi-Purpose Fungicide Ortho Garden Disease Control Dragon Daconil 2787 Monterey Fruit Tree, Vegetable, & Ornamental Fungicide
FUNGAL			
Armillaria root/stem rot Black root rot Cylindrocladium root rot Fusarium root/stem rot Ganoderma root rot	Thiophanate-methyl	Systemic	Ferti-lome Halt Systemic Fungicide Scotts Lawn Fungus Control Green Light Systemic Fungicide Dragon Systemic Fungicide 3336WP
Rhizoctonia root/stem rot Sclerotinia root rot Southern blight Verticillium Wilt	PCNB	Contact	Hi-Yield Turf & Ornamental Fungicide Terraclor (several manufacturers)

DISEASE	ACTIVE INGREDIENT (COMMON NAME)	CONTACT OR SYSTEMIC	TRADE NAME
Botrytis blight	Thiophanate-methyl	Systemic	Ferti-lome Halt Systemic Fungicide Scotts Lawn Fungus Control Green Light Systemic Fungicide Dragon Systemic Fungicide 3336WP
	Chlorothalonil (Daconil)	Contact	Ferti-lome Broad Spectrum Liq. Fungicide Hi-Yield Daconil Garden Tech Fungicide Disease Control Bonide Fung-Onil Multi-Purpose Fungicide Ortho Garden Disease Control Dragon Daconil 2787 Monterey Fruit Tree, Vegetable, and Ornamental Fungicide
Diplodia tip blight Kabatina dieback Phomopsis dieback Phomopsis needle blight Sclerotinia stem rot Tip blight	Thiophanate-methyl	Systemic	Ferti-lome Halt Systemic Fungicide Scotts Lawn Fungus Control Green Light Systemic Fungicide Dragon Systemic Fungicide 3336WP
Powdery mildew	Sulfur	Contact	Safer Garden Fungicide Monterey Sulfur 90W Bonide Sulfur Plant Fungicide Hi-Yield Wettable Dusting Sulfur Dragon Wettable or Dusting Garden Sulfur Top-Cop w/ Sulfur
	Neem oil	Contact	Green Light Powdery Mildew RTU Ferti-lome Triple Action RTU
	Jojoba oil	Contact	Monterey E-Rase RTU
	Myclobutanil	Systemic	Ferti-lome F-stop Lawn Fungicide Green Light Fung-Away Systemic Granules Spectracide Immunox 3-in-1 Spectracide Immunox Fungicide Spectracide Lawn Disease Spray Spectracide Lawn Disease Control Granules Spectracide Multi-purpose Fungicide Spectracide Immunox Plus Insect and Disease Control
	Triforine (see label for plant list)	Systemic	Ortho Rose Pride-Rose and Shrub Disease Control Ortho Orthenex Insect and Disease Control
	Potassium bicarbonate soluble powder	Contact	Monterey Bi-Carb Old Fashioned Fungicide
	Chlorothalonil (Daconil)	Contact	Ferti-lome Broad Spectrum Liq. Fungicide Hi-Yield Daconil Garden Tech Fungicide Disease Control Bonide Fung-Onil Multi-Purpose Fungicide Ortho Garden Disease Control Dragon Daconil 2787 Monterey Fruit Tree, Vegetable, & Ornamental Fungicide

DISEASE	ACTIVE INGREDIENT (COMMON NAME)	CONTACT OR SYSTEMIC	TRADE NAME
Rust	Myclobutanil	Systemic	Ferti-lome F-stop Lawn Fungicide Green Light Fung-Away Systemic Granules Spectracide Immunox 3-in-1 Spectracide Immunox Fungicide Spectracide Lawn Disease Spray Spectracide Lawn Disease Control Granules Spectracide Multi-purpose Fungicide Spectracide Immunox Plus Insect and Disease Control
	Triadimefon	Systemic	Green Light Fung-Away Fungicide Green Light Fung-Away Systemic Lawn Spray Hi-Yield Lawn Fungicide Granules
	Triforine (asters, carnations, & roses)	Systemic	Ortho Rose Pride-Rose and Shrub Disease Control Ortho Orthenex Insect and Disease Control
	Tebucanazole	Systemic	Bayer Disease Control
	Chlorothalonil (Daconil)	Contact	Ferti-lome Broad Spectrum Liq. Fungicide Hi-Yield Daconil Garden Tech Fungicide Disease Control Bonide Fung-Onil Multi-Purpose Fungicide Ortho Garden Disease Control Dragon Daconil 2787 Monterey Fruit Tree, Vegetable, and Ornamental Fungicide
Leaf spots (Alternaria, Anthracnose, Cercospora, Cylindrocladium, Entomosporium, Gnomonia, Heterosporium, Macrophoma, Mycosphaerella, Phyllosticta, Purple-eye, Septoria, Zonate) Black spot (ROSE) Curvularia leaf blight Leaf streak (daylily) Scab Spot anthracnose Volutella blight Web blight	Propiconazole Ortho Lawn Disease Control Ferti-lome Liquid Systemic Fungicide	Systemic	Bonide Infuse
	Chlorothalonil (Daconil)	Contact	Ferti-lome Broad Spectrum Liq. Fungicide Hi-Yield Daconil Garden Tech Fungicide Disease Control Bonide Fung-Onil Multi-Purpose Fungicide Ortho Garden Disease Control Monterey Fruit Tree, Vegetable, and Ornamental Fungicide Dragon Daconil 2787
	Mancozeb	Contact	Dragon Mancozeb Disease Control Bonide Mancozeb Flowable
	Maneb	Contact	Hi-Yield Maneb Garden Fungicide
	Captan	Contact	Bonide Captan Dragon Captan Wettable Powder
	Copper hydroxide	Contact	Hi-Yield Copper Fungicide Kocide 101 Nu-Cop 50DF
	Copper salts	Contact	Monterey LIQUI-COP Bonide Liquid Copper Fungicide Dragon Copper Fungicide
	Thiophanate-methyl	Systemic	Ferti-lome Halt Systemic Fungicide Scotts Lawn Fungus Control Green Light Systemic Fungicide Dragon Systemic Fungicide 3336WP
	Triforine (Black spot on roses)	Systemic	Ortho Rose Pride-Rose and Shrub Disease Control Ortho Orthenex Insect and Disease Control

DISEASE	ACTIVE INGREDIENT (COMMON NAME)	CONTACT OR SYSTEMIC	TRADE NAME
Leaf/flower gall	Chlorothalonil (Daconil)	Contact	Ferti-lome Broad Spectrum Liq. Fungicide Hi-Yield Daconil Garden Tech Fungicide Disease Control Bonide Fung-Onil Multi-Purpose Fungicide Ortho Garden Disease Control Monterey Fruit Tree, Vegetable, and Ornamental Fungicide Dragon Daconil 2787
	Mancozeb	Contact	Dragon Mancozeb Disease Control Bonide Mancozeb Flowable
Flower/petal blight	Myclobutanil	Systemic	Ferti-lome F-stop Lawn Fungicide Green Light Fung-Away Systemic Granules Spectracide Immunox 3-in-1 Spectracide Immunox Fungicide Spectracide Lawn Disease Spray Spectracide Lawn Disease Control Granules Spectracide Multi-purpose Fungicide Spectracide Immunox Plus Insect and Disease Control
	Chlorothalonil (Daconil)	Contact	Ferti-lome Broad Spectrum Liq. Fungicide Hi-Yield Daconil Garden Tech Fungicide Disease Control Bonide Fung-Onil Multi-Purpose Fungicide Ortho Garden Disease Control Monterey Fruit Tree, Vegetable, and Ornamental Fungicide Dragon Daconil 2787
Cankers (various fungal pathogens)	There are various fungal pathogens that cause cankers on woody/herbaceous ornamentals and trees. For the most part, fungicides are not an effective or practical means of control. Keeping plants healthy is the key to preventing and controlling cankers on plants. Avoid stress on the plants (over/under-watering and fertilization). PRUNE infected branches at least one inch below infected area and sterilize pruning tools between cuts (10% bleach or alcohol). AVOID WATER STRESS and TREE WOUNDING.		
BACTERIAL			
Fire Blight Bacterial Blight Soft rot	Copper	Contact	Bonide Copper Spray or Dust
	Copper hydroxide	Contact	Hi-Yield Copper Fungicide Kocide 101 Nu-Cop 50DF
	Copper Salts	Contact	Monterey LIQUI-COP Bonide Liquid Copper Fungicide Dragon Copper Fungicide
	Copper oxinate	Contact	Concern Copper Soap
	Fosetyl-Al	Systemic	Monterey Aliete
	Streptomycin sulfate	Contact	Bonide Fire Blight Spray Ferti-lome Fire Blight Spray
Crown gall	Important to purchase healthy plants. Biological controls are available. Check with County Agents. Can use copper compounds but may be phytotoxic.		
NEMATODE	Chitin		Hi-Yield Nem-A-Cide Clandosan
	This product is soil amendment that increases the growth of naturally occurring micro-organisms which feed on nematodes (nematode bodies are composed of chitin).		
VIRAL	No chemical controls for viral diseases.		

PART B: LIST OF COMMONLY GROWN ORNAMENTAL PLANTS AND TREES AND SOME OF THE DISEASES THAT OCCUR ON THEM *This is not an all-inclusive list.

ORNAMENTAL PLANTS (HERBACEOUS & WOODY) and TREES & THEIR DISEASES	
PLANT - Scientific name (Common Name)	**DISEASES**
Abelia	No major pests...leaf spots, powdery mildew, root knot nematode
Abies (Fir)	Botrytis blight, Cytospora canker, oedema (cultural), Phytophthora root/crown rot
Abutilon (Velvet leaf/Flowering Maple)	Rhizoctonia root rot, web or aerial blight; root knot nematode; stem rot; root rot; rust
Acer (Maple, Box Elder)	Anthracnose, Bacterial scorch, Bacterial Wetwood, Botryosphaeria dieback, Cytospora canker, Ganoderma root rot, leaf spot (various fungi), Nectria canker, Phomopsis dieback, tar spot, Valsa canker, Verticillium wilt, Phyllosticta leaf spot
Achillea (Yarrow)	powdery mildew
Aconitum (Monkshood)	Southern blight
Aegopodium (Goutweed)	Leaf spot
Aesculus (Horse Chestnut, Buckeye)	Guignardia blotch
Agave (Century plant)	Crown rot, Anthracnose, Leaf spot
geratum (Floss Flower)	Southern blight, Pythium & Phytophthora root rots, Botrytis blight; rust; powdery mildew
Ailanthus (Tree-of-Heaven)	Fusarium stem/root rot
Ajuga (Bugleweed)	Phomopsis dieback, Phytophthora root rot, Pythium root rot, Rhizoctonia root/crown rot, root knot nematode, Southern blight, viral disease, web blight
Albizia (Mimosa)	Fusarium wilt, Crown dieback (Fusarium)
Alcea (Hollyhock)	Root knot nematode, Rust
Allium (Ornamental Onion)	White rot
Aloe	Root rot (*Pythium*)
Amelanchier (Service berry)	Rust, Entomosporium leaf spot; bacterial fire blight; powdery mildew
Anemone	Foliar nematode, Phytophthora root rot, Rust, leaf spot; downy mildew
Anise-tree	sooty mold, leaf spot (algal)
Antirrhinum (Snapdragon)	Cercospora leaf spot, downy mildew, Phytophthora root/crown rot, Pythium root rot, Rhizoctonia stem rot, Rust, Verticillium Wilt, viral diseases, Botrytis blight
Aquilegia (Columbine)	Pythium root rot, crown rot, Powdery mildew
Arctostaphylos (Bearberry)	Pythium root rot, Phytophthora root rot
Arisaema (Jack-in-the-pulpit)	Rust
Armeria (Sea thrift)	Web blight
Aronia (Chokeberry)	Pythium root rot
Artemisia (Dusty miller)	Rhizoctonia root/stem rot
Asclepias (Milkweed)	Anthracnose
Asclepias tuberosa (Butterfly weed)	Rhizoctonia stem rot
Asimina (Pawpaw)	Nectria canker; leaf spots
Aster	Powdery mildew, Rust, leaf spot
Astilbe	Pythium root rot, root knot nematodes

PLANT - Scientific name (Common Name)	DISEASES
Aucuba	Anthracnose, Botryosphaeria dieback, leaf spots, Phomopsis dieback, ring nematode
Bamboo	Pythium root rot
Bedding plants	Damping off (Pythium)
Begonia	Anthracnose, Botrytis blight, Fusarium stem rot, Powdery mildew, Rhizoctonia root/stem rot, root knot nematode
Berberis (Barberry)	Phytophthora root rot
Bergenia	Pythium root rot
Betula (Birch)	Anthracnose, Botryosphaeria dieback, Botrytis blight, red heart, Septoria leaf spot, rust
Buddleia (Butterfly bush)	Phytophthora root rot, Rhizoctonia root rot
Buxus (Boxwood)	Botryosphaeria dieback, Boxwood decline, Lesion nematode, Macrophoma leaf spot, Phytophthora root rot, Volutella blight
Cactus	Pythium root rot
Caladium	Pythium root rot
Calibrachoa (Million bells)	Phytophthora crown rot, Rhizoctonia root rot, Southern blight
Callicarpa (Beauty berry)	No serious problems
Calocedrus (Incense Cedar)	Seiridium canker
Camellia	Anthracnose, Botryosphaeria dieback, leaf/flower gall, leaf spot, oedema (nutritional), petal/flower blight, Phytophthora root rot, Pythium root rot, viral disease
Campanula (Bellflower)	Fusarium crown rot, leaf spots
Campsis (Trumpet vine)	Anthracnose; mistletoe; powdery mildew
Canna (Cannalily)	Lesion nematodes, Pythium root rot, bacterial bud rot
Carpinus (Hornbeam)	Pythium root rot, cankers
Capsicum (Ornamental pepper)	Verticillium wilt
Carya (Hickory)	Downy leaf spot, Gnomonia leaf spot, phomopsis gall, Powdery mildew, Zonate leaf spot
Caryopteris (Bluebeard)	Phytophthora stem/root rot, Pythium root rot
Castanea (Chestnut)	Chestnut blight canker
Catalpa	Bacterial wetwood, Verticillium wilt, Cercospora leaf spot
Catharanthus (Madagascar periwinkle)	Black root rot, Botrytis blight, Phytophthora blight, Pythium root rot, Rhizoctonia stem/root rot
Cattleya (Orchid)	Bacterial brown spot
Cattleya (Orchid)	Bacterial brown spot
Cedrus (Cedar)	Armillaria root rot, Phomopsis needle/twig blight
Celosia (Cockscomb)	Pythium root rot, Rhizoctonia root rot, leaf spot
Cercis (Redbud)	Botryosphaeria dieback, Botrytis blight, Fusarium canker, leaf spot, Verticillium wilt
Chamaecyparis (Falsecypress)	Phytophthora root rot, Seiridium canker, web blight
Chionanthus (Fringe tree)	Leaf spot
Chrysanthemum (Shasta Daisy, Mum)	Pythium root rot, web blight, Rust, powdery mildew, foliar nematode, Verticillium wilt
Chrysogenum (Goldenstar)	Southern blight

PLANT - Scientific name (Common Name)	DISEASES
Cladastris (Yellow wood)	Anthracnose
Clematis	Leaf spot, Phytophthora root rot
Clivia (Kaffir lily)	leaf spot, Southern blight
Coleus	Botrytis blight, downy mildew
Consolida (Larkspur)	Pythium root rot, Rhizoctonia root/crown rot
Coreopsis (Tickseed)	Botrytis blight, Rhizoctonia root/stem rot, rust, viral disease
Cornus (Dogwood)	Anthracnose, Botryosphaeria dieback/canker, Botrytis blight, Disculaanthracnose, Fusarium canker, leaf spot, phomopsis dieback, powdery mildew, Pythium root rot, Septoria leaf spot, spot anthracnose, viral disease
Corylus (Filbert)	Eastern Filbert bligh
Cosmos (Mexican aster)	Botrytis blight, Phomopsis stem canker, powdery mildew, white smut
Cotinus (Smoke tree)	Anthracnose, Verticillium wilt
Cotoneaster	Leaf spot, Phytophthora root rot, web blight, fire blight
Crassula (Jade plant)	Oedema, Pythium root rot
Crataegus (Hawthorn)	Cercospora leaf spot, Entomosporium leaf spot, rust, fire blight
Cryptomeria (Japanese cedar)	Needle blight, Phomopsis twig blight, Phytophthora root rot
Cupressus (Cypress)	Botryosphaeria dieback, Kabatina dieback, tip blights, Phytophthora root rot, Seiridium canker
Cyclamen	Fusarium Wilt
Cymbidium (Orchid)	Viral disease
Dahlia	Crown gall, powdery mildew, tuber rot (fungal-Fusarium and Botrytis), root rot, viral disease (mosaic)
Daphne	Anthracnose, Phytophthora root/stem rot, crown rot (Sclerotium spp.)
Davidia (Dove tree)	Phomopsis dieback
Delosperma (Ice plant)	Pythium root rot
Dendranthema (Chrysanthemum)	Bacterial leaf spot, Botrytis blight, Mycosphaerella ray blight, Phytophthora root rot, pozdery mildew, Pythium root/stem rot, Rhizoctonia root rot, Septoria leaf spot, leaf rust, Verticillium wilt
Dianthus (Carnation)	Alternaria leaf spot, Botrytis blight, Fusarium stem rot, powdery mildew, Rhizoctonia stem rot, rust, aster yellows, viral disease
Digitalis (Foxglove)	Black root rot, Fusarium root rot, Pythium root rot, Anthracnose
Dimorphotheca (African Daisy)	Botrytis blight
Dracaena	Fusarium blight, Pythium root rot
Duchesnea (Indian Strawberry)	Rust
Echinacea (Coneflower)	Aster yellows, foliar nematodes, Pythium root rot, viral disease
Eichhornia (Water hyacinths)	Leaf spots
Elaeagnus (Autumn Olive)	Phytophthora root rot
Epiphyllum (Cereus)	Oedema (nutritional)

PLANT - Scientific name (Common Name)	DISEASES
Epipremnum (Pothos)	Phytophthora stem rot
Erica (Heather)	Phytophthora root rot
Eucalyptus	Anthracnose, Botryosphaeria dieback, crown gall, Fusarium canker, Phomopsis dieback, Phytophthora root rot, powdery mildew, Pythium root rot
Euonymus	Powdery mildew
Euphorbia (Spurge)	Anthracnose, Botryosphaeria dieback
Euphorbia pulcherima (Poinsettia)	Bacteria blight, bacterial leaf spot, Botrytis blight, powdery mildew, Pythium root rot, scab
Eustoma (Lisianthus)	Botrytis blight, Fusarium stem/root rot
Exacum (Persian violet)	Viral disease
Fagus (Beech)	Anthracnose, Botryosphaeria canker, Hypoxylon canker, viral disease
Fatsia	Leaf Spot
Fatshedra (Bush ivy)	Botrytis blight, Fusarium root/stem rot, Phomopsis blight, Rhizoctonia root rot, Powdery mildew, scab
Ficus (Fig)	Anthracnose, Phytophthora root rot
Ficus benjamina (Weeping fig)	Anthracnose, Phomopsis gall
Forsythia	Botryosphaeria dieback, crown gall, Phomopsis gall, Phytophthora root rot, ringer nematodes, Sclerotinia twig blight, web blight
Fraxinus (Ash)	Anthracnose, ash yellows, Botryosphaeria canker, rust
Gaillardia (Blanket flower)	Pythium root rot, White smut
Galium (Sweet woodruff)	Rhizoctonia stem/root rot, Southern blight
Gardenia	Anthracnose
Gerbera (African daisy)	Pythium root rot, Botrytis blight
Gladiolus	Botrytis leaf blight, Curvularia leaf blight, Fusarium yellows, Penicillium corm rot, Rhizoctonia corm rot, aster yellows, scab
Gleditsea (Honeylocust)	Botryosphaeria canker, Thyronectria canker
Gloxinia (Sinningia)	Viral disease
Gomphrena (Globe amaranth)	Leaf spot, root knot nematode
Gypsophila (Baby's breath)	Bacterial soft rot
Hamamelis (Witchhazel)	Botryosphaeria dieback, leaf spot, powdery mildew
Hedera helix (English ivy)	Anthracnose, Bacterial leaf spot, oedema, Phyllosticta leaf spot, Phytophthora root rot, Pythium root rot, Rhizoctonia root ro
Helianthemum (Rock rose)	Botrytis blight
Helianthus (Sunflower)	Alternaria leaf/stem spot, powdery mildew
Helichrysum (Strawflower)	Fusarium stem rot
Helleborus (Hellebore)	black leaf spot, Botrytis blight, Pythium root rot, Rhizoctonia root rot, Southern blight
Hemerocallis (Daylily)	Anthracnose, rust, leaf streak, Southern blight

PLANT - Scientific name (Common Name)	DISEASES
Heuchera (Coral bells)	Pythium root rot, leaf spot, downy mildew
Hibiscus	Phytophthora root rot, Pythium root rot, viral disease
Hibiscus syriacus (Rose-of-sharon)	Leaf spot
Hosta	Anthracnose, Botrytis blight, leaf spot, root rot, soft rot, Southern blight, virus X
Hyacinth (Hyacinthus)	bacterial soft rot, root rot, gray mold
Hydrangea	Anthracnose, Armillaria root rot, bacterial leaf spot, Botrytis blight, Cercospora leaf spot, Phytophthora root rot, Pythium root rot, powdery mildew
Hypericum (St Johnswort)	Phytophthora root/stem rot, rust, Rhizoctonia root rot, leaf spots
Iberis (Candytuft)	Anthracnose, Pythium root rot
Ilex (Holly)	Anthracnose, Bacterial Blight, Black root rot, Botryosphaeria dieback, leaf spot, root knot nematodes, oedema (nutritional), Phomopsis dieback, Phytophthora root rot, Pythium root rot, Rhizoctonia root rot, rust, tar spot, web blight
Ilex glabra (Inkberry)	Black root rot, Phytophthora root rot
Impatiens	Alternaria leaf spot, bacterial fasciation, Botrytis blight, Fusarium crown rot, powdery mildew, Pythium root/stem rot, Rhizoctonia root/stem rot, root knot nematodes, Verticillium wilt, viral diseases
Ipomoea (Morning glory)	Rust, white rust
Iris	Botrytis blight, Heterosporium leaf spot, soft rot, viral disease (mosaic)
Juniperus (Juniper)	Kabatina tip blight, Pestalotia dieback, Phytophthora root rot, Pythium root rot, rust
Juniperus virginiana (Eastern red cedar)	Cercospora blight, Kabatina tip blight, Pestalotia blight, Phomopsis tip blight, rust
Kalmia (Mountain laurel)	Botryosphaeria dieback, Cercospora leaf spot
Lagerstroemia (Crape myrtle)	Leaf spot, powdery mildew, sooty mold
Lantana	Leaf spot; root knot nematode; fusarium wilt
Laurus nobilis (Bay laurel)	Cercospora leaf spot
Lavandula (Lavender)	Phytophthora root rot, Pythium root rot
Leucothoe (Drooping Leucothoe)	Botryosphaeria dieback, Cylindrocladium leaf spot, Phyllosticta leaf spot, Phytophthora root rot
Ligustrum (Privet)	Anthracnose, Cercospora leaf spot, Phytophthora root rot
Lilium (Lily)	Anthracnose, Botrytis blight, Pythium root rot, viral disease (mosaic)
Limomium (Statice)	Phytophthora root rot, Pythium root rot, Rhizoctonia root rot
Liquidambar (Sweet gum)	Cercospora leaf spot, Sphaeropsis gall
Liriodendron (Tulip tree)	Powdery mildew, sooty mold
Liriope (Lilyturf)	Anthracnose, foliar nematodes, Mycosphaerella leaf spot, Phytophthora leaf spot, viral disease
Lobelia	Pythium root rot, viral disease
Lobularia (Sweet alyssum)	Rhizoctonia root ro
Lonicera (Honeysuckle)	Botryosphaeria dieback, Botrytis blight, Herpobasidium leaf blight, powdery mildew, witches' broom

PLANT - Scientific name (Common Name)	DISEASES
Lupinus (Lupine)	Anthracnose, brown spot, Pythium root rot
Lysimachia (Loosestrife)	Rhizoctonia root/stem rot, Southern blight
Magnolia	Bacterial leaf spot, powdery mildew
Malus (Crabapple)	Coniothyrium leaf spot, fire blight, frog-eye leaf spot, powdery mildew, rust, scab
Malva (Mallow)	Rust
Miscanthus	Blight
Morus (mulberry)	Berry blight, bacterial leaf blight, bacterial wetwood
Myosotis (Forget-me-not)	Web blight
Myrica (Bayberry)	Botryosphaeria dieback, Phytophthora root rot
Myrica cerifera (Wax myrtle)	Anthracnose, Botryosphaeria dieback, Phytophthora root rot, Septoria leaf spot
Myrtle (Myrtus)	Leaf spot; stem rot (Sclerotinia)
Nandina (Heavenly bamboo)	Cercospora leaf spot, Phytophthora root rot, Pythium root rot
Narcissus (Daffodil, Jonquil)	Fusarium bulb rot & various other fungal bulb rots; leaf spot & blight; virus
Nelumbo (Water lily)	Cercospora leaf spot
Nerium (Oleander)	Leaf spot; anthracnose; bacterial blight; sooty mold
Nyssa sylvatica (Black gum)	Anthracnose, Botryosphaeria dieback, leaf spot
Ocimum basilicum (Basil)	Alternaria leaf spot, Fusarium crown rot
Ophiopogon (Mondo grass)	Anthracnose
Oxalis (Wood sorrel)	Rust; leaf spots; root knot nematode
Oxalis (Wood sorrel)	Rust; leaf spots; root knot nematode
Oxydendrum arboreum (Sourwood)	Leaf spots
Pachysandra	Leaf spot, Pythium root rot, southern blight, Volutella blight; virus
Paeonia (Peony)	Botrytis blight, Cercospora leaf spot, Cladosporium leaf/stem blotch, Rhizoctonia root rot, Phytophthora blight
Parthenocissus (Boston ivy)	Phyllosticta leaf spot
Parthenocissus quinquefolia (Virginia creeper)	Downy mildew; leaf spots
Pelargonium (Geranium)	Bacterial blight, bacterial leaf spot, bacterial wilt, Botrytis blight, oedema (nutritional), Pythium root rot, blackleg, Rhizoctonia root rot, rust, viral disease
Petunia	Botrytis blight, Fusarium root/crown rot, Phytophthora root/crown rot and foliage blight, Pythium crown/root rot, Rhizoctonia root/stem rot, viral disease
Phalaris (Canarygrass)	Web blight
Phlox	Bacterial leaf spot, black root rot, Colletotrichum stem canker, powdery mildew, Pythium root rot, southern blight, viral disease, web blight
Photinia (Japanese photinia red-tip)	Bacterial blight, Botryosphaeria canker, Entomosporium leaf spot, powdery mildew, Armillaria root rot
Physocarpus (Ninebark)	Powdery mildew, Rhizoctonia root rot
Picea (Spruce)	Cytospora canker, Phytophthora root rot, Pythium root rot, needle blight, tip blight

PLANT - Scientific name (Common Name)	DISEASES
Pieris (Japanese Pieris)	Botryosphaeria dieback, Phomopsis canker, Phytophthora root rot
Pinus (pine)	Armillaria root rot, Atropellis twig canker, Cenangium dieback, Cytospora canker, Diplodia tip blight, Dothiostroma needle blight, Eastern gall rust, Fusiform rust, needle cast, needle rust, Phacidiopycnis canker, Phytophthora root rot, pinewood nematodes
Pistacia (Pistache)	Verticillium wilt
Platanus (Sycamore)	Anthracnose, Bacterial scorch, Botryosphaeria dieback, powdery mildew
Platycodon (Balloon flower)	Rhizoctonia crown rot
Polygonatum (Solomon seal)	Penicillium rot
Populus (Poplar)	Botryosphaeria canker, leaf spot
Portulaca (Purslane)	Rhizoctonia stem rot; root knot nematode
Potentilla (Cinquefoil)	Foliar nematodes, rust
Pratia	Southern blight
Primula (Primrose)	Leaf spots, Pythium and Rhizoctonia root/stem rot
Prunus (flowering apricot/cherry/peach/plum)	Bacterial blossom blight, bacterial leaf spot, bacterial shot hole, bacterial scorch, black knot, blossom blight/brown rot, Cytospora canker, Nectria canker, peach leaf curl, Phomopsis canker, white rot
Prunus laurocerasus (Cherry laurel)	Anthracnose, bacterial leaf spot, bacterial shot hole, Botryosphaeria dieback, Phomopsis dieback, leaf spots, Phytophthora root rot, Pythium root rot, zonate leaf spot
Pseudotsuga (Douglas fir)	Botryosphaeria canker, Swiss needle cast
Pyracantha (Firethorn)	Botryosphaeria dieback, fire blight, Phomopsis dieback, scab
Pyrus calleryana (Flowering pear)	Botryosphaeria canker, Entomosporium leaf spot, fire blight, rust
Quercus (Oak)	Anthracnose, Armillaria root rot, bacterial scorch, bacterial wetwood, Botryosphaeria canker, Cylindrocladium root rot, Discula anthracnose, Hypoxylon canker, leaf blister, Phomopsis dieback, powdery mildew, rust, smooth patch, spot anthracnose, Tubakia leaf spot
Ranunculus (Buttercup)	Bacterial blight, web blight, viral disease (mosaic), Verticillium wilt
Rhaphiolepis (Indian hawthorn)	Entomosporium leaf spot
Rhododendron (Azalea)	Anthracnose, Armillaria root rot, Botryosphaeria dieback, Botrytis blight, Cercospora leaf spot, Colletotrichum leaf spot, leaf and flower gall, lesion nematodes, oedema (nutritional), Pestalotia leaf spot, petal blight, Phomopsis dieback, Phyllosticta leaf spot, Phytophthora dieback, Phytophthora root/stem rot, powdery mildew, web blight
Rhus (Sumac)	Verticillium wilt; Bot canker & dieback; powdery mildew, root rot
Rosa (Rose)	Anthracnose, black spot, Botryosphaeria dieback, Botrytis blight, crown gall, downy mildew, Phomopsis Canker, powdery mildew, Pythium root rot, rose rosette disease, viral disease
Rosmarinus (Rosemary)	Botrytis blight, crown gall, Phytophthora root rot, Pythium root rot
Rudbeckia (Black-eyed susan)	Pythium root rot, Rhizoctonia stem rot, Septoria leaf spot
Sagittaria (Arrowhead)	Leaf spot; leaf smut
Salix (Willow)	Armillaria root rot, Botryosphaeria dieback, Botrytis blight, black canker, Cercospora leaf spot, crown gall, rust, scab, white rot
Salvia	Bacterial leaf spot, downy mildew, Pythium root rot, Rhizoctonia stem rot, Botrytis blight

PLANT - Scientific name (Common Name)	DISEASES
Sansevieria (Snake Plant)	Bacterial soft rot; leaf spots; root knot nematode; Fusarium rot
Scabiosa (Pincushion flower)	Botrytis blight
Schefflera (Umbrella tree)	oedema (nutritional), Pythium root rot
Sedum (Stone crop)	Anthracnose, bacterial soft rot, bacterial stem rot, Diplodia stem rot, leaf spot, Phytophthora stem rot, Pythium root rot, Rhizoctonia stem/root rot, root knot nematodes, web blight
Setcreasia (Purple heart)	Leaf spot
Solidago (Goldenrod)	Rust; powdery mildew; leaf spot
Spiraea	Leaf spot
Styrax (Silverbell)	Leaf spots
Syringa (Lilac)	Anthracnose, bacterial blight, Botrytis blight, Cercospora leaf spot, Phytophthora root rot, powdery mildew
Tagetes (Marigold)	Alternaria blight, Botrytis blight, crown gall, Fusarium stem/root rot, Pythium root rot, Rhizoctonia stem rot
Taxus (Yew)	Botryosphaeria dieback, Phytophthora root rot
Thuja (Arborvitae)	Armillaris root/stem rot, Cytospora canker, Kabatina tip blight, Phomopsis twig/needle blight, Phytophthora root rot, Pythium root rot, Seiridium twig canker, web blight; Diplodia canker/dieback
Thymus (Thyme)	Pythium root rot
Tilia (Linden)	Spot anthracnose, white rot
Tradescantia virginica (Spiderwort)	Southern blight
Tsuga (Hemlock)	Armillaria root rot, damping-off, rust
Tulipa (Tulip)	Botrytis blight, Fusarium basal rot, bulb rot (various fungi), virus color breaking
Ulmus (Elm)	Bacterial wetwood, bacterial leaf scorch, Botryosphaeria canker, Cytospora canker, Dutch elm disease, Verticillium wilt
Verbena (Vervain)	Powdery mildew, Pythium root rot, bacterial wilt
Veronica (Speedwell)	Phytophthora root rot; rust; powdery mildew
Viburnum (Snowball bush)	Spot anthracnose, bacterial scorch, Botryosphaeria dieback, Botrytis blight, phoma leaf spot, Phytophthora root rot, Rhizoctonia root rot
Vinca minor (Periwinkle)	Oedema (nutritional), Phoma dieback, Phomopsis dieback, Phyllosticta stem rot/leaf spot, Pythium root rot, Rhizoctonia root rot, Southern blight, Botrytis blight,
Viola (Pansy)	Anthracnose, black root rot, Botrytis blight, Cercospora leaf spot, Phytophthora root/crown rot, Pythium root/crown rot
Weigala	Phytophthora root rot, Pythium root rot
Wisteria	Botryosphaeria dieback
Yucca	Bacterial soft rot, Mycosphaerella leaf spot
Zinnia	Alternaria blight, bacterial leaf spot, Botrytis stem canker, powder mildew, Pythium root rot

HOMEOWNER FUNGICIDE GUIDE

Elizabeth Little, Extension Homeowner IPM Specialist

The following is a supplemental guide to fungicides which are readily available to homeowners. This guide is not intended to take the place of the individual product labels which are the best resource concerning the use of any pesticide. Most but likely not all of the current brand names are listed here. Follow label recommendations for application rates, methods and safety precautions when using all pesticides.

COMMON NAME (i.e. Active Ingredient)	BRAND NAME(S)	DISEASES CONTROLLED	COMMENTS
Aluminum tris	Monterey Aliette	Downy mildew on roses, Pythium and Phytophthora in ornamentals, bedding plants, conifers and turf, Fire blight on pear, pyracantha, and hawthorne.	Apply as spray or drench.
Bordeaux mixture (copper sulfate + hydrated lime)	Hi-Yield Bordeaux Mix Fungicide and others	Various diseases of fruits, vegetables and ornamentals including leaf curl on peaches and bitter rot, black rot and scab on apples. Labeled for many plants including apples, boxwoods, chrysanthemums, dahlias, iris, lilies, and tulips.	Protectant fungicide. This is a contact fungicide. Some sensitive plants require diluting the product to one half strength (depending on the product used – see label) to avoid phytotoxicity. These include geraniums, ivy, pansy, celery, strawberry, azaleas, dogwood, juniper, and rhododendron. Can cause phytotoxicity when applied to young, tender leaves of peach, plum, rose and apple. Should not be used during cool, wet weather as it can cause spotting or burning of leaves.
Captan	Ortho Home Orchard Spray, Dragon Fruit Tree Spray, Ferti-lome Fruit Tree Spray, Bonide Captan 50W, Bonide Rose Insect & Disease Control, and Hi-Yield Captan 50% WP	Good general fruit fungicide used for bitter rot, black rot, *Botryosphaeria* rot, flyspeck, sooty blotch, frog-eye leaf spot and scab control on apples, brown rot and scab on peaches and plums, Botrytis rot on strawberries, downy mildew, and black rot of grape. Also used for black spot of rose, powdery mildew on tuberous begonias, rust and leaf spot on carnations, Botrytis flower blight on chrysanthemums, petal blight of camellias, rot and/or damping off of cuttings (azaleas, carnations, chrysanthemums) and bulbs (gladiolus, tuberous begonias). General soil drench treatment for grass seedlings, cuttings and flower beds for damping off and root rot (*Rhizoctonia* spp.). Some products include grass (non- pasture/ grazing) label for brown patch, leaf spot, seedling blights and melting out (*Helminthosporium*) on St. Augustinegrass..	Broad spectrum protectant fungicide. This is a contact fungicide. Label indicates control of difficult to control diseases (i.e. root rots, petal blight of camellias) product actually gives suppression only. Does not control cedar apple rust. Combination fruit spray home orchard products also contain insecticides (usually malathion and methoxychlor) for control of home orchard insect pests. Do not combine with lime, lime-sulfur or Bordeaux mixture as fungicidal activity will be reduced. Do not apply Captan in combination with oil or near the time of oil sprays.
Chitin (organic)	Hi-Yield Nem-A-Cide	Nematodes	This is a soil amendment that increases growth of beneficial microorganisms that feed on chitin (nematode eggs and nematodes contain chitin). This is considered an ORGANIC product. A single application/year is usually sufficient.

COMMON NAME (i.e. Active Ingredient)	BRAND NAME(S)	DISEASES CONTROLLED	COMMENTS
Chlorothalonil	Ortho Garden Disease Control (Daconil 2787), Hi- Yield Daconil Lawn Vegetable Flower Fungicide, Fertilome Lawn & Garden fungicide, Ferti-lome Broad Spectrum Liquid Fungicide, and Bonide Fung-onil	Many common fungal diseases including anthracnose, downy mildew, gray mold (*Botrytis*), powdery mildew, early blight and late blight on man y vegetables including tomatoes. Downy mildew, anthracnose, fungal leaf spots, shot-hole, rusts, scab and powdery mildew on ornamentals. Some fruit diseases, including brown rot and scab on stone fruits. Listed vegetables, fruit trees, roses, flowers, shrubs and shade trees	The most widely used broad spectrum protectant fungicide. This is a contact fungicide. Not recommended for **pittosporum** or **schefflera** as phytotoxicity may result. Discoloration of blooms may occur, especially with roses. NO LONGER LABELED FOR HOMEOWNER <u>TURF</u> USE.
Copper compounds	Bonide Copper Spray or Dust, Bonide Liquid Copper, Dragon Copper Fungicide, Hi- Yield Cop per Fungicide, Ferti-lome Black Spot & Powdery Mildew control, and others	Many fungal and bacterial diseases, including powdery and down y mildew, fungal leaf spots, anthracnose, bacterial leaf spot and/or blight, fire blight and rust on a wide variety of fruits, vegetables and ornamentals.	Broad spectrum protectant fungicide. Although considered "safe" by many organic growers, copper is toxic to humans so label directions and harvest intervals should as always be followed carefully. Discoloration of blooms can occur on certain varieties of ornamentals. To avoid this problem, do not spray prior to or during the flowering period. Foliage discoloration may occur with some plants as well. Refer to individual product label for plants which may be treated.
Liquid lime-sulfur (calcium polysulfides)	Ortho Dormant Disease Control Lime-Sulfur Spray, Hi-Yield Improved Lime Sulfur Spray, Lilly Miller PolySul Summer and Dormant Spray Concentrate, Bonide Lime- Sulfur Spray, Bonide Oil Lime & Sulfur spray, and others	Used in the dormant season to kill overwintering fungal spores of black spot, powdery mildew and rust of rose, leaf curl and shot-hole of peach, cane blight and leaf spot of brambles. Some brands labeled for delayed dormant and/or growing season applications for scab and powdery mildew of apple, anthracnose, rust and powdery mildew of blackberry and powdery mildew and scab on pear. During the growing season used for powdery mildew on many ornamentals and black spot of rose.	Broad spectrum protectant fungicide. The is a contact fungicide. Labeled for roses, peaches, pears, brambles, fruit trees, deciduous hedge plants, delphinium, lilacs, euonymous, columbine, crepe myrtle, sweet peas, zinnias, fruits, ornamentals, and tuberous begonias. Do not spray when temperature is expected to exceed 80F within 24 hours. Spray early in the morning or late in the evening to avoid burning of foliage. Also controls mites and scale.
Mancozeb	Bonide Mancozeb Flowable with Zinc	Many vegetable diseases including anthracnose, fungal leaf spots, downy mildew, early blight, gummy stem blight, late blight, scab, rust and smut. Many ornamental diseases including anthracnose, b lack spot, Botrytis, cedar-apple rust, downy mildew, fungal leaf spots, and other rusts. A few brands are labeled for common fungal lawn diseases.	Broad spectrum protectant fungicide. This is a contact fungicide. When applied to plants not on the label the product should be tested on a small area of the plant or small area of the planting first. Most small container products are not labeled for use on home fruit trees. Treated ornamentals should not be used for food purposes. Be sure to observe harvest intervals on label when applied to vegetables.
Maneb	Hi-Yield Maneb Lawn and Garden Fungicide	Diseases of shrubs, flowers, and turfgrass in the home landscape; various diseases of the following vegetables: beans, cucumbers, peppers, tomatoes, and watermelons.	General protectant fungicide. This is a contact fungicide.

COMMON NAME (i.e. Active Ingredient)	BRAND NAME(S)	DISEASES CONTROLLED	COMMENTS
Myclobutanil	Spectracide Immunox (several), Ferti-lome F-Stop Granular Fungicide, Green Light Fung-Away Systemic Granules	Good for powdery mildew, black spot of rose, fungal leaf spots, rusts, anthracnose and other diseases of flowers and ornamental shrubs and trees. Controls brown patch, dollar spot, melting out, rust, large patch, fusarium blight, and anthracnose on lawns. Also controls powdery mildew, scab and rust on apples, brown rot and other diseases on stone fruits and anthracnose, b lack rot and powdery mildew on grapes.	Systemic fungicide. Provides better powdery mildew control than most other fungicides. Overdosage to ornamentals can result in foliar greening, shortened internodes and/or thickened leaves. For use on turf, proper identification of the causal disease organism is key. Contact local county agents for more information. Not labeled for vegetable crops. Avoid exclusive use of this product for resistance management.
PCNB	Terraclor 75WP, Ferti-lome Azalea, Camellia, Crape Myrtle Insecticide and Fungicide, Hi-Yield Turf and Ornamental Fungicide (containing 10% PCNB), Hi-Yield Terraclor Granular Fungicide	Turf, ornamental and vegetable diseases caused by basidiomycetes, including brown patch, dollar spot, southern blight (white mold), *Helminthosporium* leaf spot and melting out, damping off (*Rhizoctonia* spp. only), *Sclerotinia,* azalea (Ovulinia) and camellia flower blight, *Rhizoctonia* root and crown diseases. Specific vegetable diseases on label include *Rhizoctonia* root and stem rot of beans, Southern blight of peanuts, tomatoes and peppers, club root (*Plasmodiophora*) of broccoli, brussel sprouts, cabbage and cauliflower and scab and *Rhizoctonia* of potatoes.	Protectant preventative fungicide, specific for basidiomycetous fungi. Usually formulated as wettable powder or granules. Should be lightly watered in after applying to turf. For ornamentals drench or incorporate the product thoroughly into the soil for best results. Do not apply to **Philodendron** or **Pilea.** For vegetables application must be at planting or transplanting either by soil drench, incorporation, or in furrow.
Propiconazole	Ortho Lawn Disease Control and Ferti-lome Liquid Systemic Fungicide	Turf, ornamental, flower, shrub care against powdery mildew, dollar spot, anthracnose, rust, scab, tip blight, brown spot, etc.	A water-based systemic fungicide that prevents major diseases on roses, flowers, lawns, trees, and shrubs. Do not apply this product to African violets, Begonia, Boston ferns, or Geraniums.
Streptomycin sulfate	Ferti-lome Fire Blight spray, Bonide Fire Blight spray, Agri-mycin 17	Controls fire blight of apple and pear. Some brands also labeled for fire blight of pyracantha, bacterial wilt of chrysanthemum, bacterial stem rot of Dieffenbachia cuttings, bacterial leaf spot on philodendron, crown gall on roses, and bacterial spot on tomatoes and peppers.	Actually a bactericide/antibiotic compound. Has no fungicidal activity. When used for fire blight control of apples and pears it must be applied du ring bloom prior to symptoms appearing to be effective. Sprays should begin at 20-30% bloom and continue every 3-4 days until petal fall. Do not apply when fruit is visible. Do not apply within 30 days of harvest for pears. Do not apply within 50 days of harvest for apples. within 50 days of harvest for apples.

COMMON NAME (i.e. Active Ingredient)	BRAND NAME(S)	DISEASES CONTROLLED	COMMENTS
Sulfur	Ferti-lome Dusting Sulfur, Bonide Liquid Sulfur, Bonide Sulfur Plant Fungicide, Safer Garden Fungicide, others	Controls diseases of fruit including powdery mildew, cedar apple rust and scab of apples, brown rot and scab of peach, plum and nectarine, powdery mildew on brambles and strawberry. Also labeled for powdery mildew, leaf spots, rust and Botrytis on many vegetables and ornamentals (includes black spot of rose).	Broad spectrum protectant fungicide. This is a contact fungicide. Formulated as a wettable powder or dust. Should not be used when the temperature is above 90 degrees or within four weeks of an oil spray as injury to the foliage may occur. Refer to individual product label for plants which may be treated. Do not use on **apricots, cucumbers, d'Anjou pears, melons, spinach, squash** or **viburnum** as sulfur causes injury and defoliation to these plants. Also controls mites. Residue may be a problem.
Tebuconazole	Bayer Advanced All-in-One Rose & Flower Care; Bayer Advanced 3-in-1 Insect, Disease, & Mite control, Bayer Advanced Disease Control for Flowers, Roses, and Shrubs	Controls black spot, powdery mildew, rust, and southern blight on roses, flowers, azaleas, rhododendrons, camellias and other landscape ornamental shrubs.	Systemic fungicide, insecticide, fertilizer- all-in-one. Protects against insects and disease for up to 6 weeks. No spraying, just mix & poor.
Thiophanate methyl	Cleary's 3336, Ferti-lome Halt Systemic Rose and Flower Fungicide, Scott's Lawn Fungus Control, Green Light Systemic Fungicide	Anthracnose, dollar spot, Rhizoctonia (Brown patch), Helminthosporium leaf spot (melting out), Fusarium patch on lawns. Foliar diseases of ornamentals including anthracnose, black spot of rose, Botrytis, fungal leaf spots, powdery mildew, Ovulinia blight and Phomopsis blight on juniper. Soil/ root diseases of flowering & bedding plants and woody ornamentals caused by Fusarium, Rhizoctonia, Sclerotinia, and Thielaviopsis spp. Bulb diseases caused by Botrytis, Fusarium, Rhizoctonia, Sclerotinia, Fusarium and Penicillium spp.	Broad spectrum systemic fungicide. Usually available as wettable powder. Does **not** control Pythium or Phytophthora spp. A preliminary trial is suggested on a small scale when applying to a plant not listed on the label but for a listed disease problem. Wait 5-7 days before evaluating any potential injury. Not recommended for **Nephrolepis exhalta, Plectranthrus austrailis**, and **Hatiora gaertneri.** Repeated, exclusive use of thiophanate methyl may lead to buildup of resistant fungi and loss of control.
Triadimefon	Green Light Fung-Away Systemic Fungicide (several products), Bonide Bayleton Systemic Fungicide, Bayer Advanced Fungus Control for Lawns, Hi-Yield Lawn Fungicide Granules containing Bayleton	Turf diseases including brown patch, dollar spot, rusts, anthracnose, southern blight, and Fusarium patch. Ornamental diseases including flower blights (Ovulinia and Sclerotinia spp.), fungal leaf spots, powdery mildew and rusts.	Systemic fungicide. Provides better powdery mildew control than most other fungicides. Can cause some foliar discoloration and distortion on roses. Bayleton 50%DF is labeled for use on bearing apple trees for cedar apple rust and powdery mildew and grapes and pears for powdery mildew. However, most homeowner brands/ repackages of triadimefon are **not** labeled for use on bearing fruit and nut trees or any part of plants used for consumption. Check the individual product label.
Triforine	Ortho Rose Pride Orthenex Insect & Disease Control, Ortho RosePride Funginex	Black spot, powdery mildew, and rust of roses, powdery mildew on azaleas, begonias, delphinum, kalanchoe, plane tree, calendula, crepe myrtle, dahlia, euonymous, jerusalem thorn, lilac, phlox, snapdragons, Photinia, and zinnias, rust on aster, carnation and oxalis, petal blight on azaleas and rhododendron and Entomosporium leaf spot on Photinia.	Locally systemic fungicide. Triforine voluntarily cancelled by manufacturer, may become increasingly difficult to find as existing product supply is used.

ORGANIC STRATEGIES FOR THE GARDEN AND HOME LANDSCAPE

Paul Guillebeau, Extension Entomologist and Elizabeth Little, Homeowner IPM/Sustainable Agriculture Extension Specialist

What is Organic Gardening? Generally accepted organic practices comprise soil management, fertilization, and pest management.

The USDA National Organic Program established rules for commercial organic production. These rules do not apply to home gardeners, but they are a useful guide to choosing organic pest management alternatives. The chemicals listed in this section are recognized as organic insecticide, fungicide and bactericide alternatives by the National Organic Program.

Organic pest management is not simply replacing a conventional pesticide with another chemical that is labeled 'organic'. Knowledge and planning are the keys to successful organic gardening. Consider a Master Gardener Class offered through your local Extension Service. Additionally, your local library offers books on organic gardening.

Principles for Organic Gardening

- Healthy plants are less susceptible to pests and disease. Stressed plants attract some pests.
    - Choose plants that are adapted for your local climate.
    - When you buy plants, inspect them carefully for signs of pest infestation.
    - Test the soil to make sure the plants are receiving the nutrients they need to stay healthy.
    - Plant at the right date and under the proper light/water conditions.
    - Consult your local Cooperative Extension agent for advice about choosing plants and creating healthy growing conditions.

- Anticipate problems.
    - Find out what pests and pathogens are common in your area.
    - Look for plant varieties resistant to regular pests and pathogens.
    - Learn the life cycles of the pests and pathogens you expect.
        - When/how do they arrive?
        - Are any stages of the life cycle vulnerable (or protected)?
    - Cooperative Extension is your best source.

- Scout for pest and disease problems regularly.
    - It is much easier to manage young insects, early infections, and small populations.
    - Scout at least three times per week in warm weather.
    - Look at the whole plant, under leaves, and along stems.

- Practice good sanitation.
    - Dispose of diseased or spent plant materials promptly.
    - Many pests and pathogens will persist over the winter in crop debris.

- Use crop rotation.
    - Do not plant the same type of plants in the same place each year.

- Encourage natural controls.
    - An assortment of flowers and herbs will attract beneficial insects.

- Use mechanical controls.
    - Row covers and hand-picking are practical on a small scale.
    - Water spray is effective against many insects if the plants are hardy enough to withstand a vigorous spray.

- Utilize cultural controls.
    - An appropriate planting date may avoid peak pest populations.
    - Mulch helps keep plants healthy and controls some pests and pathogens.
    - Avoid plants or particular varieties that have a lot of pest problems.

- Use chemical controls sparingly. An "organic" listing does not eliminate all risks.
  - Spot treat instead of spraying a large area.
  - Use pesticides only when other options are not practical.

ORGANIC INSECTICIDE/MITICIDE OPTIONS

Except for spinosad products, nearly all organic insecticides have little or no residual activity. Repeated applications may be necessary before you see results.

Nearly all organic pesticides have a very broad range of use sites, which means you can use them nearly anywhere in the garden or landscape. Check the label to be sure it is labeled for the site you need to treat.

USE ALL PESTICIDES ACCORDING TO THE LABEL INSTRUCTIONS!
If used improperly, even natural products may injure your family or pets.

To use this guide, locate your pest problem and identify the chemical options. Review the chemical options for additional information and potential risks. If you need help choosing among several options, consult your local Extension agent.

Caterpillars	– pyrethrins, *Bacillus thuringiensis* kerstaki, spinosad, neem
Fire ants	spinosad (fire ant bait formulation)
Thrips	spinosad
Aphids, whiteflies, other soft bodied pests	pyrethrins, oils, insecticidal soap, neem
Stink bugs	neem, pyrethrins, spinosad
Beetles	spinosad, pyrethrins, neem
Scale insects	oils
Mites	oils, sulfur, insecticidal soap
Mosquito larvae	*Bacillus thuringiensis* israelensis
Yellow jackets	traps, pyrethrins
Slugs/snails	iron phosphate

Pyrethrins (pyrethrum) are produced by some varieties of chrysanthemum. Pyrethrins are often combined with piperonyl butoxide (PBO), which significantly increases the effectiveness of pyrethrins. The PBO is a synthetic chemical; some people do not consider PBO combinations an organic alternative.

Pyrethrins are also available in product combinations with oil or sulfur to give the products greater activity against mites and diseases.

Risks: May kill bees and other beneficials. Extremely toxic to aquatic species. Pyrethrins can be toxic to cats.

NOTE: Very short (hours) residual activity. Insects may recover from pyrethrin exposure unless PBO is added to the product.

Pyrethrin products – Garden Safe, Ortho Ecosense, Bonide, others.

Horticultural oils and dormant oils are highly refined petroleum products. Oils must be applied to the insects/mites to kill them. No residual activity.

Risks: May kill nontarget arthropods if they are covered with oil. May cause plant injury, particularly if the weather is hot or the plant is water stressed.

NOTE: Be sure you are using the right oil and the right concentrations to minimize the risk of plant injury.

Petroleum oil products – Bonide All Seasons and many others

Other oils include sesame oil, soybean oil, and canola oil. We have limited information about their efficacy, but their activity will be similar to the petroleum oils. They can also cause phytotoxicity.

Neem (azadirachtin) is derived from the Neem tree. Leaf extracts and oils pressed from nuts are available. Neem is an insecticide, an insect growth regulator, and a repellent. An insect growth regulator prevents juvenile insects from maturing properly.

Risks: High concentrations can harm fish. Low risk to bees and other beneficial insects.

Neem products: Green Light, others

Spinosad comes in two forms. The organic form is derived a soil bacterium, Saccharopolyspora spinosa. The other form is a synthesized version of the same chemical; it is not considered to be organic.

Risks: May harm bees. Low risks for other nontarget species.

Spinosad products: Fertilome, Bulls Eye

Iron phosphate is the only organic slug bait in U.S. Used for many years in Europe.

Risks: Low risks to nontarget species.

Iron Phosphate products: Ortho Ecosense, Worryfree

Insecticidal soap may also be called Potassium Salts of Fatty Acids. They must be applied directly to the insects. They have no residual activity.

Risks: May cause plant injury, particularly when weather is hot or plant is water stressed.

Insecticidal Soap products: Ortho Ecosense, Safer, others.

Sulfur is commonly found in combination with other organic products to provide control of fungal diseases.

Risks: Low risks to nontargets. May cause irritation of skin, eyes, and throat tissue.

Sulfur products: many.

Bacillus thuringiensis **kerstaki** is a strain of *Bacillus* bacteria that only infects caterpillars. The caterpillars must consume the bacteria. Birds, fish, pets, people, etc. catch this strain of bacteria.

Risks: Very low risks to nontarget species (except other caterpillars).

Bacillus thuringiensis kerstaki products: Dipel, Thuricide, others.

Bacillus thuringiensis **israelensis** is a similar strain of bacteria that controls mosquito larvae. Use it water containers or ponds where mosquitoes are a problem.

Bacillus popillae is a bacterial strain that infects Japanese beetle larvae. It will not affect adult insects. There is no clear evidence that using *Bacillus popillae* will reduce Japanese beetle damage in your yard.

Japanese beetle traps catch large numbers of Japanese beetle adults attracted from a large area. There is no clear evidence that using Japanese beetle traps will reduce Japanese beetle damage in your yard. On a large property, it may be possible to attract Japanese beetles away from desirable plants; however this strategy is unproven.

Yellow jacket traps can help to reduce the number of yellow jackets in a local area. May seem ineffective if other foods are nearby that are also attractive to yellow jackets.

Diatomaceous earth is not recommended. It loses most of its effectiveness in damp/humid conditions, and it is difficult to avoid inhaling the dust.

Home brews are commonly used and widely touted on the internet. Common brews include garlic, hot pepper, ground insects, etc. Because there is no consistency among brews, there are no reliable data to gauge their effectiveness. Garlic and hot pepper are known to repel some insects.

http://www.omri.org/ Organic Materials Review Institute and the National Organic Standard. Includes a list of all of the pest management chemicals accepted as organic.

http://attra.ncat.org/organic.html National Sustainable Ag Information Service. This site has a great deal of information about organic production, including pest management.

http://www.ams.usda.gov/AMSv1.0/NOP - USDA National Organic Program.

ORGANIC FUNGICIDE/BACTERIACIDE OPTIONS

The products listed in this section are registered by the EPA and are "approved" for use in organic production. However, most of these products are non-specific and are toxic to humans, plants, and many non-target invertebrates and aquatic life. In addition, the effectiveness of most of these products is generally limited when compared to "conventional" pesticides. With this in mind, organic pesticides should not be considered as substitutes for or used as conventional fungicides in a pest control program, and should only be used judiciously and as a last resort in an integrated pest management program. Most plant diseases in the home garden do not cause sufficient harm to the plant to justify the use of pesticides.

Type of diseases controlled	Compound	Notes
Coppers:		
Many fungal and bacterial diseases, including powdery and downy mildew, fungal leaf spots, anthracnose, bacterial leaf spot and/or blight, fire blight and rust on a wide variety of fruits, vegetables and ornamentals. Effectiveness against most pathogens is often limited. Labeled for many plants.	Copper sulfate and fixed coppers (copper hydroxide, copper oxide, copper oxychloride)	Copper is toxic to fish, aquatic invertebrates, and humans. Label directions and harvest intervals should be followed carefully. Copper is a heavy metal and must be used in a manner that minimizes accumulation in the soil Coppers have the potential to burn the foliage and flowers of many plants. To avoid this problem, do not spray prior to or during the flowering period, or during prolonged cold, wet weather. Refer to individual product label for plants which may be treated.
Various diseases of fruits, vegetables and ornamentals including leaf curl on peaches and bitter rot, black rot and scab on apples. Labeled for many plants.	Bordeaux Mixture (hydrated lime/copper sulfate)	Lime added to copper sulfate increases the effectiveness of the copper. Phytotoxicity (burning of foliage and flowers) can occur on many plants including the young, tender leaves of peach, plum, rose and apple. Some sensitive plants require diluting the product to one half strength (depending on the product used – see label) to avoid phytotoxicity. Should not be used during cool, wet weather since this can increase damage to plant foliage.
Sulfurs:		
Used in the dormant season to kill overwintering fungal spores of black spot, powdery mildew and rust of rose, leaf curl and shot-hole of peach, cane blight and leaf spot of brambles. Some brands labeled for delayed dormant and/or growing season applications for scab and powdery mildew of apple, anthracnose, rust and powdery mildew of blackberry and powdery mildew and scab on pear.	Liquid lime-sulfur (calcium polysulfides)	Labeled for roses, peaches, pears, brambles, fruit trees, deciduous hedge plants, delphinium, lilacs, euonymous, columbine, crepe myrtle, sweet peas, zinnias, fruits, ornamentals, and tuberous begonias. Do not spray when temperature is expected to exceed 80°F within 24 hours. Spray early in the morning or late in the evening to avoid burning of foliage. Also controls mites and scale.

Type of diseases controlled	Compound	Notes
Sulfurs: (cont.)		
Controls fungal diseases including powdery mildew, scab, and cedar apple rust of apples, brown rot and scab of peach, plum and nectarine, powdery mildew on brambles and strawberry. Also labeled for powdery mildew, leaf spots, rust and botrytis on many vegetables and ornamentals (includes black spot of rose).	Elemental sulfur (Dry wettable sulfurs of flowable sulfurs)	Should not be used when the temperature is above 90 degrees or within four weeks of an oil spray as injury to the foliage may occur. Refer to individual product label for plants which may be treated. Do not use on apricots, cucumbers, d'Anjou pears, melons, spinach, squash or viburnum as sulfur causes injury and defoliation to these plants. Sulfur is lethal to beneficial insects, spiders and mites leading to increased problems with certain pests including mites. Residue may be a problem.
Other compounds:		
Some control of insect vectors of viruses and a few fungal diseases such as powdery mildews and black spot.	Oils, horticultural, narrow range oils as dormant, suffocating, and summer oils	Do not apply when sulfur compounds have or will be used. This combination is toxic to the plant. Repeated use can cause build-up in the soil.
Controls various foliar fungal diseases, in particular powdery mildew on various hosts.	Potassium bicarbonate	Diluted in water and often mixed with insecticidal soap (surfactant) and horticultural oil to increase effectiveness.
Fire blight control in apples and pears only	Streptomycin	Bactericide/antibiotic compound. Has no fungicidal activity. Fire blight bacteria can develop resistance with prolonged use. When used for fire blight control of apples and pears it must be applied during bloom prior to the appearance of symptoms to be effective. Sprays should begin at 20-30% bloom and continue every 3-4 days until petal fall. Do not apply when fruit is visible. Do not apply within 30 days of harvest for pears. Do not apply within 50 days of harvest for apples.

TURF
HOME TURF INSECT CONTROL

Will Hudson, Extension Entomologist

PEST	INSECTICIDE AND FORMULATION	AMOUNT PER 1,000 SQ. FT.*	REMARKS AND PRECAUTIONS
Ants (also see Imported fire ants)	Various pyrethroids		See note below.
Armyworms, cutworms, sod webworms	trichlorfon (Bayer Advanced) carbaryl (Sevin) 50WP *Bacillus thuringiensis* (Dipel WP) Various pyrethroids	6 1/2 ozs. 3/4-1 1/2 ozs.	Apply as a coarse spray in sufficient water for good coverage. Repeat as needed. See note below.
Chinch bugs	carbaryl (Sevin, etc.) bifenthrin cyfluthrin (Bayer Advanced Lawn and Garden)	See label 3 fl. ozs./gal.	Apply as a coarse spray in 4-5 gallons water per 1000 ft.². Irrigation of lawn prior to application will give better control.
Digger wasps, earwigs, sowbugs	carbaryl (Sevin) 50WP Various pyrethroids	6 ½ ozs.	
Ground pearls	All suggested practices regarding fertilization, watering, mowing, etc., should be carried out to keep grass growing ahead of damage. At the present time, there is no practical, effective, pesticide treatment.		
Imported fire ant	**Individual Mound Treatments** acephate (Orthene TTO) carbaryl (Sevin) 50WP Various pyrethroids acephate (Orthene TTO)	1 1/2 Tbs. 4 ozs. See label 2 tsp./mound	Mix with 2 gal. water. Sprinkle the entire amount on and around one mound. Do not disturb mound during treatment. Dust evenly over top of mound. Do not water in.
	Bait Treatments Amdro B Award Ascend or Varsity Distance Fire Ant Bait, Spectracide, Once 'n' Done Extinguish Firestar Fire Ant Bait		Fire ant bait should be used at 1-1 1/2 lbs. per acre. Bait should be used as soon as possible after opening package. Apply baits when ants are actively foraging for food. Follow label directions.
	Broadcast Treatments Over 'N' Out bifenthrin (Talstar, others) Various pyrethroids	2 lb. See label	See note below.
Millipedes	carbaryl (Sevin) 50WP Various pyrethroids	6 ozs.	Apply to turf 6 to 10 feet around building to provide a barrier treatment. Water thoroughly after application of granules. See note below.
Mole crickets	bifenthrin carbaryl (Sevin) 20B imidacloprid (Bayer Advanced Lawn Product)	See label 2-4 ozs. 2.87 lbs.	Water lawn before applying bait if soil is dry.
Spittlebugs	Various pyrethroids		Cut grass to its recommended height and remove clippings prior to application. Various pyrethroids may also provide some control. See note below.
White grubs (such as Japanese beetle larva, European chafer, Southern chafer, Billbugs)	trichlorfon (Bayer Advanced) imidacloprid 1.47% (Bayer Advanced) carbaryl (Sevin SL) halofenozide (Grub-B-Gon)	4-6 ozs.	Water lawn before application of any control material. Water thoroughly following insecticide application. For Green June beetle only. Apply as directed on label. Identification of pest grub species is important for effective control recommendations. Consult your local County Extension Agent.

NOTE: A number of pyrethroid materials are available in a variety of homeowner formulations for use as broad-spectrum contact insecticides. Common names include bifenthrin, cyfluthrin, cypermethrin, deltamethrin, lambda-cyhalotin, permethrin and tralomethrin. Active ingredients are listed on the label.

Most of the materials listed in the Commercial Landscape Insect Control section of this handbook are not Restricted Use Pesticides, and so are available for homeowner use. They are not marketed for homeowners, in small quantities at retail garden centers, but they could provide options for some homeowners. Consult your county Cooperative Extension Agent for advice on alternatives.

* Unless otherwise specified, mix with six gallons of water/1,000 square feet.

HOMEOWNER TURF DISEASE CONTROL

Elizabeth Little, Extension Homeowner IPM Specialist

Proper management is of utmost importance in preventing turf disease. Most of the time, culture and environment are the key reasons diseases develop, since potential turf pathogens are virtually always present. Disease problems are encouraged by improper watering, improper fertilization, nutrient deficiencies, excessive thatch, and improper mowing. Effective disease management centers on avoiding these problems through sound turf management and prevention of plant stress. In most cases, presence of a disease indicates an underlying cultural and/or environmental problem that needs to be addressed. Fungicides are not always necessary and when used should be part of a total management program. Follow label recommendations for rates and safety precautions when using all pesticides.

BROWN/LARGE PATCH (*Rhizoctonia solani*)
DOLLAR SPOT (*Sclerotinia homeocarpa*)

Management Tips:
- Use low to moderate amounts of nitrogen, moderate amounts of phosphorous and moderate to high amounts of potash.
- Avoid nitrogen applications when the disease is active.
- Increase the height of cut.
- Increase air circulation.
- Minimize the amount of shade.
- Irrigate turf early in the day.
- Improve the drainage of the turf.
- Reduce thatch.
- Remove dew from the turf early in the day (drag a hose over the turf).
- Warm season grasses — FALL preventative applications are BEST/MOST EFFECTIVE (Sept-Oct), with a follow-up SPRING application.

PESTICIDE	RATE	REMARKS
Captan (Hi-Yield Captan Fungicide 50% WP)	Use 5 tsp/gal water for Brown Patch.	Apply 1 gal/100ft^2. Begin application when new growth starts in the spring. Do NOT exceed 2 applications/year.
Maneb, Mancozeb (Hi-Yield Maneb Lawn & Garden)	See individual product labels.	Apply every 7-14 days as needed.
Myclobutanil (Immunox Lawn Disease Control-RTU, Concentrate, and Granules)	4-8 lbs/1000 sq. ft.	Apply every 14-28 days as needed.
PCNB (Terraclor 75WP, Hi-Yield Terraclor Granular Fungicide, Hi-Yield Turf & Omamental Fungicide containing 10% PCNB, Hi-Yield PCNB Granular Fungicide)	Brown Patch: 16 oz/1000 sq. ft. In 10-15 gals. Of water for warm season turfs. 3-4 oz/1000sq.ft. In 3-6 gals of water for cool season turfs. Dollar Spot: 7-10 oz/1000 sq. ft. In 5-10 gals of water.	Treated areas should be watered following application to move material to soil. Caution on cool season turfs for phytotoxicity. Retreat in 3-4 weeks if disease reappears.
Thiophanate methyl (Cleary's 3336, Scotts Lawn Fungus Control)	wettable powder(50%)-2 oz/3-5 gals water/1000sq.ft. flowable (46.2%)-1-2 oz/1000 sq. ft.	Apply every 7-14 days as needed.
Triadimefon (Bayleton, Green Light Systemic Lawn Spray Hose-end Concentrate, Hi-Yield Lawn Fungicide Granules, Bayer Advanced Fungus Control for Lawns)	See individual product labels.	Apply at 15-30 day interval as needed. Protective activity can be longer than 30 days depending on environmental conditions.

FADING OUT (*Curvularia sp.*)
MELTING OUT (*Helminthosporium sp.*)
LEAF SPOTS, RUST, ANTHRACNOSE

Management Tips:
• Increase the height of cut.
• Reduce turf stress by using lightweight equipment.
• Increase air circulation to speed turf's drying process.
• Avoid application of high rates of water-soluble nitrogen in the spring.
• Minimize the amount of shade.
• Irrigate turf deeply and as in frequently as possible.
• Reduce thatch in the early spring or fall for cool-season turfgrass and in the summer for warm-season turfgrass.

PESTICIDE	RATE	REMARKS
Maneb, Mancozeb (Hi-Yield Maneb Lawn & Garden)	See individual product labels.	Apply every 7-14 days as needed.
Myclobutanil (Immunox Lawn Disease Control- RTU, Concentrate, and Granules)	4 lb./1000 sq.ft.	Apply every 14-28 days as needed.
PCNB (Terraclor 75WP, Hi-Yield Terraclor Granular Fungicide, Hi-Yield Turf & Omamental Fungicide containing 10% PCNB, Hi-Yield PCNB Granular Fungicide)	7-10 oz/1000 sq.ft. In 5-10 gals of water.	Treated areas should be watered following application to move material to soil. Caution on cool season turfs for phytotoxicity. Retreat in 3-4 weeks if disease reappears.
Thiophanate methyl (Cleary's 3336, Scotts Lawn Fungus Control)	1-2 oz/1000 sq.ft. In 3-5 gals of water (anthracnose of cool season turfs).	Apply 10-14 days as needed.
Triadimefon (Bayleton, Fung-Away, Procide, Hi-Yield Lawn Fungicide Granules, Bayer Advanced Fungus Control for Lawns)	See individual product labels.	Apply at 15-30 day interval as needed. Protective activity can be longer than 30 days depending on environmental conditions.

FUSARIUM (*Fusarium sp.*)

Management Tips:
• Maintain balance fertility.
• Avoid using lime. Alkaline soils enhance disease development.
• Increase air circulation to speed turf's drying process.
• Minimize the amount of shade.
• Reduce thatch.

PESTICIDE	RATE	REMARKS
Myclobutanil (Immunox Lawn Disease Control Granules)	4-8 lb/1000 sq.ft.	Apply 14-21 days, when conditions are favorable for disease development.
Thiophanate methyl (Cleary's 3336, Scotts Lawn Fungus Control)	Patch: 2oz/1000sq.ft. Repeat at 5-14 day intervals. Blight: 4-8oz/1000sq.ft. Apply 2 applications at 10-14 day intervals.	Apply every 7-14 days as needed.
Triadimefon (Bayleton, Fung-Away, Hi-Yield Lawn Fungicide Granules, Bayer Advanced Fungus Control for Lawns)	See individual product labels.	Apply first in mid-June or 30 days prior to time blight normally becomes evident.

FAIRY RING (*various fungi*)

Management Tips:
• Avoid using root zone mixes with high levels of undecomposed organic materials.
• Reduce thatch.
• Irrigate deeply.
• Use nitrogen fertilizer to mask symptoms on some types of fairy ring.
• Use soil wetting agents to help penetrate hydrophobic areas.
• **NO PESTICIDES FOR HOMEOWNER USE.**

GRAY LEAF SPOT *(Pyricularia grisea)*

Management Tips:
- Avoid medium to high nitrogen levels during mid-summer.
- Irrigate turf deeply and as infrequently as possible to avoid water stress.
- Allow water to remain on leaves for only a short period of time.
- Reduce thatch.
- When possible, plant turfgrass that is resistant to gray leaf spot.
- Avoid using herbicides or plant growth regulators when disease is active

PESTICIDE	RATE	REMARKS
Propiconazole (Banner Max)	Refer to label for rates (1-2 fl. oz./1000 sq. ft.)	Local systemic; provides some control, best used in rotation or tank mix with other chemistries.
Thiophanate methyl (Cleary's 3336)	Refer to label for rates (1-2 fl. oz./1000 sq. ft.)	Local systemic; provides some control, best used in rotation or tank mix with other chemistries.

PYTHIUM BLIGHTS
PYTHIUM ROOT ROTS
(Pythium sp.)

Management Tips for Pythium Blight:
- Avoid mowing wet turf when temperature is over 70°F to minimize spreading the disease.
- Reduce thatch.
- Apply less than ½ pound of nitrogen per 1000 square feet a month during hot weather.
- Increase air circulation to speed the drying process of the turf.
- Minimize the amount of shade.
- Irrigate turf early in the day.
- Improve the drainage of the turf.
- Irrigate turf deeply and as in frequently as possible.

Management Tips for Pythium Root Rot:
- Increase the height of cut.
- Apply optimum amounts of nitrogen, phosphorous and potash.
- Reduce mowing frequency and use lightweight mowers.
- Avoid overwatering.
- Apply low amounts of nitrogen in the spring when roots are forming.
- Minimize the amount of shade.
- Improve the drainage of the turf.
- Reduce soil compaction through aerification by using lightweight equipment.

PESTICIDE	RATE	REMARKS
Maneb, Mancozeb (Hi-Yield Maneb Lawn & Garden)	See individual product labels.	Apply every 5 days as needed.
Aluminum tris (Monterey Aliette)	4 oz./1000 sq. ft.	Every 14 days

SPRING DEAD SPOT *(Leptosphaeria)*

Management Tips:
- Avoid late summer or fall applications of nitrogen fertilizers which may enhance disease severity.
- Use ammonium sources of nitrogen for fertilizer from spring through early August.
- Control weeds in affected turf to enhance recovery from spring dead spot.
- Apply moderate to high levels of phosphorous, potash, and minor elements.
- Improve drainage of turf.
- Reduce thatch.
- Use preventive fungicides applications in late September and October.

PESTICIDE	RATE	REMARKS
Myclobutanil (Immunox Lawn Disease Control - Ready to Spray Concentrate)	See Label.	Start treating when grass begins to turn green in spring or when signs of disease are first noticed.

TAKE-ALL PATCH (*Gauemannomyces graminis*)
TAKE-ALL ROOT ROT
BERMUDAGRASS DECLINE

Management Tips:
- Maintain soil pH below 6.5, preferably between 5.5 and 6.0.
- Manganese deficiency enhances development of take-all patch. Supplemental applications of this in fall or spring should reduce disease severity (rate of 2lb/acre).
- Avoid excessive irrigation and nitrogen applications.
- Improve surface and subsurface drainage.
- Reduce thatch.
- Aerate the soil.
- Application of sphagnum peat moss (3.8 cu ft./1000 sq ft).
- Use preventive fungicides (in fall, prior to dormancy, and early spring). FALL FUNGICIDES (Sept-Oct for Warm Season grasses) and follow-up early spring application — most effective. Summer applications NOT effective.

PESTICIDE	RATE	REMARKS
Myclobutanil (Immunox Lawn Disease Control- RTU, Concentrate, and Granules; Green Light Fung-Away Systemic Granules)	8 1b/1000 sq.ft.	Spring/Fall: 28 day intervals. Optimum disease control is achieved when the product is applied preventively. To reduce the severity of take-all, make 1 to 2 applications in Sept/Oct when night temps. drop below 55°F and 1 to 2 applications in the spring.
Triadimefon (Bayleton, Fung-Away, Hi-Yield Lawn Fungicide Granules; Green Light Systemic Lawn Spray Hose-end Concentrate, Bayer Advanced Fungus Control for Lawns)	See individual product labels.	Apply at 15-30 day interval as needed. Protective activity can be longer than 30 days depending on environmental conditions.

NEMATODES

Management tips:
- Promote root growth.
- Reduce stress.
- Clean all equipment.
- If suspect nematodes are a problem, contact local extension office to have a sample sent.

AMENDMENT (non-chemical)	RATE	REMARKS
Chitin	Depends upon soil analysis	A single annual application is usually sufficient for nematode control. Chitin is a non-chemical soil amendment that promotes growth of beneficial soil microorganisms which in turn feed on nematodes, whose body is made of chitin. This may not be practical for large turf areas.

TURFGRASS WEED CONTROL FOR HOMEOWNERS

Patrick McCullough, Extension Agronomist – Weed Science

The herbicides recommended in this section are available in small containers at most lawn and garden, hardware and discount stores. The herbicides listed in the section entitled "TURFGRASS WEED CONTROL RECOMMENDATIONS FOR PROFESSIONAL MANAGERS" are not usually available in small containers at stores that homeowners purchase lawn and garden pesticides.

USE STAGE AND HERBICIDE	TURFGRASSES	AMOUNT OF FORMULATION PER 1,000 SQ.FT.	REMARKS AND PRECAUTIONS
PREEMERGENCE HERBICIDES: Applications must be made prior to weed emergence or poor control will result. Recommended dates of application for crabgrass and other annual grasses are February 15 - March 5 in South GA and March 1-20 in North GA. Recommended dates for annual weeds are September 1-1 5 in North GA and October 1-15 in South GA.			
PREEMERGENCE (Established Grasses)			
oryzalin (Surflan) 4AS	Bermudagrass centipede, tall fescue, zoysia, St. Augustine	1.0 to 1.5 fl.oz.	Controls annual grasses and certain annual broadleaf weeds. Apply 1.5 oz./1,000 sq . ft. for summer annual grass control, or apply 1.0 oz./1,000 sq. ft. and apply an additional 1.0 oz./1,000 sq. ft. 8 to 10 weeks after the initial application. Split applications are recommended for improved goosegrass control and for tall fescue. Use the low rate for annual bluegrass control. **DO NOT** apply to newly sprigged grasses until well established. **DO NOT** make a spring application to fall planted turfgrasses. Surflan is recommended for use on healthy, established turf. Delay reseeding for 3 to 4 months after applications.
benefin (Balan) 2.5G (Crabgrass Preventer) 2.5G (Crabgrass Preventer) 1.72G	Ky. Bluegrass, bermudagrass, centipede, tall fescue, zoysia, St. Augustine	1.5 to 3.0 lbs.[1] 1.8 to 2.8 lbs.[1] 2.0 to 2.7 lbs.[1]	Controls annual grasses and certain annual broadleaf weeds. An additional application may be made 8 weeks after the initial treatment for continued weed control. **DO NOT** apply to newly sprigged grass until well established. **DO NOT** make a spring application to fall planted turfgrass. Delay reseeding for 6 weeks after application for the low rate, and for 12 to 16 weeks at the high rate. Benefin is available on a dry fertilizer carrier under various trade names.
pendimethalin (Halts) 1.71G	Ky. Bluegrass, bermudagrass, centipede, tall fescue, zoysia, St. Augustine	2.0 lbs.[1]	Controls annual grasses and certain annual broadleaf weeds. **DO NOT** use on newly sprigged grasses. On newly-seeded lawns, delay the application until after the fourth mowing. An additional application may be made 8 weeks after the first application to improve control of crabgrass and goosegrass. NOT recommend for turfgrass that has been severely thinned due to winter stress. **DO NOT** reseed within 4 months of application. Pendimethalin is available on a dry fertilizer carrier under various trade names.
benefin + trifluralin (Team) 2G	Ky. Bluegrass, bermudagrass, centipede, tall fescue, St. Augustine, zoysia,	2.5- to 3,5 lbs.[1]	Controls annual grasses and certain annual broadleaf weeds. **DO NOT** make a spring application to fall planted turfgrasses. **DO NOT** apply to newly sprigged grasses until full soil coverage is achieved. Under conditions of heavy goosegrass or annual bluegrass infestations, a second application should be made 10 weeks after the initial application. Delay reseeding for 8 weeks (low rate) to 12 weeks (high rate) after application.
benefin + oryzalin (XL) 2G	Bermudagrass, centipede, tall fescue, St. Augustine, zoysia,	2.5- to 5 lbs.[1]	Controls annual grasses and certain annual broadleaf weeds. **DO NOT** apply to newly sprigged grasses until well established. **DO NOT** make a spring application to fall planted Augustine turfgrasses. Delay reseeding for 6 weeks (low rate) and for 12 to 16 weeks (high rate).
atrazine (Bonus S) Southern Lawn Fertilizer plus Weed Control	Carpetgrass, centipede, St. Augustine, zoysia	4.3 lbs.[1] 5.0 lbs.[1 1]	Atrazine controls annual bluegrass and a wide range of broadleaf weeds. These products are formulated on a dry fertilizer carrier. **DO NOT** apply to newly seeded carpetgrass or centipedegrass until after two mowings. **DO NOT** sprig for one month or seed for six months after application. Atrazin will provide preemergence and postemergence control of many annual weeds. If centipede has been fertilized with more than 1.0 lb./1,0 00 sq. ft. of a nitrogen containing fertilizer, the use of these product is NOT recommended. These products are not Restricted Use Herbicides.

[1] Apply granules directly to the soil surface.

USE STAGE AND HERBICIDE	TURFGRASSES	AMOUNT OF FORMULATION PER 1,000 SQ.FT.	REMARKS AND PRECAUTIONS
PREEMERGENCE (Established Grasses) (continued)			
(Hi-Yield Atrazine) 4.0% (Image for St. Augustine & Centipedegrass) 4.0%	Centipedegrass, St. Augustine	8.0 fl. oz. 8.0 fl. oz.	Controls a wide range of broadleaf weeds, sandspur (sandbur) and suppresses crabgrass. May be applied in all 12 months for postemergence control of various weeds. Use in the fall or spring for the preemergence control of a wide range of annual grass and broadleaf weeds. Delay application to newly sodded or sprigged lawns until the sprigs have rooted and are actively growing. May be applied up to two times per year
dithiopyr (Turf & Ornamental Weed & Grass Stopper) 0.125GR	Ky. Bluegrass, bermudagrass, centipedegrass, tall fescue, St. Augustine, zoysia	4.6 to 9.2 lbs.[1]	Controls annual grasses and certain annual broadleaf weeds. A sequential application of 4.6 lbs. followed by a second application at 4.6 lbs. may improve control of annual grasses. Apply the second treatment 8 weeks after the first application. **DO NOT** apply to newly sprigged grasses until full soil coverage is achieved. Delay reseeding for 10 weeks (low rate) to 16 weeks (high rate) after application.
POSTMERGENCE (Established Grasses)			
sethoxydim (Segment) 1.0 lb./gal	centipede, fine fescue	0.5- to 0.75 fl. oz.	Apply only to centipede, and fine fescues (Creeping red, Chewing, Hard fescue). Other turfgrasses will be severely injured by this herbicide. Controls annual grasses and suppresses bahiagrass growth. Apply no sooner than 3 weeks after spring green-up. May be applied at the low rate to seedling centipede. **DO NOT** mow 7 days prior to or after application. Two applications per season may be utilized in established centipede. For bahiagrass suppression, repeat treatment 10 to 14 days after the first application.
fenoxaprop (Bermudagrass Control for Lawns) 0.41% fenoxaprop	Ky. Bluegrass, tall fescue, zoysia		Controls bermudagrass, crabgrass, Japanese stiltgrass, sandbur and numerous other grass weeds. **DO NOT** apply to bermudagrass, centipedegrass or St. Augustinegrass lawns. Apply at monthly intervals during the summer months to suppress/control bermudagrass. Plan on doing this program annually for at least two years. Annual grass weeds are usually controlled with a single application.
MSMA (Crabgrass Killer) 1 lb./gal. (529 Weed Killer) 4 lb./gal. (Crabgrass & Nutgrass Killer) 1.6 lb./gal. (Image with MSMA) 4 lb./gal.	Ky. Bluegrass, tall fescue, zoysia, bermudagrass	6.0 fl. oz. 2.0 fl. oz 4.0 fl. oz. 2.0 fl. oz.	These herbicides provide good control of emerged annual grasses, bahiagrass and dallisgrass, and fair control of nutsedge. Multiple applications sp aced 7 to 10 days apart are needed for acceptable control. Temporary turf discoloration will occur. Zoysiagrass cultivars vary in their tolerance to MSMA. 'Meyer' is more tolerant to MSMA than 'Matrella' and 'Emerald'. **DO NOT** apply to St.Augustine, carpetgrass, or centipede..
2,4-D + MCPP + dicamba (33 Plus) (Ace Lawn Weed Killer) (Wipe-out), (Trimec) (Southern Weed Killer for Lawns)	Ky. Bluegrass, tall fescue, zoysia, bermudagrass	2.67 fl. oz. 4.0 fl. oz 5.0 fl. oz. 4.0 fl. oz 4.0 fl. oz..	Controls a broader spectrum of weeds than 2,4-D alone. Newly-seeded lawns may be treated after a minimum of 3 mowings. Use one-half rates and spot treatments to minimize injury on centipede and St. Augustine. Applications during spring transition (green-up) should be avoided unless temporary (2 to 4 weeks) delays in green-up is acceptable. **DO NOT** apply at air temperatures>90°F.
carfentrazone + 2,4-D + MCPP + di-camba (SpeedZone Lawn Weed Killer)	Ky. Bluegrass, tall fescue, bermudagrass, zoysia-grass	0.75 to 1.0 fl. oz.	Controls a wide range of broadleaf weeds, including spotted spurge. May be applied after the second mowing in newly-established cool-season turfgrasses, or 4 weeks after sprigging or sodding warm-season turfgrasses. **DO NOT** reseed until 2 weeks after application. **DO NOT** apply at air temperatures > 90°F.

[1] Apply granules directly to the soil surface.

USE STAGE AND HERBICIDE	TURFGRASSES	AMOUNT OF FORMULATION PER 1,000 SQ.FT.	REMARKS AND PRECAUTIONS
POSTMERGENCE (Established Grasses)			
MCPP + 2,4-D + dicamba (Weed-B-Gon Max Ready-to-Use) (Weed-B-Gon for Southern Lawns)	Ky. Bluegrass, bermudagrass, centipedegrass, tall fescue, zoysiagrass, St. Augustine	Ready-to-Use 2.5 -5.0 fl. ozs.	Controls a broader spectrum of weeds than 2,4-D alone. Use the low rate on bermudagrass. Newly-seeded lawns may be treated after a minimum of 3 mowings. **DO NOT** reseed within 3 weeks of application. **DO NOT** apply at air temperatures >90°F. Use the lowest recommended rate on centipede and St. Augustine. **DO NOT** use on 'Floratam' St. Augustine
triclopyr (Weed-B-Gon Chickweed, Clover and Oxalis Killer) 8%	Ky. Bluegrass, tall fescue, zoysiagrass	2.5 fl. oz..	Controls numerous broadleaf weeds. Particularly effective for control of violets and ground ivy. Apply twice, at an interval of 3 to 4 weeks for improved control. NOT recommended for use on bermudagrass, centipedegrass and St. Augustinegrass. Newly-seeded lawns may be treated after a minimum of 3 mowings. **DO NOT** reseed for 3 weeks after application.
MSMA + 2,4-D + MCPP + dicamba (All-in-One Weed Killer for Lawns) (Trimec+++Plus)	Ky. Bluegrass, bermudagrass, tall fescue, zoysiagrass	3.0 - to 7.0 fl. oz. 3.0 to 4.0 fl. oz.	Controls both annual broadleaf weeds and certain annual grass weeds. Apply 1 to 3 days after mowing. **DO NOT** apply at air temperatures >90° F. Not recommended for use on centipedegrass, carpetgrass and St. Augustinegrass. Repeat applications 14 days apart will be necessary to control certain perennial broad leaf weeds, annual grasses and nutsedge. Newly-seeded lawns may be treated after a minimum of 4 mowings. **DO NOT** reseed for 3 to 4 weeks after application.
2,4-D + quinclorac + dicamba (All-in-One Lawn Weed and Crabgrass Killer) (Weed-B-Gon Max Plus Crabgrass Control Concentrate)	Ky. Bluegrass, bermudagrass, tall fescue, zoysiagrass	Product is designed to be applied by connecting bottle to garden hose. One quart will treat 5,000 sq. ft. 6.0 fl. ozs.	Controls both annual broadleaf weeds and crabgrass. Apply 1 to 3 days after mowing. **DO NOT** mow for 1 to 2 days after spraying. **DO NOT apply at air temperatures >85° F. Not recommended** for use on centipedegrass, carpetgrass and St. Augustinegrass. A repeat application at 14 days after the first application may be necessary to control certain perennial broadleaf weeds and annual grasses. Newly- seeded lawns may be treated after a minimum of 4 mowings. **DO NOT** reseed for 4 weeks after application.
atrazine (Hi-Yield Atrazine) 4.0% (Image for St. Augustine & Centipedegrass) 4.0% (Weed-B-Gon Spot Weed Killer for St. Augustine) 0.6% GR	Centipedegrass, St. Augustine	8.0 fl. oz. 8.0 fl. oz. Spot treatment.	Controls a wide range of broadleaf weeds, sandspur (sandbur and suppresses crabgrass. May be applied in all 12 months for postemergence control of various weeds. Use in the fall or spring for the preemergence control of a wide range of annual grass and broadleaf weeds. Delay application to newly sodded or sprigged lawns until the sprigs have rooted and are actively growing. May be applied up to two times per year. Weed-B-Gon Spot Weed Killer for St. Augustine is a granular product used as spot treatment (1.0 tablespoon per 4.0 sq. ft,) to control broadleaf weeds in centipedegrass, carpetgrass, St. Augustinegrass and zoysia. **DO NOT** overseed 4 months before or 6 months after treatment. **DO NOT** apply within the active zone of azaleas, ammellias, boxwoods, etc. **DO NOT** apply to any cool-season turfgrass or severe injury will occur.
imazaquin (Image Consumer Concentrate) 0.3 lbs./gal.	bermudagrass, centipedegrass, St. Augustinegrass, zoysia	3.75 fl. oz.	Controls nutsedge(s), wild garlic and selected broadleaf weeds. **DO NOT** apply when turfgrass is emerging from winter dormancy. **DO NOT** apply to newly planted or sprigged turfgrasses. This product is not recommended for use on St. Augustinegrass during the winter months.

[1] Apply granules directly to the soil surface.

USE STAGE AND HERBICIDE	TURFGRASSES	AMOUNT OF FORMULATION PER 1,000 SQ.FT.	REMARKS AND PRECAUTIONS
POSTMERGENCE (Established Grasses)			
bentazon (Basagran T/O) 4.0 lbs./gal. (Hi-Yield Basagran) 4.0 lbs./gal.	Ky. Bluegrass, bermudagrass, centipedegrass, tall fescue, St. Augustine, zoysia	0.75 to 1.5 fl. oz.	Apply bentazon to emerged yellow nutsedge that is actively growing and under good soil moisture conditions. Follow 10 to 14 days later with an additional application. Crop oil concentrate at 0.75 fl. oz./1,000 sq.ft. should be added to the spray mix. **DO NOT** mow 3 days before of after application. **DO NOT** apply to newly seeded or newly sprigged turfgrass until the seedlings or sprigs are well established.
potassium soap of fatty acids 22.1% (Bayer 2-in-1 Moss & Algae Killer)	Ky. Bluegrass, bermudagrass, centipedegrass, tall fescue, St. Augustine, zoysiagrass,	Product is designed to be applied by connecting bottle to garden hose.	Controls moss and algae in established lawns. Rinse treated areas with water 15 to 30 minutes after treatment to lower risk of turfgrass injury. **DO NOT** heavily irrigate turf for 6 hours after treatment. For best results apply in spring or fall months. This product should not be applied at air temperatures > 85° F. Treated areas can be reseeded 5 days after treatment.
iron sulfate (Scotts Turf Builder Fertilizer with Moss Control) 17.5%	Ky. Bluegrass, bermudagrass, centipedegrass, tall fescue, St. Augustine, zoysiagrass,		This product contains iron sulfate formulated on a 22-2-2 fertilizer carrier. One bag will treat up 5,000 sq. ft. This application rate will supply 1/1 lbs. N per 1,000 sq. ft. Apply in winter or spring months to moist turf when moss is actively growing. This product may cause turfgrass foliage to temporarily blacken. Subsequent mowing will alleviate this condition. **DO NOT** apply to a newly seeded or sodded lawn until it has been mowed four times. Brush or rinse particles from cement, stone, clothing, or shoes to prevent staining.

[1] Apply granules directly to the soil surface.

TURFGRASS HERBICIDES COMMONLY FOUND IN RETAIL LAWN AND GARDEN STORES/CENTERS

Patrick E. McCullough, Extension Agronomist – Weed Science

I. Preemergence Herbicides

Trade Name	Active Ingredient
Balan	benefin
Bonus S	atrazine
Southern Lawn Fertilizer plus Weed Control	atrazine
Gallery	isoxaben
Green Light Amaze	benefin + oryzalin
Green Light Betasan	bensulide
Halts	pendimethalin
Hi-Yield Crabgrass Preventer	benefin + trifluralin
Surflan	oryzalin
StaGreen CrabEx	dithiopyr
Hi-Yield Turf & Ornamental Weed & Grass Stopper	dithiopyr
StaGreen Crabgrass Preventer	prodiamine
Lawn Fertilizer plus Weed Control	prodiamine
StaGreen Crabgrass Preventer with Fertilizer	benefin + trifluralin
Team	benefin + trifluralin
XL	benefin + oryzalin

II. Postemergence Herbicides

Trade Name	Active Ingredient
Ace Lawn Weed Killer	2,4-D + MCPP + dicamba
Acme Super Chickweed Killer	2,4-D + MCPP + dicamba
Basagran T&O	bentazon
Bayer Advanced All-in-One Weed Killer	MSMA + 2,4-D + MCPP + dicamba
Bayer Advanced Southern Lawn Weed Killer	2,4-D + MCPP + dicamba
Dragon Lawn Weed Killer	2,4-D + MCPP + dicamba
Drexel MSMA 6 Plus	MSMA
Enforcer Weed Stop	2,4-D + MCPP + dicamba
Fertilome Crabgrass, Nutgrass & Dallisgrass Killer	MSMA
Fertilome Weed Out Lawn Weed Killer	2,4-D + MCPP + dicamba
Green Light Wipe Out	2,4-D + MCPP + dicamba
Green Light DSMA Crabgrass Killer	DSMA
Green Light MSMA Crabgrass Killer	MSMA
Green Light Spot Weed Killer	MCPA + MCPP + dicamba

Trade Name	Active Ingredient
Hi-Yield Basagran	bentazon
Hi-Yield 529 Crabgrass Killer	MSMA
Hi-Yield Atrazine	atrazine
Ortho Spot Weed Killer for St. Augustine Lawns	atrazine
Image	imazaquin
Image for St. Augustine and Centipede	atrazine
Image with MSMA	MSMA
Rigo's Best Crabgrass Killer	MSMA
Rigo Super Lawn Weed Killer	2,4-D + MCPP + dicamba
Safer Weed Away	2,4-D + MCPP + dicamba
Sethoxydim G-Pro	sethoxydim
Spectrum Lawn Weed Killer 33 Plus	2,4-D + MCPP + dicamba
Speed Zone Lawn Weed Killer	2,4-D + MCPP + dicamba + carfentrazone
Spectracide Weed Stop	2,4-D + MCPP + dicamba
Trimec Classic	2,4-D + MCPP + dicamba
Trimec Southern	MCPP + 2,4-D + dicamba
Weed-B-Gon Chickweed, Clover & Oxalis Killer	triclopyr
Weed-B-Gon Crabgrass Killer Formula II	CAMA
Weed-B-Gon Max	MCPA + triclopyr + dicamba

Web sites for homeowner lawn and garden herbicide labels (and other pesticides):

Bayer: http://www.bayeradvanced.com/lawn/

Enforcer: http://www.enforcer.com/

GreenLight: http://www.greenlightco.com/

Hi-Yield: http://www.v-p-g.com/

Lebanon: http://www.lebsea.com/newlebsea/index.jsp

Monsanto: http://lawncare.roundup.com/index.cfm/event/Home.Normal

Ortho: http://www.ortho.com/

PBI Gordon: http://www.pbigordon.com/homefarm/lawncare_weed.php

Scotts: http://www.scotts.com/

Southern Ag: http://www.southernag.com/

Spectracide: http://www.spectracide.com/

96

TURFGRASS WEED RESPONSE TO HERBICIDES – HOMEOWNER PRODUCTS

	atrazine	benefin	dithiopyr	oryzalin	prodiamine	pendimethalin
Time of application				PREEMERGENCE		
PERENNIAL WEEDS						
bahiagrass	F	P	P	P	P	P
bermudagrass	P	P	P	P	P	P
dallisgrass	P	P	P	P	P	P
nutsedge, purple	P	P	P	P	P	P
nutsedge, yellow	P	P	P	P	P	P
tall fescue	F	P	P	P	P	P
wild garlic/onion	P	P	P	P	P	P
ANNUAL GRASSES						
annual bluegrass	E	E	G	G	E	G
crabgrass	F	E	G-E	E	E	E
crowfootgrass		G		G		G
goosegrass	P	F	F	F-G	G	F-G
sandbur		F		G		G
BROADLEAF WEEDS						
carpetweed	E		G-E	G-E	G-E	G-E
chamberbitter (niruri)	G					
common chickweed	E	G	G	G	G	G
corn speedwell	E	E	G			E
cudweed	E	P		P		P
dandelion	F	P	P	P	P	P
dichondra	F	P	P	P	P	P
docks	G	P	P	P	P	P
doveweed	G	P		P		P
Florida betony	E	P		P		P
ground ivy		P	P	P	P	P
henbit	E	G	G	G	G	G
hop clovers	E	P				
knotweed	E			F		
lespedeza	E					
mallow, bristly		P	P	P	P	P
mock strawberry		P	P	P	P	P
mouseear chickweed		E		P		G
mugwort		P	P	P	P	P
mustards	E					
parsley piert	E	P				P
pennywort	F	P		P		P
plantains	G	P	P	P	P	P
spurges	E	P	G			F
spurweed (burweed)	E	P	P	F	P	G
VA buttonweed		P	P	P	P	P
violets		P	P	P	P	P
white clover	E	P	P	P	P	P
yellow woodsorrel	E	P	P	F	P	F

Key to response symbols: E = Excellent control (90 to 100 %), G = Good control (80 to 89%), F = Fair control (70 to 79%), P = Poor control (< 70%). A blank space indicates weed response is not known.

	atrazine	bentazon	2,4-D	2,4-D + MCPP + dicamba	imazaquin	MSMA CAMA	sethoxydim	triclopyr
Time of application	POSTEMERGENCE							
PERENNIAL WEEDS								
bahiagrass	P-F	P	P	P	P	F	F-G	P
bermudagrass	P	P	P	P	P	P	F	P
dallisgrass	P	P	P	P	P	F-G	P	P
nutsedge, purple	P	P	F	P	G	F	P	P
nutsedge, yellow	P	G	F	P	F-G	F	P	P
tall fescue	F	P	P	P	P-F	P	P-F	P
wild garlic/onion	P	P	G	G	E	P	P	F
ANNUAL GRASSES								
annual bluegrass	E	P	P	P	P-F	P	P	P
crabgrass	F	P	P	P	P	E	E	P
crowfootgrass	P	P	P	P	P	E	F-G	P
goosegrass	P	P	P	P	P	F	G	P
sandbur	F	P	P	P	F	G	G	P
BROADLEAF WEEDS								
carpetweed	E		G	G-E			P	G
chamberbitter (niruri)	G-E	P	P		P	P-F	P	
common chickweed	E	G	P	G	E	P	P	E
corn speedwell	E	P	F	F	P	P	P	G
cudweed	G		G-E	E	F	F-G	P	F
dandelion	F	P	E	G		P	P	G
dichondra	F	P	G	G		P	P	F-G
docks	G	P	F	G		P	P	F-G
doveweed	G-E	P	F	F-G			P	F
Florida betony	F-G	P	F	G		P	P	G
ground ivy		P	P-F	F		P	P	G
henbit	E	P	P	G		P	P	E
hop clovers	E		F	G		P	P	E
knotweed	E		P	G		P	P	F
lespedeza	E		P-F	G		P	P	G
mallow, bristly		P	F	F-G		P	P	G
mock strawberry		P	P	G		P	P	
mouseear chickweed	G	P	P-F	G	G	P	P	G
mugwort		P	P	P-F		P	P	P-F
mustards	E	G	E	G		P	P	G
parsley piert	E	G	P	F-G	G	P	P	E
pennywort	E	P	G	G		P	P	F
plantains	F	P	E	G		P	P	F
spurges	E	P	F	G		P	P	F
spurweed (burweed)	E.	E	G	G	E	P	P	F-G
star-of-Bethlehem	P	P	P	P	P	P	P	P
VA buttonweed		P	P	F		P	P	F
violets		P	P	P-F		P	P	F-G
white clover	E	P	F	G	G	P	P	G
yellow woodsorrel	G	P	P	F		G	P	F

Key to response symbols: E = Excellent control (90 to 100 %), G = Good control (80 to 89%), F = Fair control (70 to 79%), P = Poor control (< 70 %). A blank space indicates weed response is not known.

ANIMALS
PETS (Companion Animals) EXTERNAL PARASITE CONTROL

Nancy Hinkle, Extension Veterinary Entomologist

Numerous external parasites infest our pets. Dogs and cats can become infested with fleas, ticks and mange mites and pet birds with mites and lice. Often these parasites infest our homes and yards. Thus control measures should focus on the infested pet and the pet's roaming area as well.

Pet owners should seek professional advice and assistance from Veterinarians, Professional-Licensed Pest Control Operators and University Extension Agents when dealing with external parasite control on pets and the home environment. This will help prevent problems when using chemicals to treat pets, as well as indoor and outdoor areas. Pets can be poisoned and even killed by external parasiticides if they are used improperly. Rugs, carpets and home furnishings can be damaged by the improper use of insecticides. Humans can be allergic to external parasiticides used on pets and insecticides used in the home. For these reasons, when treating pets and the home environment, one should always seek professional advice and adhere to instructions provided on drug and insecticide labels.

Many of the insecticides listed in this section will control or aid in control of other external dog parasites and offer temporary relief from flies. Mites are difficult to control and only those products labeled for mites can be expected to provide acceptable results. Only those insecticides that have labels specifically permitting feline treatment can be used to treat cats; exercise extreme caution when treating cats to avoid toxicity. See Household Pest Control section for recommendations on treating indoor flea infestations.

DOGS AND CATS – EXTERNAL PARASITE CONTROL

Common Name (Trade Names)	Parasite Controlled	Formulation	Indoor	Pets	Outdoor
allethrin (SP)	fleas, ticks	Aerosol	X		
		Shampoo		X	
amitraz (Preventic Tick Collar, Mitaban)[1]	fleas, mites	Collar		X[2]	
		Dip		X[2]	
carbaryl (Sevin) (CR)	fleas, ticks. lice	Shampoo		X	
		Dust	X	X	X
d-limonene (Flea and Tick Spray, Dip and Shampoo) (BOT)	fleas, ticks	Aerosol	X	X	
		Dip		X	
		Shampoo		X	
deltamethrin (SP)	fleas, ticks	Collar		X	
fipronil (Frontline)[1]	fleas, ticks	Spot-on		X	
		Spray		X	
imadacloprid (Advantage)[1]	fleas	Spot-on		X	
ivermectin[1]	mites	Suspension		X	
limonene (BOT)	fleas / Spray	Shampoo		X	
		Dust	X	X	
linalool (BOT)	fleas, ticks / Dust	Spray	X	X	
		Dust	X		
lufenuron (Program, Sentinel)[1] (IGR)	fleas	Suspension		X	
		Tablet	X	X	
		Injection		X	
methoprene (Precor) (IGR)	fleas, ticks	Aerosol	X		
		Spot-on	X	X	
		Shampoo		X	
		Collar		X	
		Emulsifiable concentrate (Spray)	X		
		Spray	X	X	
milbemycin oxime (Milbemite)[1]	mites	Suspension		X	
nitenpyram (Capstar)[1]	fleas	Tablet		X	

Common Name (Trade Names)	Parasite Controlled	Formulation	Indoor	Pets	Outdoor
permethrin (SP)	fleas, ticks, lice, mites	Aerosol	X		
		Spot-on		X^2	
		Emulsifiable concentrate (Spray)	X		
		Shampoo		X^2	
		Spray		X^2	
phenothrin (SP)	fleas, ticks	Shampoo		X^2	
		Fogger	X		
		Collar		X	
		Spot-on		X^2	
		Spray	X		
propoxur (Sendran) (CR)	fleas	Collar		X	
pyrethrins + piperonyl butoxide (NP) (BOT)	fleas, ticks, lice	Spray	X	X	
		Shampoo		X	
		Dip		X	
		Emulsifiable concentrate (Spray)	X		
		Dust		X	
		Fogger	X		
	mites	Suspension		X	
pyriproxyfen (IGR)	fleas, ticks	Spray	X		
		Collar		X	
		Shampoo		X	
		Spot-on		X	
		Fogger			
resmethrin (SP)	fleas	Spray		X	
		Emulsifiable concentrate (Spray)	X		
		Shampoo		X	
rotenone[1] (BOT)	mites	Spray		X^2	
		Supension		X	
		Cream		X^2	
selamectin (Revolution)[1]	fleas, ticks, mites	Spot-on		X	
tetrachlorvinphos (OP)	fleas	Collar		X	
		Fogger	X		
tetramethrin (SP)	fleas	Spray	X		

PET BIRDS (mites, lice, fleas)

carbaryl (Sevin) (CR)		Dust	X	X	
pyrethrins + piperonyl butoxide (many available) (NP)		Aerosol	X	X	

[1] Some formulations for veterinary application or prescription only.

[2] Treat dogs only.

Abbreviations: CR - carbamate, IGR - insect growth regulator, INO - inorganic, NP - natural pyrethrins, OP - organophosphate, SP - synthetic pyrethroid.

FLEA CONTROL PRODUCTS

Nancy Hinkle, Extension Veterinary Entomologist

Adult fleas spend their entire lives on the dog or cat. As they are laid, flea eggs fall off the animal and collect in the environment (carpet or dirt). Flea larvae emerge from eggs within a couple of days and crawl around, eating their parents' feces. In about two weeks, the larva has completed its development and is ready to spin a cocoon within which it will change into an adult. Once this metamorphosis has taken place, the adult flea remains within the cocoon until it is stimulated to emerge. If a host is not present, an unemerged flea can remain within its cocoon for months, allowing a flea infestation to persist for long periods without an animal around. Cues that signal a nearby host include movement, heat, and carbon dioxide (exhaled by all mammals). Upon detecting one of these stimuli, the flea bursts from the cocoon and hops toward the host. It repeatedly flings itself against the host until its claws catch. To avoid being groomed off or knocked loose, the flea burrows into the host's coat. Adult fleas must suck blood once an hour, so never leave the host. Once on the host, fleas live for two or three weeks.

Fleas can live on wild animals such as opossums, raccoons, foxes, skunks, etc., so it is important to discourage wild animals from visiting your yard and sharing their fleas. Do not leave pet food outside at night, and seal garbage cans to prevent attracting wildlife. Screen openings to crawl spaces and do not allow wild animals to den under the house, in the attic, or in outbuildings.

Because flea eggs, larvae, and pupae are dispersed in the environment, they are very difficult to control. Daily vacuuming helps suppress fleas indoors. The most efficient flea control method is to treat the host (dog or cat) and kill adult fleas before they can reproduce. Pets should be treated early in the spring, before fleas become a problem, to prevent large populations becoming established in the environment. Over-the-counter products, while less expensive, do not contain the same ingredients as those obtained through veterinarians and may be more toxic. Always read and follow label directions. Pesticides can sicken or kill pets and people if used incorrectly.

HOST-APPLIED FLEA PRODUCTS

Product	Manufacturer	Active Ingredient	Formulation	Dosage	Pet	Effective Against
Advantage	Bayer	Imidacloprid	Topical Spot-on	Once/mo.	Dogs & Cats	Fleas
Advantix	Bayer	Imidacloprid and Permethrin	Topical Spot-on	Once/mo.	Dogs	Fleas, Ticks, Mosquitoes
Capstar	Novartis	Nitenpyram	Tablets	Once/day	Dogs & Cats	Fleas
Comfortis	Lilly	Spinosad	Tablet	Once/mo.	Dogs	Fleas
Frontline	Merial	Fipronil	Topical Spot-on Spray	Once/mo Once/mo..	Dogs & Cats Dogs & Cats	Fleas, Ticks Fleas, Ticks
Program	Novartis	Lufenuron	Tablets Liquid Injectable	Once/mo. Once/mo. Once/mo.	Dogs & Cats Cats Cats	Fleas (immatures)
ProMeris for dogs	Fort Dodge	Metaflumizone, amitraz	Topical Spot-on	Once/mo.	Dogs	Fleas, Ticks
ProMeris for cats	Fort Dodge	Metaflumizone	Topical Spot-on	Once/mo.	Cats	Fleas
Revolution	Pfizer	Selamectin	Topical Spot-on	Once/mo.	Dogs & Cats	Fleas, Ear Mites, Heartworm, Intestinal Worms
Sentinel	Novartis	Milbemycin oxime and Lufenuron	Tablets	Once/mo.	Dogs	Fleas (immatures), Heartworm, Intestinal Worms
Vectra 3D	Summit VetPharm	Dinotefuran, permethrin and pyriproxyfen	Topical Spot-on	Once/mo.	Dogs	Fleas, Ticks, Mosquitoes
Vectra	Summit VetPharm	Dinotefuran, pyriproxyfen	Topical Spot-on	Once/mo.	Cats	Fleas

HONEY BEE DISEASE AND PEST CONTROL

Keith S. Delaplane, Extension Entomologist

PEST	MATERIAL AND FORMULATION	RATE	REMARKS AND PRECAUTIONS
American foulbrood (AFB)	Terramycin	Mix one 6.4 oz. packet of Terramycin with 2.7 lb. powdered sugar. For each treatment, apply 2 tablespoons to top bars. Repeat at 4-5 day intervals for a total of 3 treatments.	Antibiotics are strictly for preventing disease. Treat in February and September and never within 4 weeks of a marketable nectar flow. Diseased colonies must be burned. Dig a p it and burn all bees, combs, and frames. Bottom boards, supers, and lids can be salvaged by scorching their interiors. With medicated extender patties, re-move all uneaten portions after 4 weeks of treatment and never treat within 4 weeks of a marketable nectar flow. The use of genetically AFB - resistant queens expressing hygienic behavior can reduce or eliminate the need for antibiotic treatments.
	Tylosin	Honey bee colonies should receive three treatments administered as a dust in confectioners/powder sugar. Mix 200 mg tylosin in 20 g confectioners/ powdered sugar. The 200 mg dose is applied (dusted) over the top bars of the brood chamber. Apply 3 single doses, each one week apart. For use in limited amounts, mix 1 tablespoon with 2 boxes (1.93 lbs.) of powdered sugar. This will provide treatment for 44 colonies with single doses or 15 colonies with 3 doses (for a complete treatment)	
Chalkbrood	None		Keep hives well ventilated. Prop lid slightly to exhaust warm, damp air. Lean hive forward to drain rain water from interior. Use hygienic selected bee stock.
European foulbrood (EFB)	Terramycin Tylosin	Same as for American foulbrood	Drug is for preventing and treating disease. Treat in February and September and never within 4 weeks of a marketable nectar flow. Help infected colonies by adding unsealed brood and feeding 1: 1 sugar syrup. Use hygienic — selected bee stick.
Nosema	Fumagilin B	Dissolve 1 teaspoon of Fumagilin B in 1.1 gallons of sugar syrup.	Feed medicated syrup in spring and fall and never immediately before a marketable nectar flow. Keep hives well ventilated. Prop lid slightly to exhaust warm, damp air. Lean hive forward to drain rain water from interior.
Beetles		1. For treatment inside colonies: Adult beetles can be trapped and drowned in vegetable oil with any of the numerous in-hive adult beetle traps available by bee suppliers.	
	2. Permethrin (GardStar 40% E.C.)	2. For treatment outside colonies: Mix 5 mi GardStar concentrate with 1 gal water. Thoroughly wet ground in an area 18-24 in. wide in front of each hive (1 gal per 6 hives).	2. GardStar: Product is designed to kill immature beetles when they leave hive in order to pupate in the soil. Product is highly toxic to bees. Avoid direct spray onto hive surfaces. Apply in late evening after bees become in active. For pre-placement cleanup of new apiary site, apply thoroughly to ground surface 24-48 hours prior to hive placement.

PEST	MATERIAL AND FORMULATION	RATE	REMARKS AND PRECAUTIONS
Beetles (cont.)	3. Predatory soil nematodes especially *Heterohabditis indica*	3. For treatments outside colonies: Mix 1 million infective juveniles in 2 gal. water per colony. Strain out gelatin globules and trickle solution on ground in front of hive. Treat ground under hive if screen bottoms are used.	3. Predatory nematodes have been shown to effectively kill SHB pupae in soil in front of hives.
Tracheal mites	menthol	one 1.8 oz. packet per colony	Do not use on hives containing marketable honey. Enclose 1.8 oz. menthol in a 7-inch square plastic (or other porous) screen packet. Treat colonies in fall and early spring and only when daytime highs range from 60° -90° F. If daytime high is $\geq 80^\circ$ F., place packet on bottom board. If daytime high is 60° -79° F., place packet on top bars. Replace menthol as needed. Remove all menthol 10-12 weeks after first treatment and at least 1 month before nectar flows. Vegetable oil such as in the medicated extender patty described above for AFB and EFB helps control tracheal mites.
	oil patties	Mix patties with 2 parts sugar: 1 part vegetable cooking shortening. Each patty should be ½ lb.	Place oil patty on top bars of brood frames. Spring treatments (February-April) are most effective.
Varroa mites			Treatable threshold for varroa mite is 60-180 mites recovered in one 24-hour exposure with a bottom board sticky sheet, without use of miticide.
	fluvalinate (Apistan)	1 strip for each 5 combs of bees in each brood chamber	1. Apistan: Do not use on hives containing marketable honey. Hang one strip between frames 3 and 4, and another strip between frames 7 and 8. Leave strips in hive for 42 to 56 days. Apistan treatments are usually most effective if given in early fall. Supplement Apistan with Terramycin treatments as described above for AFB.
	coumaphos (CheckMite+ Strip)	1 strip for each 5 combs of bees in each brood chamber	2. CheckMite: Hang the strips within two combs of the edge of the bee cluster. If two deep supers are used for the brood nest, hang CheckMite+ Strips in alternate corners of the cluster, in the top and bottom super. Remove honey supers before application of Check-Mite+ Strips and do not replace until 14 days after the strips are removed. Treat all infested colonies within yard. The treatment is most effective when brood rearing is lowest. Do not treat when surplus honey is being produced. Leave the strips in the hive for at least 42 days (six weeks). Do not leave strips in hive for more than 45 days. Do not treat more than twice a year for varroa mites.
	Apiguard	1 tray per colony, repeated after 2 weeks	3. Apigard: Open the hive. Peel back the foil lid of the APIGUARD tray leaving one corner of the lid attached to the tray. Place the open tray centrally on top of the brood frames, gel side up. Ensure that there is a free space of at least ¼ inch between the top of the tray and the hive cover board, for example, by placing an empty super on top of the brood box. Close the hive. After two weeks replace the first tray with a new one, according to the same instruction. Leave the product in the colony until the tray is empty. Remove the product when in stalling the supers on the colony. The efficacy of APIGUARD is maximized if the product is used in late summer after the honey harvest (when the amount of the brood present is diminishing). However, in the case of severe infestations, APIGUARD can also be used during springtime, when temperatures are above 60°F. Efficacy will vary between colonies due to the natural of the application. Therefore, APIGUARD should be used as one treatment among others within an Integrated Pest Management program, and mite fall regularly monitored. If further significant mite fall is observed during the following winter or spring, use an additional secondary winter or spring treatment for varroa.

PEST	MATERIAL AND FORMULATION	RATE	REMARKS AND PRECAUTIONS
Varroa mites (cont.)	Api-Life VAR	1 treatment consists of 3 wafers over 2-32 days	4. Api-Life VAR: Applications can be made in any season (spring, summer, fall, winter) in which all applicable restrictions, precautions and directions for use can be followed. Do not use when surplus honey supers are in place. Use when average daily temperatures are between 59°F and 69°F. Do not use ApiLife VAR at temperatures above 90°F. Two treatments per year may be made. A treatment (3 tablets) consists of the following: Take one tablet and break into four equal pieces. Place pieces on the top corners of the hive body. Avoid placing pieces directly above the brood nest. After 7-10 days, replace with a fresh tablet broken in to pieces as above. Repeat procedure again, 7-10 days later and leave last tablet for 12 days. After 12 days, remove residuals from the colony. To prevent the bees from gnawing the tablet either enclose each piece of tablet in an envelope of screen wire (8 mesh/inch) or place the uncovered pieces above a sheet of metal screen that prevents bees from contacting it. Remove ApiLife VAR tablets from hive at least 1 month (30 days) prior to harvesting the honey.
Wax moths	PDB crystals	Stack stored supers, cover stack and make air-tight with newspaper or duct tape. At intervals equal to the height of 5 deep supers or 10 shallow supers, insert 6 tablespoons of PDB. Put crystals on a small piece of cardboard placed on top bars of frames. Replace crystals as they evaporate. Air-out supers before using on live bee hives.	Wax moths are secondary scavengers. Wax moths in living colonies indicate an underlying problem. Check for queenlessness, disease, or mites. Protect stored combs by: (1) storing them on top of strong colonies, (2) freezing combs and supers, then stacking them and taping shut all cracks to exclude moths, (3) stacking combs so they are constantly exposed to air and daylight, (4) operating an electronic "bug zapper" in the super storage room to kill adult moths, (5) using PDB crystals.

HOUSEHOLD AND STORED PRODUCTS
HOUSEHOLD AND STRUCTURAL INSECT CONTROL

Dan Suiter, Extension Entomologist

Document Pest Identification and Habits

It is important that pests be accurately identified. An Extension Specialist's recommendation(s) for chemical and non-chemical pest control are largely dependent on the pest's identification and a full description of the circumstances surrounding its collection and appearance— i.e., its habits, food, description, where it was found, and what it was found infesting (if anything). In some cases, the chemical control of pests is not needed, and indeed of no use. In other cases, only the use of pesticides will solve the problem. Many cases, however, require a combination of both chemical and non-chemical control techniques.

Contact a local county Extension Service agent for help in identifying specimens. An Extension agent can identify samples by visual observation or by looking at a photograph. If the homeowner has access to a digital camera, a photograph(s) can be taken and emailed to the Extension Service for immediate identification. Specimens can also be collected, placed in a leak-proof vial filled with rubbing alcohol, and mailed to the nearest county Extension Service office.

Hiring a Professional Pest Control Company

It is often best to hire a professional pest control company to tackle pest control problems. It is especially important to select a company committed to customer service, especially if the homeowner is considering entering a long-term service contract. Some tips on hiring a pest control company include:

- Ask friends, neighbors, and co-workers about their experiences and interactions with pest control companies. Selecting a professional pest control company is not unlike selecting other service providers, such as electricians and plumbers. Consistently good recommendations are still the most reliable means of selecting a quality pest control professional.

- Avoid going to the yellow pages and selecting a company based solely on an advertisement. Furthermore, do not hire a pest control company based on treatment price alone. A variety of factors should be considered when making a decision on which company to hire.

- Contact the appropriate state regulatory agency to ensure that prospective companies are licensed. In Georgia, the Department of Agriculture (www.agr.state.ga.us) is the agency that regulates the pest control industry.

- Ask prospective companies to describe their commitment to the continuing education of their pest control technicians. Although all technicians in Georgia are required to attend State-approved continuing education seminars, some companies provide in-house training or send their employees to University- or State-sponsored training programs and workshops that are above and beyond that required by the State.

- Ask prospective companies whether they are a member of their state and/or national pest control organization(s). Membership in these organizations suggests that the firm is well-established, and that the owners are active in their profession. Membership also suggests that owners and managers attend national and state conferences where insight into key issues facing the pest control industry are highlighted and discussed, and the most recent findings on pest control research and application technology are presented.

Homeowners and Termite Control

Homeowners should not attempt to treat their home for an existing termite infestation. The treatment techniques, products, and equipment needed to rid a home of termites are available only by hiring a professional. The most important challenge confronting anyone attempting to control termites lies in locating and properly treating the area(s) where termites are entering the structure. This goal can best be accomplished by a professional. To learn more about subterranean termites and their control see Georgia Cooperative Extension Service publications at http://www.ent.uga.edu/pubs.htm.

Where to Treat

Before selecting chemically-based pest control measures (see Table below), a thorough **inspection** of the outdoor and/or indoor premises should be conducted to determine the extent of the infestation and to highlight those areas where control approaches should be focused. Many indoor infestations of urban pests can be tracked to areas of pest activity (harborage) on the outside of the structure, while still other pests are found only indoors.

Moisture Management

The most important condition conducive to pest infestation in and around the home is **excessive moisture**. Since all life forms are dependent upon moisture, its excess not only attracts pests but allows them to thrive. Some common sources of excessive moisture in and around homes include improper grade/drainage; standing water in the crawlspace; broken drainpipes; roof leaks; interior plumbing leaks; improperly installed flashing around fireplaces, windows and doors; improper ventilation in the crawlspace; lack of a vapor barrier in the crawlspace; misdirected sprinklers; clogged gutters and downspouts; and downspout exhaust within 5 feet of the structure.

The property owner should ensure that water flows away from structure (i.e., grade is appropriate and gutters and downspouts are operating properly), that the structure is properly ventilated, that water leaks are fixed in a timely manner, and that a vapor barrier is in place in the crawlspace. Homeowners should keep groundcovers, shrubs, vines, and mulch several feet away from outside foundation walls as these horticultural practices often hold excessive moisture close to the structure. For instance, **mulch** retains moisture in the soil, thereby creating a zone that provides conditions (high moisture) urban pests need to explore and thrive in an area. Although no scientific data specifically addresses the affect that mulch has on pest infestation rates, it is known that mulch placed against a structure's outside walls allows pests easy access.

How to Use Various Product Types

Bait Products. Over-the-counter bait products are generally limited to ant, cockroach, rat, and mouse control, and can be used both inside and outside the home. Baits are available in the form of **gels/pastes, granules, liquids, stations, or blocks,** and most come ready-to-use.

Baits are products that kill pests only after being consumed. As such, they are comprised of a toxicant (i.e., active ingredient) incorporated into a food source (i.e., the bait material) that is both palatable and preferred by the target species. Since baits contain food materials, they are susceptible to spoilage; read the product's lab el do determine if the bait has an expiration date. Baits are target-specific, and thus considered more environment ally-sensitive, than the other chemically-based control tactics discussed hereafter.

When **baiting for ants,** a few recommendations should be followed. First, place baits where ants are seen foraging (inside and/or outside structures) and if possible always in the shade when baiting outdoors. Ants do not forage in the direct sun or during the heat of the day, but may be found foraging in the same area in shaded locations. Second, it is often advantageous to purchase and use, at the same time, several different baits to discover one that ants will readily consume since no single bait is consistently eaten by all ant species. Third, baiting species whose colonies are comprised of a large number of ants (such as Argentine ants) requires that a large quantity of bait be offered. In these cases, it is advantageous to place a large number of baits or bait placements (at least several dozen), no matter the type of bait used, throughout the area(s) where ants are seen. Fourth, when using granular baits (use them only outdoors), they should be delivered from a number of small piles (about the size of a quarter) placed on the ground in areas where ants have been seen. Finally, during drought or extended periods of moisture stress liquid baits (use them inside and outside) may be used to take advantage of the ants' natural propensity for sweet liquids. To use liquid baits, completely soak a small cotton ball with liquid bait and place it on a piece of foil or wax paper in areas where ants have been seen. As the liquid bait evaporates from the cotton ball (1-2 days), simply add water to 'recharge' the liquid bait.

When **baiting for cockroaches** use gel/paste baits and/or bait stations and when treating for rats and mice use block and/or throw packages of bait granules. Indoors (i.e., for German cockroaches), use a combination of **sticky traps** (no toxicant) and gel/paste baits and /or bait stations placed throughout each room where German cockroaches are found. German cockroaches are most common in the kitchen, where 12-15 strategically-placed bait stations may be needed in cases of severe infestation. Additionally, gel/paste bait may be used by placing small 'dabs' (each about the size of pencil eraser) in hidden locations (up to 2-3 dozen sites per baiting). Each dab should be placed in an out of sight crack, crevice, or corner where cockroaches live. Whether using gel/paste bait and/or bait stations, it is often advantageous to introduce a large number of bait placements throughout the baited room since cockroaches generally do not move far from the area(s) where they live.

Place baits on flat surfaces in dark locations in corners (e.g., in cabinets and drawers) and a long walls. Since research shows that most German cockroaches are found near the garbage can, refrigerator, and under the stove and sink, concentrate bait placement in these areas. Never hang stations vertically or otherwise bait vertically, and never place baits in the middle of a floor or cabinet— i.e., away from a corner or wall.

Sticky traps (10-12) can be placed in locations similar to that of baits, checked weekly for the presence of cockroaches, and replaced as needed. Since German cockroaches do not move far, traps that consistently catch the largest number of cockroaches often highlight 'focal points' of cockroach infestation.

For large cockroach species (i.e., not German cockroaches) use mainly gel/paste baits. Place bait wherever cockroaches are seen foraging, particularly at night. The breeding site of large cockroach species are those locations characterized by a protected, moist environment— typically crawlspaces or attics with a moisture problem, or outdoors in clogged rain gutters, treeholes, decorative crossties, hollow retaining walls, and similarly protected habitats. Concentrate gel/paste baiting in these areas. Again, it is most advantageous to introduce a large number of small bait placements since cockroaches generally do not move very far from the area(s) where they live.

Granular Products. Granulars are formed by impregnating or coating insecticide onto a small granule of non-active carrier (e.g., clay, corncob, sand, silica, clay, sawdust, etc.). Granules are applied only on the outside, and are used to control a wide variety of crawling pests by application to places pests live— that is mulch, leaf litter, lawn, etc. Granular products are sometimes purchased in large bags (pounds) as a ready-to-use product.

After application, the insecticide must be released from the granule by allowing water to wash over it. Thus, granular 'activation' requires lawn-watering or natural rain. Unlike liquid sprays (discussed below), granular products may remain active for as long as six to eight weeks. Like liquid sprays, granular products act by contact (killing) and by keeping foraging pests out of treated areas (repellency).

Granular products exhibit one distinct advantage over other formulation types— their weight. The weight of the granule allows the chemical to reach deeper into treated areas than would be expected from a liquid spray treatment (discussed below) applied directly to the surface of the same substrate. *It is important to note that pests do not eat granular products, as they do some baits that are delivered as small granules. In fact, a granular product is never a bait, but bait can be delivered in the form of a granule.*

Dust Products. Dust products have the consistency, look and feel of powder and are purchased ready-to-use. They are not mixed with water, and are applied dry. Dusts are comprised of small particles of active ingredient mixed with equivalently small particles of an inactive carrier material such as talc or clay. Most dusts work because insects pick up the minute particles and ingest them, while others severely desiccate the insect, causing it to dehydrate and die.

Generally, dusts should be used only in dry voids such as behind brick veneer, drywall, electrical switch-plates, and synthetic stucco to remedy existing pest problems indoors and to prevent the reinvasion of pests into voids from the outside. For example, if ants can be seen coming from an electrical switch-plate a small quantity of dust can be applied behind the plate.

Many homeowners make the mistake of over-applying dust. Too much can be repellent, causing insects to avoid dusted areas. Apply dusts so that a very thin film settles in treated voids and on treated surfaces. Ideally, the quantity of dust applied should be only slightly visible in comparison to undusted areas. Some dusts never degrade, while others remain effective for up to a year.

Some dusts contain a high concentration of active ingredient, and should n ever be applied where or when they can injure or sicken non-target organisms— including the applicator. Misapplication of dusts can result in accidental inhalation and thus unnecessary exposure. Since dusts become airborne very easily, it is advisable to always wear a protective mask and preferably eye protection when applying them.

Aerosol and Fogger Products. The contents of aerosol cans and tot al release aerosol foggers are pressurized, usually contain a propellant and the pesticide(s), and emerge as a fine mist or smoke (i.e., microscopic droplets). Aerosol cans are very popular among homeowners because they result in 'revenge' killing— i.e., direct spraying and immediate knock down and kill of the target pest. Although aerosol cans may be effective in the short-term, they should not be relied upon as the sole means of chemic al pest control in and around the home.

Some aerosol cans shoot their contents in a jet stream, and are a good choice when there is a need to treat pests from a distance (e.g., yellow jackets). Although aerosol cans may be used both indoors and outdoors, the use of foggers is restricted to indoor use especially when treatment requires that a room be filled with pesticide for an extended period of time.

If aerosols are used indoors, never use them in voids or near fires. Wet formulations not only damage drywall, insulation, and wood molding but there is a danger of electrical shock and/or fire when using liquids a round electricity. Furthermore, man y aerosols and foggers are flammable.

Liquid Spray Products. Liquid spray products most commonly available to homeowners are **emulsifiable concentrates (ECs).** Emulsifiable concentrates are available as *concentrates* (these products must be diluted with water before use) and *ready-to-use (RTU)* products (these products are usable without further dilution., and usually come in 1 gallon jugs).

Emulsifiable concentrates are composed of an insecticide dissolved in a petroleum-based solvent which, when mixed with water, forms a milky-white emulsion that can be sprayed. Emulsifiable concentrates do not require agitation (shaking). The main hazard with undiluted emulsifiable concentrates is that t hey are readily absorbed should the material come in contact with unprotected ski n. They do, however, protect against inhalation hazard. Emulsifiable concentrates are readily absorbed by porous materials, making them fairly unsuitable for treating concrete, brick, unpainted wood, mulch, and other porous substrates.

Liquid spray treatments are commonly applied to the outside of infested homes in either of two ways. To conduct a **perimeter treatment** spray the outside walls two to three feet high and spray the ground (including shrubbery, mulch, flower beds, etc.) for three to five feet away from each wall around the entire perimeter of the home. Spray as many areas where pests live or are traveled or potentially traveled as possible. Concentrate spray treatments to areas where pests might enter the structure, such as around doors and windows, inside weep holes, and inside wall penetrations such as gas, plumbing, and exhaust pipes. Perimeter treatments should be re-applied every four to six weeks during the summer and within a week following a heavy rain. Perimeter treatments may require up to 10 gallons of spray, depending on the size of the structure treated.

Spot treatments are limited to those areas where pests are found living an d breeding. Typically, no one spot requires more than a quart or so of spray — sometimes less, depending ultimately on the severity of the pest infestation. When spot treating, only those areas considered nests and/or breeding sites or areas where pests are found entering the structure are treated. Breeding sites should be exposed prior to treatment. For example, exposure of breeding sites in mulch can be accomplished by pulling back the mulch with a stiff rake or similar instrument held in one hand while treating exposed nest sites with the other.

Unfortunately, research has shown that liquid-based spray treatments applied outdoors provide only temporary relief (about 30 days) against invading pests. Many sprays break down quickly when exposed to intense sunlight, heat, and moisture — dominant outdoor conditions when pest infestations are greatest.

How to Use This Table

Use of the following table is based on proper identification of the pest — see section above, *Document Pest Identification and Habits*. Once the pest has been identified, locate its name in the table. The table provides a list of product types and names available to homeowners at home improvement, grocery, and consumer warehouses. For additional help, the above section, *How to Use Various Product Types*, provides tips and recommendations on how to use the various products listed in the table. Additional information on urban and structural pest biology and control can be found at http://www.ent.uga.edu/pubs.htm.

PEST	PRODUCT TYPE	PRODUCT NAME	% ACTIVE INGREDIENT
Ants (including Argentine [i.e., "sugar" ants] & odorous house ants) First, bait both indoors and outdoors at the same time if ants are found in both areas. Often, indoor ant problems originate outdoors. Indoors, bait wherever ants are seen with bait gel, liquid, and stations. Do not use Bait granules, sprays, or granulars indoors. If ants are found out doors, use baits wherever ants are seen (especially next to trails). Use all types of bait products listed. Second, if baiting is not successful (give it one week), apply a perimeter spray and/or spot-treat outdoors only (i.e., windows, doors, nest sites). In addition, apply a granular to soil/mulch where ants nest. TIP: The application of many small bait spots is preferred to the application of a few large bait spots. If feasible, apply baits in shaded areas. TIP: After applications of granulars, water thoroughly.	Bait Gel	Combat Ant Killing Gel	0.001% fipronil
	Bait Granules	Amdro Ant Block Home Perimeter Ant Bait	0.88% hydramethylnon
	Bait Liquid	Terro The Liquid Ant Killer	5.4% Borax
		Hot Shot Ultra Liquid Ant Bait	0.05% dinotefuran
	Bait Station	Combat Quick Kill Formula-Ants	0.01% fipronil
		MaxAttrax Ant Bait	0.05% indoxacarb
		Grants Kills Ants	1% hydramethylnon
		Real Kill Ant Bait	0.04% indoxacarb
		Raid Ant Baits III	0.01% avermectin B1
		Raid Double Control Ant Baits	0.05% avermectin B1
		Spectracide Ant Shield Outdoor Killing Stakes	0.05% indoxacarb
		Raid Outdoor Ant Spikes	0.05% avermectin B1

PEST	PRODUCT TYPE	PRODUCT NAME	% ACTIVE INGREDIENT
Ants (including Argentine [i.e., "sugar" ants] & odorous house ants) (continued)	Sprays	Any ready-to-use or concentrated liquid spray labeled for this pest(s).	Various
	Granular	Any granular product labeled for this pest(s).	Various
		Greenlight Yard Safe Insect Repellent Granules	2% cedar oil
Bedbugs Capture several bugs, place them in a vial filled with alcohol, and acquire positive identification from an entomologist. If a positive ID is made, contact a pest control professional skilled and experienced in the treatment and elimination of bedbug infestations. Bedbug elimination is very difficult, an d should be left to an experienced individual. For more information: See publication, *Bed Bugs*, at ht tp://www.uky.edu/ Agriculture/ Entomology/entfacts/struct/ef636.htm	None	None	None
Booklice (Psocids) Indoors: The presence of booklice is an indication of excessive moisture. Psocids feed on fungi, which grow on substrates such as books, paper, and cardboard. Fungi thrive only in environments where humidity is excessive. As a result, the ultimate remedy to infestation is a reduction in humidity (see section above on Moisture Management). Outdoors: No treatment needed.	None	None	None
Carpenter Ants Indoors: At night, when ants are most active, provide them bait. Use any of the gel, liquid, or station baits listed until one is found that the ants will consume. Outdoors: Find nest(s) at night – look for trails of big, black ants, especially on the trunk of large trees. If nest(s) are found (they'll most likely be in trees), drench with a liquid spray if feasible. If nest(s) are not found or treatment is not feasible, at night (when ants are most active) provide them any of the baits listed until one is found that the ants will consume. Place bait next to ant trails. For more information: See publication, *Biology and Management of Carpenter Ants*, at http://www.ent.uga.edu/pubs.htm	Bait Gel	Combat Ant Killing Gel	0.001% fipronil
	Bait Granules	Amdro Ant Block Home Perimeter Ant Bait	0.88% hydramethylnon
	Bait Liquid	Terro The Liquid Ant Killer	5.4% borax
	Bait Station	Raid Double Control Ant Baits	0.05% avermectin B1
		Combat Quick Kill Formula-Ants	0.01% fipronil
	Sprays	Any ready-to-use or concentrated liquid spray labeled for this pest(s).	Various

PEST	PRODUCT TYPE	PRODUCT NAME	% ACTIVE INGREDIENT
Carpenter Bees Indoors: No treatment needed. Outdoors: Apply spray or jet aerosol directly into carpenter bee holes. Begin treatment when bees are first seen (April in Georgia). Re-treat every two weeks while bees are active. In August (when all bees have left their nest sites), fill holes with wood filler, sand. and paint (or apply another finish); replace damaged wood as necessary. NOTE: Pesticides are extremely toxic to all types of bees.	Sprays	Any ready-to-use or concentrated liquid spray labeled for this pest(s).	Various
	Jet Aerosol	Any jet-spray aerosol product that shoots 20-25 feet.	Various
Carpet Beetles Indoors: Find infested article(s) and remove; spot-treat infested area (especially the floor) with a spray while freezing or fumigating article(s); return article(s) and watch for re- infestation. Outdoors: No treatment needed.	Sprays	Any ready-to-use or concentrated liquid spray labeled for this pest(s).	Various
Cockroaches Indoors (German cockroaches): Use gel baits, bait stations, and sticky traps in areas (mainly kitchen) where German cockroaches are found. In cases of extreme infestation, use a fogger or spray into cracks and crevices where cockroaches live. For details, read section **baiting for cockroaches** under the heading How to Use Various Product Types (above). Outdoors (Smokybrown cockroaches): Use gel baits in areas where cockroaches are found (attics, crawlspaces, treeholes, hollow walls, and other voids outdoors). If bait's not effective, spot-treat same areas with a spray. For details, read section **baiting for cockroaches** under the heading How to Use Various Product Types (above). If smokybrown cockroach populations are found in the attic and/or wall voids, apply a fine mist of diatomaceous earth dust into these areas. Do Not apply dust where it can be contacted by humans. TIP: When using gel baits, the application of many small bait spots is preferred to the application of a few large bait spots.	Bait Gel	Combat Platinum Roach Killing Gel	0.01% fipronil
		Amdro Kills Ants and Roaches Baits	2.15% hydramethylnon
		Hot Shot Ultra Clear Roach gel	0.05% dinotefuran
	Bait Station	Combat Quick Kill Formula-Roaches	0.03% fipronil
		Hot Shot Nest Destroyer Roach Bait	0.10% indoxacarb
		Raid Max Double Control	0.05% avermectin B1
		Raid Double Control Small Roach Baits Plus Egg Stopper (for German cock roaches only)	0.05% avermectin B1 95% hydroprene
	Spray	Any ready-to-use or concentrated liq-uid spray labeled for this pest(s).	Various
		Bengal Gold Roach Spray (aerosol can)	2% permethrin 0.05% pyrirpoxyfen
	Fogger	Raid Fumigator	12.6% permethrin
	Dust	Safer Brand Diatomeceous Earth	77.69% silicon dioxide from DE

PEST	PRODUCT TYPE	PRODUCT NAME	% ACTIVE INGREDIENT
Fire Ants Indoors: No treatment needed. Outdoors: Spread bait granules in late afternoon (when temperatures have cooled and the ground is dry) to entire yard or sprinkle one handful around (not on top of) the perimeter of each active mound; 1 0-14 days later, if active mounds remain either (1) apply granular to entire yard, or (2) treat individual mounds with dust. For more information: See publication, *Managing Imported Fire Ants in Urban Areas,* at http://www.ent.uga.edu/pubs.htm TIP: After applications of granulars, water thoroughly.	Bait Granules	Ortho Ecosense Fire Ant Bait Granules	0.015% spinosad
		Amdro Fire Strike (bag)	0.036% hydramethylnon 0.0172% methoprene
		Once & Done (red bag or black jug)	0.016% indoxacarb
		Over- N - Out Fire Ant Killer Mound Treatment (blue jug)	0.008% indoxacarb
	Dust	Orthene Fire Ant Killer	50% acephate
	Granular	Over-N-Out Fire Ant Killer Granules (blue bag)	0.0103% fipronil
Fleas Indoors: Spray or fog small areas or rooms where pets spend the most time. Use products containing pyriproxyfen or methoprene. Concurrently, treat animal(s) with one product containing either lufenuron or imidacloprid or fipronil. Keep pet resting areas clean. Outdoors: Concurrent with the above actions, spot-treat infested areas with sp ray or apply granulars to areas where pets spend the most time. For more information: See publication, *Fleas and the PCO,* at http://www.ent.uga.edu/pubs.htm TIP: After applications of granulars, water thoroughly.	Sprays	Any ready-to-use or concentrated liquid spray labeled for this pest(s).	Various
	Aerosol can	Bengal Full Season Flea Killer Plus	0.015% pyriproxyfen 0.40% tetramethrin 0.30% sumithrin
		Raid Flea Killer Plus Carpet and Room Spray (purple can)	0.14% pyrethrins 0.063% tetramethrin 0.015% methoprene
	Fogger	Hot Shot Bed Bug & Flea Fogger (Nylar)	0.10% pyriproxyfen; 0.05% pyrethrins
		Raid Flea Killer Plus Fogger	0.50% pyrethrins 0.075% methoprene
	Granular	Any granular product labeled for this pest(s).	Various
	RTU 1 gal spray	Enforcer Flea Spray for Homes	0.01% pyriproxyfen (Nylar); 0.25% permethrin
Flies Indoors: Find fly breeding site(s) and eliminate. To reduce adult fly populations in doors, use a fogger (keep all doors and windows closed) or trap. Outdoors: Find fly breeding site(s) and eliminate.	Fogger	Raid Fumigator (or equivalent fogger product)	12.6% permethrin
	Traps	Rescue Fly Trap	None
		Victor Fly Catcher Ribbon	None
		Victor Indoor Fly Trap	None

PEST	PRODUCT TYPE	PRODUCT NAME	% ACTIVE INGREDIENT
Multicolored Asian Lady Beetle First, before lady beetles begin to seek refuge indoors (October & November in Georgia), take action to (1) seal all cracks 1/8 wide or wider, and (2) apply a spray around all potential entry points; reapply treatment every 2 weeks through the end of November. It is often best to seek help and advice from a professional pest control operator experienced in lady beetle control. Contact should be made early enough (August-September) so that preventative measures are in place before the onset of beetle migration indoors. Second, if beetles get inside the best solution is to vacuum them; insecticide treatments indoors are not recommended. For more information: See publication, *Multicolored Asian Lady Beetle,* at http://ipm.osu.edu/lady/lady.htm	Sprays	Any ready-to-use or concentrated liquid spray labeled for this pest(s).	Various
Perimeter Pests: Boxelder Bugs, Centipedes, Crickets, Earwigs, Grasshoppers, Ground beetles, Millipedes, Pillbugs, Scorpions, Scuds, Sowbugs, Crawling Spiders, Springtails Indoors: No treatment needed. Outdoors: Apply granulars to soil/mulch where these pests live and breed. If granulars are ineffective, apply a complete perimeter spray, or spot-treat around windows, doors, and other potential entry points. Place glue boards along the wall-floor interface to trap these pests as they enter. TIP: Reduce moisture in areas where these pests live by directing water away from the house and by keeping mulch to a reasonable depth. See previous section on Moisture Management. Avoid excessive accumulations of leaf litter and all other forms of debris. Store firewood away from the house. Be sure that all exterior doors are equipped with operative doorsweeps. TIP: After applications of granulars, water thoroughly.	Sprays	Any ready-to-use or concentrated liquid spray labeled for this pest(s).	Various
	Granular	Any granular product labeled for this pest(s).	Various
	Glue Board	Tomcat Household Pest Glue Board	None
		Real Kill Household Pest Glue Boards	None
Rats and Mice Indoor and/or Outdoor: Bait trap with food that rats and mice like. If food baiting is ineffective, try placing a piece of cotton or several strips of yarn on the trap that these vertebrates will use to line their nest. Place snap traps out of reach of toddlers and young children to avoid injury to fingers. TIP: Place traps along routes that these pests use most.	Snap & Live Traps	Victor Snap Traps for Mice and Rats	None
		Tomcat Snap Traps for Mice and Rats	None
		Victor Live Traps for Mice	None
		Tomcat Live Traps for Mice	None

111

PEST	PRODUCT TYPE	PRODUCT NAME	% ACTIVE INGREDIENT
Silverfish & Firebrats Indoors: With a spray, spot-treat areas where these in sects live. Outdoors: No treatment needed.	Sprays	Any ready-to-use or concentrated liquid spray labeled for this pest(s).	Various
Spiders (Web-Building) Indoors: Use a broom and remove spiders and cobwebs without pesticide use. Outdoors: Spray areas where spiders live; spray spiders directly. Use long broom and remove spiders and cobwebs without pesticide use. NOTE: Brown recluse spiders do not build webs. Their occurrence in Georgia is limited and largely unknown. Control of brown recluse spiders should be conducted only by a licensed pest control firm. If an infestation is suspected, collect a spider and submit to a county extension agent for verification.	Sprays	Any ready-to-use or concentrated liquid spray labeled for this pest(s).	Various
Stored Product Pests Indoors: Find spilled and/or infested food (cereal, bird food, etc.) and throw away; only rarely is pesticide use needed. Place traps in area(s) where moths are seen. Outdoors: No treatment needed.	Trap	Safer The Pantry Pest Trap (for stored product moths only)	None
Subterranean Termites Seek help from a professional termite control comp any. Do not attempt to treat your own home for termites. The products and treatment equipment needed are not available to the novice. For more information: See publications, *Termite Control Services: Information for the Georgia Property Owner* and *Biology of Subterranean Termites in the Eastern United States,* at http://www.ent.uga.edu/pubs.htm	Concentrate	Phantom. See www.termidoronline.com for more information. Premise 75. See backed by bayer.com for more information. Termidor. See www.termidoronline.com for more information.	21.45% chlorfenapyr; 0.125% or 0. 25% application rate. 75% imidacloprid; 0.05 or 0.10 % application rate. 9.1% fipronil; 0.06% or 0.1 25% application rate.
	Bait	Advance. See www.advancetbs.com for more information. Exterra/ Labyrinth .See www.ensystex.com for more information. Sentricon/Recruit. See www.sentricon.com for more information. HexPro/Shatter. See www.dowagro.com/hexpro for more information.	0.25% diflubenzuron 0.25% diflubenzuron 0.50% noviflumuron 0.50% hexaflumuron

PEST	PRODUCT TYPE	PRODUCT NAME	% ACTIVE INGREDIENT
Wasps, Hornets & Yellow Jackets Indoors and Outdoors: Treat nest entrance with jet-stream aerosol spray; treat at night when insects are least active. If apprehensive, please seek help from a professional pest control company. In the case of yellow jackets, if the nest cannot be found, traps can be placed in areas where yellow jackets forage. It should be noted, however, that research has demonstrated that yellow jacket traps have little to no impact on population reduction. NOTE: A mistake during treatment can result in hospitalization or even death from excessive wasp stings.	Jet Aerosol	Any jet-spray aerosol product that shoots 20-25 feet.	Various
	Trap	Rescue Yellow Jacket Trap	None
		Raid RTU Disposable Yellow Jacket Trap	None
Wood-Infesting Beetles Determine if infestation is active or not active. Control recommendations, if they are needed, are first dependent upon determining whether the infestation is even active and, if so, then upon a positive beetle identification, preferably from an entomologist. If treatment is deemed necessary, seek help from a professional termite control company. *Product available for sale and use only to licensed professionals trained in the use of gas fumigants.	Wood Treatment (preventative)	Bora-Care. See www.nisuscorp.com for more information.	40% disodium octoborate tetrahydrate
	Fumigant* (remedial)	Vikane. See www.vikanegasfumigant.com for more information.	99.8% sulfuryl fluoride; For Old House Borers use 4X the drywood termite rate. For Powderpost Beetles and Death Watch Beetles use 10X the drywood termite rate.

HOUSEHOLD PESTICIDE DILUTION TABLE

Dan Suiter, Extension Entomologist

Pesticide Formulation	(Amount of Pesticide Formulation for One Gallon of Water) Percentage of Actual Chemical Wanted in Mixture								
	0.0313%	0.0625%	0.125%	0.25%	0.5%	1.0%	20%	3.0%	5.0%
15% WP	2 1/2 tsp.	5 tsp.	10 tsp.	7 Tbs.	1 cup	2 cups	4 cups	6 cups	10 cups
25% WP	1 1/2 tsp.	3 tsp.	6 tsp.	12 tsp.	8 Tbs.	1 cup	2 cups	3 cups	5 cups
40% WP	1 tsp.	2 tsp.	4 tsp.	8 tsp.	5 Tbs.	10 Tbs.	1 1/4 cups	2 cups	3 1/4 cups
50% WP	3/4 tsp.	1 1/2 tsp.	3 tsp.	6 tsp.	4 Tbs.	8 Tbs.	1 cup	1 1/2 cups	2 1/2 cups
75% WP	1/2 tsp.	1 tsp.	2 tsp.	4 tsp.	8 tsp.	5 Tbs.	10 Tbs.	1 cup	2 cups
Emulsifiable Concentrate (EC)*									
10% - 12% EC 1 lb. actual/gal.	2 tsp.	4 tsp.	8 tsp.	16 tsp.	10 Tbs.	2/3 pt.	1 1/3 pts.	1 qt.	3 1/4 pts.
15% - 20% EC 1.5 lbs. actual/gal.	1 1/2 tsp.	3 tsp.	6 tsp.	12 tsp.	7 1/4 Tbs.	1/2 pt.	1 pt.	1 1/2 pts.	2 1/2 pts.
25% EC 2 lbs. actual/gal.	1 tsp.	2 tsp.	4 tsp.	8 tsp.	5 Tbs.	10 Tbs.	2/3 pt.	1 pt.	1 3/4 pts.
33% - 35% EC 3 lbs. actual gal.	3/4 tsp.	1 1/2 tsp.	3 tsp.	6 tsp.	4 Tbs.	8 Tbs.	1/2 pt.	3/4 pt.	1 1/3 pts.
40% - 50% EC 4 lbs. actual/gal.	1/2 tsp.	1 tsp.	2 tsp.	4 tsp.	8 tsp.	5 Tbs.	10 Tbs.	1/2 pt.	4/5 pt.
57% EC 5 lbs. actual/gal.	7/16 tsp.	7/8 tsp.	1 3/4 tsp.	3 1/2 tsp.	7 tsp.	4 1/2 Tbs.	9 Tbs.	14 Tbs.	1 1/2 cups
60% - 65% EC 6 lbs. actual/gal.	3/8 tsp.	3/4 tsp.	1/2 Tbs.	1 Tbs.	2 Tbs.	4 Tbs.	8 Tbs.	12 Tbs.	1 1/2 cups
70% - 75% EC 8 lbs. actual/gal.	1/4 tsp.	1/2 tsp.	1 tsp.	2 tsp.	4 tsp.	8 tsp.	5 Tbs.	7 1/2 Tbs.	13 Tbs.

* Quantity based on a standard weight of 8.3 lbs. liquid per gallon.

MILLILITERS OF CONCENTRATE REQUIRED TO PREPARE 1-GALLON OF SPRAY USING VARIOUS PERCENT CONCENTRATES

The figures in the Table are in milliliters. To convert to fluid ounces divide by 30, to teaspoons divide by 5 or tablespoons divide by 15.

By Wt Lb AI* (%)Per Gal	Percent Concentrate Desired								
	1/4	1/2	3/4	1	2	3	4	5	6
10-12 = 1 lb.	78.9	157.8	236.7	315.6	631.1	946.7	1262.2	1577.8	1893.4
15-20 = 1 1/2	52.6	105.2	157.8	210.4	420.7	631.1	841.5	1051.9	1262.2
25 = 2 lb.	39.4	78.9	118.3	157.8	315.6	473.3	631.1	788.9	946.7
30-35 = 3 lb.	26.3	52.6	78.9	105.2	210.4	315.6	420.7	525.9	631.1
40-50 = 4 lb.	19.7	39.4	59.2	78.9	157.8	236.7	315.6	394.5	473.3
55-57 = 5 lb.	15.8	31.6	47.3	63.1	126.2	189.3	252.4	315.6	378.7
60-65 = 6 lb.	13.1	26.3	39.4	52.6	105.2	157.8	210.4	263.9	315.6
66-70 = 7 lb.	11.3	22.5	33.8	45.1	90.2	135.2	180.3	225.4	270.5
72-85 = 8 lb.	9.9	19.7	29.6	39.4	78.9	118.3	157.8	197.2	236.7

HUMANS
PUBLIC HEALTH INSECT CONTROL OUTDOORS AND PARASITES OF MAN [1]

Ray Noblet and E.W. Gray, Entomologists

PEST	PRODUCT TYPE, ACTIVE INGREDIENT & PRODUCT NAME (if specified)	METHODS AND RATE OF APPLICATION	REMARKS AND PRECAUTIONS
ANTS, FIRE	Mound drenches:		Treatments tend to be more effective when applied early morning or late morning or late afternoon after soil temperatures have warmed to 60°F. The active ingredients listed may come in various formulations — be sure to use one labeled for fire ants.
	Acephate (Orthene)	Dilute with water as instructed on the label.	Mix the proper amount into a gallon container such as a sprinkling can or gallon plastic jug with holes drilled in the screw-on cap. Mark the container POISON and use it for no other purpose or destroy after use. Pour the solution on top of and around the mound like a gentle rain. Do not otherwise disturb the mound. Use a minimum of 1-2 gallons of solution per mound. These products may not give immediate kill. Check mounds 5-7 days later and retreat if the colony has moved or new mounds are found.
	Bifenthrin		
	Carbaryl (Sevin)		
	Cyfluthrin		
	Permethrin		
	Spinosad		
	Granular products:		
	Bifenthrin	For treating individual mounds, measure out the recommended amount as specified by the label. Sprinkle on the top of, and around, the mound.	Mow area where mounds will be treated prior to treatment. Best results if treated area is thoroughly watered immediately after application. Treat as mounds appear. Residual control for up to 4 weeks. Use a sprinkler can or water hose to wet the mound and begin washing the insecticide into the mound. Allow 5-7 days for control.
	Carbaryl (Sevin)		
	Cyfluthrin		
	Deltamethrin		
	Gamma-Cyhalothrin		
	Indoxacarb		
	Imidacloprid & Beta-cyfluthrin		
	Fipronil (Over'n Out)		
	Lambda-cyhalothrin		
	Permethrin		
	Spinosad	Listed by Organic Materials Review Institute for use in organic production. Check label.	
	Dry powders:		
	Acephate	Treat mound and surrounding area, ants track insecticide into mound causing mortality.	**CAUTION:** wear protective gloves, avoid breathing the powder and contact with skin and eyes. Check area in 5-7 days and retreat new mounds.
	Cyfluthrin		
	Deltamethrin		
	Permethrin		

[1] Be certain that the insecticide that you purchase is labeled for the site desired.

PEST	PRODUCT TYPE, PRODUCT NAME, % ACTIVE INGREDIENT	METHODS AND RATE OF APPLICATION	REMARKS AND PRECAUTIONS
ANTS, FIRE (cont.)	Bait formulations: Ascend (avermectin) Amdro (hydramethyinon) Award (fenoxycarb) Enforcer (Abamectin B1) Extinguish (s-methoprene) Maxforce (fipronil) First Strike (Hydromethylnon + (s)-Methoprene) Distance, Spectracide (pyriproxyfen) Justice, Eliminator (spinosad)		Typically baits can be used at 2-5 tablespoons of bait per mound or 1-1.5 lbs. broadcast per acre. Read the label for rates. Baits are usually slower acting than other formulations. They are more effective if applied during the spring or fall, and broadcast is more economical than mound treatment. Apply baits when ants are actively foraging for food. Few baits are labeled for vegetable gardens. Check the label.
BEDBUGS	Ready to use: Bayer Advanced Home Pest Control, Cyfluthrin 0.1% Hi-Yield Garden, Pet and Livestock Insect Control. Permethrin 10% Natural Pyrethrin Conc.	Thoroughly clean the mattress, springs, bed frame and area surrounding the bed. Lightly spray (do not soak) bedsteads, slats, springs, baseboards and wall cracks. Allow to dry thoroughly (at least 4 hours) before use.	Bedbugs are typically nocturnal, feeding at night and hiding during the day in cracks and crevices near the bed. Treatments should target cracks and crevices on the bed and bedding, the structure of the bedroom itself and the decor (behind pictures). Good coverage is essential.
BEES, WASPS, HORNETS, AND YELLOW JACKETS	Aerosol: Variety of Jet Sprays available	Apply in evening when insects are at rest. With wind at back, aim at nest opening in trees, bushes, under eaves or in ground cracks and crevices. Thoroughly treat nest. Retreatment may be necessary. If possible, destroy nest, or seal nest opening.	Nuisance honey bee nests can often be removed by bee removal experts. Contact Extension Specialist for more information. Some aerosols produce a jet stream up to 20 -25 feet for the safety to the operator and the ability to reach nests high off the ground. Apply in the evening. Make sure a clear and accessible escape route is planned and available prior to initiating spraying.
	Variety of other products labeled for these pests. However, knockdown could be delayed resulting in increased hazard for the applicator.		

PEST	PRODUCT TYPE, PRODUCT NAME, % ACTIVE INGREDIENT	METHODS AND RATE OF APPLICATION	REMARKS AND PRECAUTIONS
EYE GNATS	Fogger: Cutter Bug Free Backyard Outdoor Fogger. Tetramethrin 0.2% and Permethrin 0.05% Enforcer Mosquito Killer Indoor-Outdoor Fogger, Tetramethrin 0.2% and Sumithrin 0.2%		Air movement from electric fans will give protection in a limited area. Commercial repellents are not very satisfactory. However, devices like the Thermocell Mosquito Repellent or the Off Power Pad Lamp, may provide localized relief. No suitable control for households. Fogging and space sprays give temporary relief to limited area (patio, porch, etc.). Mosquito adulticides will provide temporary relief.
	Ready to Use: Black Flag Fogging Insecticide, Resmethrin 0.2%	Fogging insecticides formulated for electric, and propane gas powered thermo-foggers to be used undiluted (hand held models for homeowners from Sears, Act Hardware, Lowes, Home Depot and probably others). Spray down wind to allow spray to drift through area to be treated.	
FLEAS (outside treatment only)		Trim vegetation and grass to reduce harborage (hiding sites) and increase contact with pests.	At time of treatment, bedding should be removed, site treated and fresh bedding provided. A comprehensive program is required to eliminate breeding on animals and in bedding and loafing/confinement areas. A follow-up treatment 7-10 days after initial treatment is suggested.
	Any Concentrate, Dust, Granular or Ready to Use Hose End Product containing Beta- cyfluthrin, Bifenthrin, Carbaryl, Cyfluthrin, Cypermethrin, Deltamethrin, Esfenvalerate, Gamma-cyhalothrin, Imidacloprid & Beta-cyfluthrin, Lambda-Cyhalothrin, Malathion, Permethrin or Tralomethrin		
	Martin's IG Regulator Concentrate w/Nylar, Pyridine 1.3%		Insect growth regulator, best if used in conjunction with an adulticide. If used with an adulticide, necessity of follow-up treatment reduced.
HOUSE FLIES, BLOW FLIES, STABLE FLIES, DEER FLIES, BLACK FLIES, AND GNATS (outside treatment only)	Aerosol Foggers: Various products available.	Use only under calm conditions in protected areas.	Can provide temporary relief in areas with limited air movement.
	Bait Granules: Methomyl Fly Baits – several products	Primarily for Houses Flies. 1/4 lb. (4 oz.)/500 sq. ft. (Scatter daily, or as needed for quick knockdown.	Avoid placing bait where children, pets or other animals will be exposed.

117

PEST	PRODUCT TYPE, PRODUCT NAME, % ACTIVE INGREDIENT	METHODS AND RATE OF APPLICATION	REMARKS AND PRECAUTIONS
HOUSE FLIES, BLOW FLIES, STABLE FLIES, DEER FLIES, BLACK FLIES AND GNATS (outside treatment only) (cont.)	Concentrates and Ready To Use Products containing Beta-cyflutrin, Bifenthrin, Cyfluthrin, Cypermethrin, Deltametherin, Esfenvalerate, Lambda-cyhalothrin, Permethrin		Residual products, spray around house foundations, outside of buildings on resting areas, garbage cans, under porches, along fences and shrubbery, border vegetation and other areas flies congregate.
	Malathion – variety of products		May do a poor job with house flies due to resistance.
	Black Flag Fogging Insecticide, Resmethrin 0.2%	To be used undiluted.	Ideal for use in electric, propane or gas powered foggers available through home improvement and hardware stores.
	Cygon 2E Dimethoate 23.4%	1 pint/3 gals. of water. Spray exposed surfaces such as walls, fences and refuse containers.	Do not contaminate water or food intended for human or animal use. Available through farm supply stores.
	Dibrom, Naled	Can be applied as a thermal fog or ULV non-thermal ground application, or aerial application.	Very corrosive to equipment. Available through mosquito control distributors.
	Traps and Pest Strips:		Suspend in area where flies are active, away from concentrations of human activity.
	No Pest Strip, Dichlorvos 18.6%	Treats 900-1200 cu. ft. area	Not for use in food handling areas. Lasts up to 4 months.
	Quick Strike Fly Abatement Strip, Nithiazine 1%		
	Variety of sticky traps and funnel/jug traps		Traps should not be placed in direct association with areas of human activity. By design, the traps draw flies to them.
LICE – HEAD, BODY AND CRAB For more information see extension publication 851.	Various products available as shampoos, cream rinse, mousse, gels or lotions. Products typically contain either Permethrin or Pyrethrins.	Follow label directions! Inspect head after 7 days, despite label claims, shampoos usually do not kill all eggs present. If live lice or eggs less than 1/4 of an inch from the scalp are seen, a second treatment should be given. Read the label carefully for additional precautions.	Head lice live on the scalp and lay small white eggs (nits) on individual hair shafts close to the scalp. Nits are most easily found on the nape of the neck or behind the ears. All personal headgear, scarves, coats and bed linen should be disinfected by machine washing in hot water and drying using the hot cycle of the dryer for at least 20 minutes. Personal combs and brushes should be disinfected by soaking in hot water (above 130°F) for 5 to 10 minutes. Vacuuming lounging areas to pickup hairs and lice is helpful. However, head lice can not live off a human host for more than 24 hours.
	Kwell Shampoo, Lindane 1% also available as a lotion and cream — all by physician's prescription only.	Apply sufficient quantity of shampoo to thoroughly wet the hair, thoroughly work into hair and allow to remain for 4 minutes. Add small quantities of water until a good lather forms, rinse thoroughly. The lotion and cream formulations are left in place for 8-12 hours. Read the label carefully.	A fine-toothed comb can be used to help remove nits (eggs) and dead lice. Avoid contact of shampoo with eyes or other mucous surfaces.

* Pesticide sprays are not recommended to control head lice populations.

PEST	PRODUCT TYPE, PRODUCT NAME, % ACTIVE INGREDIENT	METHODS AND RATE OF APPLICATION	REMARKS AND PRECAUTIONS
MIDGE LARVAE (Chironomidae)	Granular: Abate 1G or 2 G, Temephos, 1 or 2%	5-10 lbs./acre in standing water. 10-20 lbs./acre in tidal water, marshes and water high in organic content.	Shrimp and crabs may be killed at these rates.
	Provect 1G 1% Temephos	5-20 lbs./acre	Non-target concerns.
	Liquid: Strike, Methoprene 20%	**Standing water** – 10 lbs./acre for initial dose, supplemental dose for 5- 7.5 lbs./acre required every 21 days. **Waste-water treatment sites** – 5 ozs. per million gallons of flow for 14 days. Maintenance rate of 2.5-3 ozs. per million gallons will prevent reinfestation.	Will suppress mosquitoes in standing water and filter flies in water treatment sites.
	Agnique, Monomolecular Surface Film, 100%	**Fresh water** – ponds and lakes, 0.5 gallons/acre. **Polluted waters** – sewage lagoons and percolation ponds 0.5-1.0 gallons/acre.	Persistence – 5-22 days depending on conditions. 10-14 days most likely. Indicator oil provided to monitor presence of film.
	Vectobac 12AS, *Bacillus thuringiensis* var. *israelensis* (Bti) 1200 ITU's	**Standing waters** less than 6 feet deep, 1 gallon/acre every 14 days. **Waste water treatment sites** – 20 mg/liter a.i. (1.67 ml) per liter of waste water. Treat for 30 minutes, repeat applications as needed after 2-4 weeks.	Not effective against all midge species, members of the subfamilies Chironomini and Tanytarsini are generally susceptible. Will suppress mosquitoes in standing water and filter flies in water treatment sites.
	Pellet: Bactimos PT, 2-3%, *Bacillus thuringiensis* subsp. israelensis	18.0 - 26.0 lbs./acre	Target areas where larvae are developing.
MITES, CHIGGERS			See repellents. Keep grass cut short and open to the sun to help reduce chiggers. Permethrin repellent of choice for chiggers. Permethrin is for treating clothing only. Vegetation should not touch legs on walking trails.
	Variety of products available in either concentrate, granule or ready to use formulations Products containing Beta-cyfluthrin, Bifenthrin, Carbaryl, Cyfluthrin, Deltamethrin, Gamma-cyhalothrin, Imidacloprid & Beta-cyfluthrin, Lambda-cyhalothrin, Permethrin or Tralomethrin will all be effective if applied according to label.	Mow grass and trim vegetation prior to insecticide application.	Water lightly, immediately after granule applications.
	Yellow Jacket Wettable Dusting Sulfur, Sulfur 100%	2 lbs./1000 sq. ft.	Apply with enough water for thorough coverage. Treat at weekly intervals and a day or two before protection is desired.

119

PEST	PRODUCT TYPE, PRODUCT NAME, % ACTIVE INGREDIENT	METHODS AND RATE OF APPLICATION	REMARKS AND PRECAUTIONS
MITES clover mites (outside use only)	Variety of products available in concentrate granular and ready to use formulations. Products containing any of the following active ingredients (Bifenthrin, Cyfluthrin, Deltamethrin, Gamma-cyhalothrin, Imidacloprid & Beta-cyfluthrin, Lambda-cyhalothrin, Malathion, Permethrin, Pyrethrin, and Tralomethrin) will work effectively if used properly.	Spray lower foundation of house as well as ground, lawn and plants in an area 10ft. wide around the perimeter of home. Water lightly, immediately after granule applications.	Keeping the turf from 12-48 inches from the side of the building will help create a barrier for clover mites
MITES Human itch mite (scabies)	Lotions or Creams: Ellimite, Permethrin (Physician's prescription only) Kwell lotion or cream, Lindane 1% Physician's prescription only.	A physician should be consulted for diagnosis and treatment. The lotion or the cream is applied to dry skin in a thin layer and rubbed in thoroughly. Usually one ounce is sufficient for an adult. A total body application should be made from the neck down. The lotion or cream is left on for 8-12 hours then removed by thorough washing.	Scabies rarely affects the head of children or adults but may occur in infants. One application is usually curative. Read the label carefully. Some itching may continue several weeks after a successful treatment due to dead mites and tunnels still in the skin.
MITES rodent mites, bird mites	Few products specifically labeled for these pests. Products labeled for perimeter pests would be effective. Mites are not typically hard to control off their host..	Treat in cracks and crevices, attics, between walls, or other dry inconspicuous areas harboring mites.	Various mites that feed on rodents or birds will readily attack man, especially when the normal host is not available (dead, migrated, etc.) or large populations develop. Biting can cause severe itching and discomfort. Remove the nest if possible and exclude hosts.
	Total release indoor aerosol foggers will control mites entering homes. (various formulations) 8 in 1 Mite and Lice Spray, Pyrethrins 0.03%	Quick kill, but no residue.	Follow label precautions carefully. Do <u>not</u> overtreat, or an explosion is possible. Can treat birds and cages.
STRAW ITCH MITES	Pyrethrins (various formulations)	In a kitchen, spray infested area after removing food.	Mites are parasitic on the larva of grain and cereal insects. Mites readily bite man when in contact with infested hay, straw, or stored grain or flour. Can cause intense itching, and fever. Remove infested materials. To prevent, keep products dry. For a residue in a food handling area, select one of the insecticides labeled for spraying of cockroaches. Apply to infested area following label instructions.

PEST	PRODUCT TYPE, PRODUCT NAME, % ACTIVE INGREDIENT	METHODS AND RATE OF APPLICATION	REMARKS AND PRECAUTIONS
MOSQUITOES homeowner larval stage	Agnique MMF	0.2 - 1.0 gal/acre	Effective against larvae and pupae. Can be used in pet waters.
	Vectolex *(Bacillus sphaericus)*	5 - 20 lbs./acre	Very effective against the Culex species. Some residual control, reapply as needed after 1- 4 weeks.
	Water Soluble Pouch available	1 pouch/50 sq. ft.	
	Bacillus thuringiensis, subsp. *israelensis* (Bti) – Mosquito Dunks – Briquets	1/100 Sq. Ftt.	Very safe and effective.
	Bti (various formulations)	Varies by formulation	Treatments need to be repeated every 7-12 days.
	Altosid Briquets (methoprene)	1/100 sq. ft.	30 day residual.
	Pre-Strike Granules (methoprene)	1 lb./8000sq. ft.	21 day residual – available in pet stores. Can be use in pet waters.
	Temephos (several formuations)		Good choice for treating used tires.
MOSQUITOES homeowner adult mosquitoes (outside treatment only)	Aerosol Foggers: Variety of products available.	Spray areas infested with mosquitoes with a slow sweeping motion while moving away from treated area. Spray when air is still. Repeat if necessary.	For temporary relief over limited areas.
	Surface Residuals: Variety of products available. Products contain Bifenthrin, Carbaryl, Cyfluthrin, Cypermethrin, Deltamethrin, Gamma-cyhalothrin, Imidacloprid & Beta-cyfluthrin, Lambda-cyhalothrin, Malathion, Permethrim, Tralomethrin are all effective if used properly.	Wet surfaces uniformly, carefully treat vegetation, trying to coat bottom surfaces of leaves on shrubbery.	
	Black Flag Fogging Insecticide, Resmethrin 0.2%	For use in electric, propane, or gas powered thermal fogger (available from Sears, Ace Hardware, Lowes, Home Depot, and probably others).	Follow manufactures and label directions carefully. For temporary relief over limited areas.

TRAPS: Several types of insect traps are sold for mosquito control. These would include the Mosquito Magnet, Flowtron Power Trap, The Dragon-Fly and traditional "bug-zappers" as well as others. While all of these traps will usually catch and kill mosquitoes, it is important to carefully read the operating instructions to be certain that the trap you plan to purchase has been shown to be effective against the species of mosquito that you have present.

CANDLES. LAMPS & TORCHES: Typically these devices contain citronella or allethrin. These devices can be effective in repelling mosquitoes in enclosed areas or under still conditions. Moderate air movement will significantly reduce effectiveness.

PEST	PRODUCT TYPE, PRODUCT NAME, % ACTIVE INGREDIENT	METHODS AND RATE OF APPLICATION	REMARKS AND PRECAUTIONS
MOTH FLIES (larval stage)	Concentrate – EC: Strike, Methoprene	**Wastewater treatment sites –** 5 ozs. per million gallons of flow for 14 days. Maintenance rate of 2.5 - 3.0 ozs. per million gallons of flow will prevent reinfestation.	Metering pumps are the most efficient and accurate application method. Will also suppress midge larvae.
	Biological Control Agent: Vectobac 12AS, *Bacillus thuringiensis* var. isrealensis (Bti)	**Wastewater treatment sites –** 10 - 20 mg/liter a.i. (0.833-1.67 ml) per liter of wastewater. Treat for 30 minutes, repeat applications as needed after 2 - 4 weeks.	Does not damage the zoogloea in wastewater, filters and adds no chemicals to the discharges of receiving rivers and streams.
MOTH FLIES filter flies in sewage treatment plants	ULV Concentrate: Malathion, varietyof concentrations	Thermal aerosol or fog: dilute Cython in fuel oil. Non-thermal aerosols; non-diluted-ultra low volume. Check label for rates. No residue, retreat as needed.	Undiluted spray droplets can permanently damage automobile and other paint finishes unless label instructions are carefully followed. Apply only in early morning or evening when air currents are low.
	Pyrethrins, variety of concentations	Thermal aerosol of fog ready to use. Other aerosols of ULV labeled for mosquito control will also control moth flies.	
Perimeter Treatments	Concentrate – EC: Permethrin		Various formulations are available to mosquito control programs from Adapco, Clarke, and Vopak as a perimeter or barrier treatment.
Repellents for Mosquitoes, biting flies and gants, chiggers, fleas and ticks	DEET, or N, N-Diethyl-meta-toluamide (many brands and formulations)	Protect skin by applying a few drops on the palm and rub into exposed skin.	Wash hands after applying. Keep out of eyes and mouth. The higher strength DEET formulations are usually more expensive, but likewise longer lasting that lower strength formulations
		Aerosol applications: hold 6 - 8 inches form skin or clothing and apply with a slow sweeping motion. Spread over skin to spread evenly. Also spray on clothing.	May damage watch crystals. Children should use 30% concentrations or less. Product should be applied by parents, apply to parent's hand and then spread onto child's skin. Approved for use on children over 2 months of age.
	Oil of Lemon Eucalyptus		Not approved for children under 3 years of age. Skin reactions have been documented.
	Picaridin		Effective alternative to DEET.
	Permethrin, (many brands and formualations)	To be used on clothing only.	Good choice when exposed to ticks and chiggers.
PERIMETER PESTS: Centipedes, Millipedes, Scorpions, Spiders (outside treatment only)		To prevent scorpions, millipedes and spiders from entering building, spray a 5 ft. band of soil around the house next to the foundation to a height of 2 - 3 ft. Thoroughly spray any piles of firewood, debris and other outside areas where they are found.	Removing piles of wood and trash close to inhabited areas will reduce harborage areas. Removing mulch at least 3 ft. from sides of buildings will reduce millipede breeding. Do not burn sprayed firewood within 2 weeks following treatment.

PEST	PRODUCT TYPE, PRODUCT NAME, % ACTIVE INGREDIENT	METHODS AND RATE OF APPLICATION	REMARKS AND PRECAUTIONS
PERIMETER PESTS: Centipedes, Millipedes, Scorpions, Spiders (outside treatment only) (cont.)	A variety of products available in either concentrate, granular of ready to use formulations.		
	Any product with one of the following active ingredients (Bifenthrin, Carbaryl, Cyfluthrin, Cypermethrin, Deltamethrin, Esfenvalerate, Gamma-cyhalothrin, Lambda-cyhalothrin or Permethrin) will be effective if used according to the label.		
TICKS – brown dog and spot treatments outside			Tick control is best conducted as part of a comprehensive program, where the animals involved, their bedding and indoor and outdoor areas that they use are all treated.
	Concentrate – EC: Any product containing Bifenthrin, Carbaryl, Cyfluthrin, Esfenvalerate, Permethrin, Tralomethrin	Carbaryl or Permethrin suggested for Brown Dog Tick Treatments	Standard residual treatment would involve thoroughly spraying window frames, door sills, porch and patio walls, foundations, cracks and crevices. Spray 5 ft. band around the house, 2 - 3 ft. up wall.
	Dusts: 5 or 10% Carbaryl (several products available)	2 - 4 lbs/1000 sq. ft.	Best applied after rain and with no rain or irrigation for 48 hours post-treatment.
	Granules: Any products containing Bifenthrin, Imidacloprid & Beta-cyfluthrin, Deltamethrin, Gamma-cyhalothrin, Lambda-cyhalothrin, Permethrin Ready to use/hose end: Any products containing Bifenthrin, Cyfluthrin, Deltamethrin, Lambda-cyhalothrin, Permethrin or Tralomethrin		Perimeter treatment to building surfaces and ground treatment.

PEST	PRODUCT TYPE, PRODUCT NAME, % ACTIVE INGREDIENT	METHODS AND RATE OF APPLICATION	REMARKS AND PRECAUTIONS
TICKS – area-wide treatment: campgrounds, picnic areas, footpaths, recreational parks, backyards and other outside			Large scale tick control is a difficult task. It is important to keep vegetation mowed and trails cleared where the majority of human activity occurs. By eliminating the majority of vegetation that will contact hiker's legs a large percentage of tick contacts can be eliminated. Walking trails should be cut as low as possible.
	Granular:		
	Basic Solutions Lawn and Garden Insect Killer, 0.1% Bifenthrin	1.2 lbs./500 sq. ft.	Granular formulations usually work best if lightly watered after application.
	Bayer Advanced Multi-Insect Killer 0.1% Cyfluthrin	2 - 3 lbs./1000 sq. ft.	
	Bayer Advanced Lawn, Complete Insect Killer for Soil & Turf, 0.15% Imidacloprid & 0.05% Beta-cyfluthrin	2 - 3 lbs./1000 sq. ft.	
	Spectracide Triazicide Soil & Turf Insect Killer Granules, 0.04% Lambda-cyhalothrin		
	Spectracide Bug Stop Insect Control Granules, 0.25% Permethrin		
	Concentrate EC:		
	Esfenvalerate, Permethrin, various products		Uniform coverage important.
	Concentrate WP:		
	Rabon 50WP	2 lb. formulation/25 gals. to treat about one acre.	Most readily available through poultry supply dealers. This is the chemical of choice.

AQUATIC ENVIRONMENTS
FISHERY CHEMICALS — (PARASITES, PISCICIDES AND OTHER TREATMENTS)[1]

Updated by Gary J. Burtle, Extension Aquaculture and Fisheries

	CHEMICAL	APPLICATION RATE	CATEGORY OF USE[2]	COMMENTS
A. Fish Parasites	Formalin	25 ppm in ponds (7.5 gals./acre-foot)	F	Use in warm weather may cause oxygen depletion. Provide aeration during treatment to prevent low oxygen. Use with extreme caution when dissolved oxygen is 5 ppm or lower.
		125-250 ppm (1-2 pints per 1000 gal. in tanks for one hour		In tanks, if stress is excessive, flush with fresh water. Use lower rate in water above 70°F.
B. Piscicides	Antimcycin	1-10 ppb active ingredient (0.4 - 4.3 fl. oz./acre-foot)	N	Treatment rate dependent on water temperature and pH.
	Rotenone (Restricted)	1-5 ppm active ingredient (2.7-13.6 lb./acre-foot)	N	Do not use in waters colder than 65°F
C. Miscellaneous Aquatic Treatment	MS-222 (Anesthetic)	15 - 66 ppm active ingredient for 6 - 48 hours for sedation; 50-330 ppm active ingredient for 1- 40 minutes for anesthesia	F	21- day preslaughter withdrawl period.
	Romet 30 (Bactericide) Ormetropin + Sulfadimethoxine	2.3 g. active ingredient/100 lb. fish per day for 5 days in feed	F	3-day preslaughter with drawl period for catfish, do not use on trout within 6 weeks of marketing or release as stocker fish
	Terramycin (Bactericide)	2.5-3.75 g. active ingredient/100 lb. fish per day for 10 days in feed	F	21-day preslaughter withdrawl period.
	Calcium hypochlorite (Disinfectant & sterilant)	10 ppm available chlorine (38.8 lb./acre-foot)	F	Kills all fish and some parasites.
	Hydrated Lime (Disinfectant & sterilant)	1,338 lb./acre burnt lime	F	Drained pond treatment.
		1,784 lb./acre slaked lime	F	Drained pond treatment.
	Potassium permanganate (oxidizing agent)* (Cairox)	2 ppm (5.4 lb./acre-foot)	F	Drinking water treatment. Treatment may have to be repeated within 24 hours to be effective.**
	Salt (sodium chloride) (hauling aid)	0.5-3% (83 to 250 lb./1000 gal.) Dip for 30 minutes to 2 hours; for a continuous bath 1 to 2 lb./100 gal. Pond treatments of 100 ppm to 150 ppm indefinitely for osmatic enhancement.	F	

[1] Adapted from R. A. Schnick, F. P. Meyer and D. L. Gray. 1986. A Guide to Approved Chemicals in Fish Production and Fishery Resource Management. University of Arkansas Cooperative Extension Service and U.S. Fish and Wildlife Service.

[2] F - Approved for use on fish intended for human or animal consumption.

N - Not approved for use on fish intended for human or animal consumption.

*Zebra mussels, biofilm, and other biofoulants such as algae and microorganisms.

**Limit residual to less than 1 ppm. Taste, odor, zebra mussel, hydrogen sulfide, and organic pollutant oxidation control.

AQUATIC WEED CONTROL

Updated by Gary J. Burtle, Extension Aquaculture and Fisheries

| USE STAGE/ HERBICIDE | BROADCAST RATE/ACRE | | REMARKS AND PRECAUTIONS |
	AMOUNT OF FORMULATION	POUNDS ACTIVE INGREDIENT	
Algae copper sulfate (Triangle copper- sulfate) 99% Granule 99% Snow 99% Crystal, Others	2.7-5.4 lbs.* 2.7-5.4 lbs.* 2.7-5.4 lbs.* 2.7-5.4 lbs.*	1.0-2.0 ppm* 1.0-2.0 ppm* . 1.0-2.0 ppm* 1.0-2.0 ppm*	Apply at early stages in algae development (usually April or May), repeat as needed. Read and observe all label cautions and instructions. Copper algaecides may be toxic to fish at high rates. Use the low rate in acid waters and the high rate in alkaline waters. The rates suggested should not be toxic except through oxygen depletion. Under heavy infestations, treat only 1/4 to 1/3 the water body at any one time to avoid fish suffocation caused by oxygen depletion. Copper containing products may be used for spot treatments of algae. Copper sulfate, copper complexes and diquat may also be used in commercial fish production ponds.
copper sulfate – acidified liquid (Earthtec or Agritech) 5.0% as copper, 9.9 lb/gal	1.0 to 40.0 pt*	0.06 to 2.5 lbs.	Dosage is variable according to algae species, pH and water temperature.
copper complex (Cutrine-Plus) 0.9 lbs./gal. (Cutrine-Plus G) 3.7% Granule (K-Tea) 0.8 lbs./gal.	0.6-1.2 gal.* 60.0 lbs. 0.7-1.4 gal.*	0.2-0.4 ppm* --- 0.2-0.4 ppm*	Several formulations are marketed, so check labels for use restrictions.
diquat (Reward) 2 lbs./gal. (Weed-Trine D) 0.4 lbs./gal.	1.0-2.0 gal. 3.4-10.2 gal.*	2.0-4.0 lbs. 0.5-1.5 ppm*	Diquat is effective for filamentous algae control. Apply Diquat as recommended in SUBMERSED WEEDS section. Use 1.0 gal. Reward per surface acre in water with an average depth of 2.0 feet. The higher rate may be used in water with an average depth greater than 2.0 feet. Repeat applications will be necessary.
endothall (Hydrothol 191) g ranular, 11.2% (Hydrothol 191) liquid, 2 lbs. /gal.	3 to 81 lbs./A-ft 0.6 to 1.8 pts./A-ft	0.05 to 1.5 ppm 0.05 to 1.5 ppm	Hydrothol formulations are toxic to fish and should be used only on sections by a commercial applicator at rates below 0.3 ppm unless fish kills are not objectionable.
Aquashade	1.0 gal./4 acre ft.	1.0 ppm	Aquashade is a non-toxic blue dye that controls filamentous algae by blocking light penetration for up to six weeks after application. May be used in lakes, ponds, ornamental ponds and fountains and commercial fish production ponds that have little or no outflow. Apply one gallon of Aquashade per one acre of water that averages 4.0 feet deep in the early spring before weed growth begins, or apply when weeds may be seen on bottom of pond. Additional applications will be necessary through the year to maintain an acceptable level of dye in the water. May be used at any time of year, but is less effective when weed growth is near the surface. Do not apply to water that will be used for human consumption. Water may be used for swimming after complete dispersal of the dye in water. Aquashade is non-toxic to livestock. For use in ponds that are not for commercial food fish production. Elevated pH may occur.
sodium carbonate peroxyhydrate (Green Clean Pro) 50% Granular (PAK-27) 85% granular (Green Clean Liquid, 27)	8-90 lbs./A-ft 4-45 lbs./A-ft 8-16 lbs./A-ft 6.8-13.6 lbs./A-ft 1.2-12 gal./A		Mix with 50 to 100 gal. water per surface acre and spray evenly over the infested area. Use higher rates for filamentous algae. Repeat treatment for dense infestations. Not for food fish use. May elevate pH up to 1.0 point, especially if applied in the afternoon.

*Indicates rate per acre foot of water. All other formulation rates are based on amount per surface area.

USE STAGE/ HERBICIDE	BROADCAST RATE/ACRE		REMARKS AND PRECAUTIONS
	AMOUNT OF FORMULATION	POUNDS ACTIVE INGREDIENT	
Floating Weeds **diquat** (Reward) 2 lbs./gal. (Weedtrine-D) 0.4 lbs./gal.	1.0 gal. 5.0 gal.	2.0 lbs. 2.0 lbs.	Spray to wet exposed plants with 50-150 gallons of water per acre plus 1.0 pt. of nonionic surfactant per 100 gal. of spray mix. Do not apply to muddy water. Labeled also for commercial fish production ponds. Consider tank mixes with chelated copper formulations for resistant duck weeds.
fluridone (Sonar AS)	0.25 to 2.0 qt.	0.25 to 2.0 lbs.	Apply Sonar AS as a surface application to duckweed at labeled rates. Apply only once per year when duckweed is present. Apply Sonar to bladderwort as suggested in the EM ERSED WEEDS section. See REMARKS AND PRECAUTIONS for Sonar as listed in the EMERSED WEEDS AND SUBMERSED WEEDS sections. 15 0 ppb for water meal.
Floating Weeds **2,4-D** (Hardball) 1.74 lbs./gal.	2.25 gal.	3.9 lbs.	Controls water hyacinth. Do not apply to open water. Apply only to dense stands. Treat 1/3 to 1/2 of the water body to avoid oxygen depletion problems.
imazapyr (Habitat) 2 lbs./gal.	See label.		Use of spreader-stickers will improve results. Insure complete coverage by applying with 100 gallons water per acre.
carfentrazone (Stingray) 1.9 lbs./gal.	3.4-13.5 ozs.	0.025-0.2 lbs.	Use a non-ionic surfactant and 100 gallons of dilution water per surface area. 80% of foliage should be exposed to treatment. Use tank mixes with 2, 4-D, glyphosate, or diaquat products for better control at the lower rates of application.
Emersed Weeds **2,4-D** (Aqua-Kleen) 19G (2,4-D Granules) 19G (Navigate granules) 19% DP Acid equivalent (Hardball) 1.74 lbs./gal.	100.0-200.0 lbs. 100.0-200.0 lbs. 100 to 200 lbs. 2.25 gal.	19-38 lbs. 19-38 lbs. 27.6 to 55.2 lbs. 3-9 lbs.	Spray to wet foliage or spread granules uniformly in infested area in spring or early summer. Read the label for specific weeds controlled and special precautions. Do not apply to more than 1/2 the pond in any one month. Do not apply to waters used for irrigation, agricultural sprays, watering dairy animals, or domestic waters. This group of products is also labeled for commercial fish production ponds. Applications made after September may be less effective depending on water temperatures and weed growth.
glyphosate (Rodeo) 5.4 lbs./gal. (Aquaneat) (Eagre)	See label.		Apply after drawdown or when water is present. Allow 7 or more days after drawdown treatment before reintroduction of water (apply within one day after drawdown). Add 2.0 qts. of a manufacturer approved surfactant per 100 gal. of spray solution. Rodeo may be used in commercial fish production ponds.
fluridone (Sonar AS) (Sonar SRP)	Rates vary Rates vary	Rates vary Rates vary	Controls several emersed weeds. Apply Sonar AS as a surface spray, or near the bottom with weighted trailing hoses or meter into pumping system. Uniformly broadcast the SRP formulation. Trees or shrubs growing in water treated with Sonar may be injured. Thirty to 90 days are required before desired weed control is achieved. Use Sonar SRP (slow release pellet) in irrigation or drain age canals with slow moving water. Not recommended for spot treatment. Labeled also for commercial fish production ponds.
imazapyr (Habitat) 2 lbs./gal.	See label.		Use of spreader-stickers will improve results. Insure complete coverage by applying with 10 0 gallons water per acre.
carfentrazone (Stingray) 1.9 lbs./gal.	3.4-13.5 ozs.	0.025-0.2 lbs.	Use a non-ionic surfactant and 100 gallons of dilution water per surface area. 80% of foliage should be exposed to treatment. Use tank mixes with 2, 4-D, glyphosate, or diaquat products for better control at the lower rates of application.
triclopyr (Renovate 3) 3 lbs./gal.	0.25 to 3 gal.	0.75 to 9 lbs.	Do not spray open water. Use non-ionic surfactant for foliar application according to surfactant label. Not for water intended for irrigation. Avoid overspray to open water.

*Indicates rate per acre foot of water. All other formulation rates are based on amount per surface area.

USE STAGE/ HERBICIDE	BROADCAST RATE/ACRE		REMARKS AND PRECAUTIONS
	AMOUNT OF FORMULATION	POUNDS ACTIVE INGREDIENT	
Submersed Weeds diquat (Reward) 2 lbs./gal. (Weedtrine-D) 0.4 lbs./gal.	1.0-2.0 gals. 5.0-10.0 gals.	2.0-4.0 lbs. 2.0-4.0 lbs.	Apply in early season where submersed growth has not reached the surface by pouring directly from the container into the water while moving slowly over the water surface in a boat. Distribute in strips 40 feet apart. In late season or where submersed weed growth has reached the surface, use the high rate indicated on the label for the weeds present. Also labeled for commercial fish production ponds. Do not apply to muddy water.
2,4-D granular (Aquakleen) 19G (2,4-D Granules) 19G (Hardball) 1.74 lbs/gal.	100.0-200.0 lbs. 2.5-10 gal./A	19-38 lbs. 4.3-17.0 lbs./A	See comments for granular formulations in "Emersed Weeds" section. Effective on parrotfeather, coontail and Eurasian watermilfoil. Also labeled for commercial fish production ponds.
endothall (Aquathol Granular) 10.1% (Aquathol Super K Granular) 63.0% (Aquathol K) 4.2 lbs./gal. (Hydrothol Granular) 5G (Hydrothol 191) 2 lbs./gal.	13.0-81.0 lbs.* 0.3-1.9 gal.* 3.0-27.0 lbs.* 0.6 pts.-0. 7 gal.	0.5-3.0 ppm* 0.5-3.0 ppm* 0.05-0.5 ppm* *0.05-0.5 ppm*	Aquathol and Aquathol K are contact killers and must be applied as early as possible after weeds are present. Water temperature should be a minimum of 65°F. Water containing heavy weed growth should be treated in sections 5-7 days apart. Apply on a calm day. Hydrothol formulations are toxic to fish and should be used only on sections by a commercial applicator at rates below 0.3 ppm unless fish kill is not objectionable. Hydrothol formulations are not recommended for commercial fish production ponds. Aquathol formulations are also labeled for commercial fish production ponds. Apply Aquathol Super K evenly over the treatment area and as early as possible after weed growth is observed.
Submersed Weeds Aquashade	1.0 gal./4 acre ft.	1.0 ppm	Aquashade is a non-toxic dye that controls several submersed weeds, such as naiads, by blocking light penetration for up to six weeks after application. May be used in lakes, ponds, ornamental ponds and fountains and commercial fish production ponds that have little or no outflow. Apply one gallon of Aquashade per one acre of water that averages 4.0 feet deep in the early spring before weed growth begins, or apply when weeds are seen on bottom of pond. Additional applications will be necessary through the year to maintain an acceptable level of dye in the water. May be used at any time of year, but is less effective when weed growth is near the surface. Do not apply to water that will be used for human consumption. Water may be used for swimming after complete dispersal of the dye in water. Aquashade is non-toxic to livestock.
fluridone (Sonar AS) (Sonar SRP)	Rates vary Rates vary	Rates vary Rates vary	Apply fluridone to control coontail, common elodea, egeria, hydrilla, naiad, pondweeds, and watermilfoils. See directions in "Emersed Weeds" section. Trees or shrubs growing in water or having roots growing in water treated with Sonar may be injured . Thirty to 90 days will be required before desired weed control is achieved. Not recommended for spot treatment. Also labeled for commercial fish production ponds.
Floating plants Penoxsulam (Galleon SC)	2.0-5.6 oz.	0.031-0.087 lb.	Do not use if pond is used to irrigate food crops unless analyses shows less than 1 ppb residue. Do not use in successive years.
Imazamox (Clearcast)	32-64 oz.	0.24-0.5 lb.	Spot spray foliage with 0.25 to 5% solutions in water with a surfactant.
Emersed weeds Penoxsulam (Galleon SC)	2.0-5.6 oz.	0.031-0.087 lb.	Do not use if pond is used to irrigate food crops unless analyses shows less than 1 ppb residue. Do not use in successive years.
Imazamox (Clearcast)	32-64 oz.	0.24-0.5 lb.	Spot spray foliage with 0.25 to 5% solutions in water with a surfactant.
Drawdown application Penoxsulam (Galleon SC)	5.6-11.2 oz.	0.087-0.175 lb.	Mix up to 100 gpa water and a surfactant for post- or pre-emergence use.
Imazamox (Clearcast)	64 oz.	0.5 lb.	Wait two weeks before re-flooding the pond.

RESPONSE OF COMMON AQUATIC WEEDS TO HERBICIDES[1]

Aquatic Group and Weed	copper complexes, copper sulfate (various)	2,4-D (various)	diquat (Reward)	endothall (Aquathol K) (Aquathol G) (Hydrothol G) (Hydrothol 191)	fluridone (Sonar)	glyphosate (Rodeo) (Pondmaster)	carfentrazone	triclopyr	imazapyr
Algae									
planktonic	E	P	P		P	P	NR	NR	NR
filamentous	E	P	E	G²	P	P	NR	NR	NR
chara	E	P	G	G²	P	P	NR	NR	NR
nitella	E	P	G	G²	P	P	NR	NR	NR
Floating Weeds									
bladderwort	P	G³	E		E		-	P	NR
duckweeds	P	P	G⁵	P	E	P	G	P	G
water hyacinth	P	E	E		P	F	G	E	G
watermeal	P	P	P⁵		G	P	P	NR	NR
Emersed									
alders	P	E	F	P	P	E	-	-	-
alligatorweed	P	F	P	P	G	E	F	G	G
American lotus	P	E	P	P	F	G	-	G	G
arrowhead	P	E	G	G		E	-	-	-
buttonbush	P	E	F	P	P	G	-	-	-
cattails	P	G	G	P	F	E	-	F	E
fragrant & white waterlily	P	E	P	P	E	E	-	G	E
frogbit	P	E	E						
maidencane	P	P	F		F	E	-	-	-
pickerelweed	P	G	G		P	F	-	NR	E
pond edge annuals	P		G	P	F	E	-	-	E
sedges/rushes	P	F	F		P	G	-	NR	G
slender spikerush	P		G⁵		G	P	-	NR	-
smartweed	P	E	F		F	E	-	E	E
spatterdock	P	E	P		E	G-E	-	F	E
So. watergrass	P	P			G	E	-	-	-
torpedograss	P	P	P		F	G	-	NR	E
watershield	P	E	P	P	G	G	-	P	P
water pennywort	P	G	G		P	G	-	-	-
water primrose	P	E	F	P	F	E	F	G	E
willows	P	E	F		P	E	-	-	-
Submersed Weeds									
broadleaf	P		E	E	E	P	-	E	NR
watermilfoil	P	G	E	E	E	P	-	G	NR
coontail	P	P	G	F	E	P	-	NR	NR
egeria	P		E	F	E	P	-	NR	NR
elodea	P	E	E	E	E	P	G	E	NR
eurasian water-milfoil	P	F	G	E	E	P	-	NR	NR
fanwort	F⁴	P	G	G	E	P	-	NR	NR
hydrilla	P	F	E	E	E	P	-	NR	NR
naiads	P	E	E	E	F	F	-	E	NR
parrotfeather	F	E	E	E	E	NR	-	E	NR
pondweeds (Potamogeton)	P	P	G	E	E	P	NR	NR	NR

[1]E = excellent control (90 to 100%); G = good control (80 to 89%); F = fair control (70 to 79%), P = poor control (<70%).

A blank space indicates weed response is not known.

[2]Hydrothol formulations only.

[3]Granular 2,4-D formulations.

[4]Copper complexes only.

[5]Cutrine Plus: Reward, 3:2 tank mix will improve response.

NR - Not recommended

- Insufficient data

Penoxsulam and Imazamox have been recently labeled for control of floating, emergent, and submerged plants, but the labels should be consulted for a list of plants controlled or partially controlled by these herbicides.

AQUATIC WEED CONTROL USE RESTRICTIONS[1]
(Number of days after treatment before use.)

Updated by Gary J. Burtle, Extension Aquaculture and Fisheries

(Common Name) Trade Name	Company	Conc. PPM	HUMAN		
			Drinking	Swimming	Fish Consumption
copper sulfate[2] Copper Sulfate G	Tenn. Chem.	-	0	0	0
Copper Sulfate Snow	Tenn. Chem.	-	0	0	0
Copper Sulfate Crystal	Tenn. Chem.	-	0	0	0
Triangle Copper Sulfate	Triangle		0	0	0
(copper complexes) Cutrine-Plus	Applied	-	0	0	0
Cutrine-Plus G	Biochemists	-			
K-Tea	Griffin	-			
AquaCure	PBI Gordon	-			
(2,4-D) Aquakleen	Rhone-Poulenc	-	NL	0	0
2,4-D Granules	Riverdale	-	NL		
Hardball	Helena	-	NL		
(diquat) Reward[5]	Zeneca	-	1-3	0	0
(endothall) Aquathol G	Atochem	-	7	1	3
Aquathol K		0.5	7	1	3
		1.0 -3.0	14	1	3
Hydrothol 191 &	Atochem	< 0.3	7	*	3
Hydrothol 191G		0.5	14	*	3
(fluridone3) Sonar AS	DowElanco	-	0	0	0
Sonar SRP	DowElanco	-	0	0	0
(glyphosate[4]) Rodeo	Monsanto	-	0	0	0
Pondmaster	Monsanto	-			
(trichlopyr) Renovate 3	Dow Agrosciences	2-8 qt./A	**	0	0
carfentrazone (Stingray)	FMC	-	0	0	0
imazapyr	BASF	-	2	0	0
Galleon SC	Seapro Corp.	10-30 ppb	0	0	0
Clearcast	BASF Corp.	0-500 ppb	0	0	0

[1] Algae control may result in a fish kill due to oxygen depletion if herbicides are applied to large areas, or when dissolved oxygen levels are low, or if fast-acting contact herbicides are used (diquat, copper sulfate, etc.). Similar hazards exist when vascular plants or floating weeds are rapidly killed in large masses with diquat or other herbicides used on emersed or submersed weeds.

[2] If water is used for drinking, the elemental copper concentration should not exceed 1.0 ppm (i.e. 4.0 ppm copper sulfate.)

[3] Do not apply within 0.25 mile of any potable water intake.

[4] Do not apply within 0.5 mile upstream of potable water intakes.

[5] Drinking water restriction depends on rate of application. Refer to Reward label.

NL = NOT LABELED FOR APPLICATION TO BODIES OF WATER WITH THIS INTENDED USE.

*Herbicide label does not prohibit use of water for this intended use.

**Drinking water restrictions depend on laboratory analysis, see Garlon 3A label.

(Common Name) Trade Names	Company	Conc. PPM	ANIMAL DRINKING		IRRIGATION		Agric. Sprays
			Dairy	Livestock	Turf	Crops	
(copper sulfate[2]) Copper Sulfate G	Tenn. Chem.	-	0	0	0	0	0
Copper Sulfate Snow	Tenn. Chem.	-		0	0	0	
Copper Sulfate Crystal	Tenn.Chem.	-		0	0	0	
Triangle Copper Sulfate	Triangle						
(copper complexes) Cutrine-Plus	Applied Biochem-ists Griffin	-	0	0	0	0	0
Cutrine-Plus G		-					
K-Tea	PBI Gordon	-					
AquaCure		-					
(2,4-D) Aquakleen	Rhone-Poulenc	-	NL	0	NL	NL	NL
2,4-D Granules	Riverdale	-	NL		0	NL	NL
Hardball	Helena	-				NL	
(diquat) Reward[5]	Zeneca	-	1	1	1-3	5	5
(endothall) Aquathol G	Atochem	-	7	7	7	7	7
Aquathol K		0.5	7	7	7	7	7
		1.0 -3.0	14	14	14	14	14
Hydrothol 191 & Hydrothol 191G	Atochem	< .03	7	7	7	7	7
		0.5	14	14	14	14	14
(fluridone[3]) Sonar AS	DowElanco DowElanco	-	0	0	30	30	*
Sonar SRP		-		0	30	30	*
(glyphosate[4]) Rodeo	Monsanto	-	0	0	0	0	0
Pondmaster	Monsanto	-		0			
(trichlopyr) Renovate 3	Dow Agrosciences	2-8 qts./A	0	0	NL	NL	NL
carfentrazone (Stingray)	FMC	-	0-1	0-1	1-14	1-14	0
imazapyr	BASF	-	0	0	120	120	0
Galleon SC	Seapro Corp.	10-30 ppb	0	0	0	1 ppb	1 ppb
Clearcast	BASF Corp.	0-500 ppb	0	0	1 d pr 50 ppb	1 d pr 50 ppb	0

[1]Algae control may result in a fish kill due to oxygen depletion if herbicides are applied to large areas, or when dissolved oxygen levels are low, or if fast-acting contact herbicides are used (diquat, copper sulfate, etc.). Similar hazards exist when vascular plants or floating weeds are rapidly killed in large masses with diquat or other herbicides used on emersed or submersed weeds.

[2]If water is used for drinking, the elemental copper concentration should not exceed 1.0 ppm (i.e. 4.0 ppm copper sulfate.)

[3]Do not apply within 0.25 mile of any potable water intake.

[4]Do not apply within 0.5 mile upstream of potable water intakes.

[5]Irrigation water use restriction for turfgrasses and ornamentals depends on rate of application. Refer to Reward label. NL = NOT LABELED FOR APPLICATION TO BODIES OF WATER WITH THIS INTENDED USE.

*Herbicide label does not prohibit use of water for this intended use.

CALCULATING PESTICIDE CONCENTRATIONS IN AQUATIC SITUATIONS[1]

Updated by Gary J. Burtle, Extension Aquaculture and Fisheries

Depending up on the chemical, pesticides a re applied as a surface acre, bottom acre-foot or total water volume treatment. Total water volume treatments are expressed on a part per million by weight (ppmw) basis. Water volume can be measured in gallons, cubic yards, cubic feet, etc.; however, the most commonly used unit of water volume measurement is acre-feet. The following formula may be used to determine the amount of pesticide formulation required to obtain a desired final concentration (ppmw) in the water of a pond or lake on an acre-feet basis:

1. Concentration based on part per million by weight (ppmw)

$$\text{Amount of formulation} = \frac{A \times D \times CF \times ECC}{I}$$

A = area of the water surface in acres (Use precise measurement or measure from aerial photos).

D = average depth of the pond or lake in feet.

CF = 2.72 lbs./acre foot. The Conversion Factor (CF) when total water volume is express on an acre-feet basis. 2.72 lbs. of a pesticide per acre-foot of water is equal to one ppmw.

ECC = Effective Chemical Concentration of the active ingredient of a pesticide needed in the water to achieve control of the pest.

I = The total amount of active ingredient divided by the total amount of active and inert ingredients. Liquid products usually list the amount of active ingredients as pounds per gallon. For such products:

$$I = \frac{\text{pounds of active ingredients}}{\text{one (1) gallon}}$$

Non-liquid formulations usually list active ingredients as a percentage of the total formulation. For non-liquid formulations:

$$I = \frac{\text{percent active ingredients}}{100\%}$$

The following formula may be used to determine the amount of pesticide formulation on a surface acre basis.

1. Amount of pesticide formulation per surface acre.

Amount of formulation = Surface acres X Broad cast formulation rate/ acre.

[1] **For additional information, refer to Bulletin 866 — "Using Chemicals in Pond Management."**

VERTEBRATE PEST CONTROL

Mike Mengak, Wildlife Specialist

NOTE: For recommendations on the use of chemicals to control vertebrate pests, contact your Extension Service agent.

It is necessary to obtain a permit prior to killing protected animals in Georgia. Get a permit by writing the Wildlife Resources Office of the Georgia Department of Natural Resources, 2070 U.S. Highway 278, S.E., Social Circle, Georgia 30279; or call (404) 656-4994.

In the following section non-game animals include pocket gophers, chipmunks, bats, amphibians, and reptiles. A permit is also required to take furbearing animals or game animals out of season. A current hunting or trapping license is required to take game or furbearing animals in season.

To begin the permit process for taking protected birds call the USDA Wildlife Services at (706) 546-5637. For permits to kill other protected animals call the Wildlife Resources office of the Georgia Department of Natural Resources (770) 761-3044.

MAMMALS

Species	Habitat Modification	Exclusion	Frightening	Repellents	Toxicants/ Fumigants	Trapping	Other
Beaver	Eliminate food, trees, woody vegetation where feasible Continually destroy dams Install water control device (Clemson beaver pond leveler)	Fence small areas along stream and yard Fence around valuable trees	Continual destruction of lodges and dams	None are registered	None are registered	Very effective if done by a trained Wildlife Control Expert	None
Chipmunk	Store food such as bird seed and dog food in rodent-proof container Ground cover, shrubs, and wood piles should not be located adjacent to structural foundation	Seal all cracks and holes in foundations ¼ inch mesh hardware cloth buried 1-2 feet deep to exclude from gardens and flower beds	Not effective	Area repellent such as Naphthalene (moth balls) may work in confined area but only outside (like in a shed—never in a house) Taste repellents containing Bitrex or Thiram applied to seeds, bulbs, or vegetation not meant for human consumption	None are registered	Very effective; using standard mouse or rat snap traps baited with peanut butter	None
Gray squirrel or flying squirrel	Trim trees away from house Remove diseased trees or trees with cavities	Sheet metal bands on isolated trees to prevent climbing in order to protect developing nut crop Seal all openings to buildings especially around chimney, eaves, and soffets Install excluder in attics to allow squirrel to escape and prevent re-entry	Not effective	Some products containing hot sauce (capsaicin) and other distasteful compounds may work (may also be used with deer)	None are registered	Can be very effective but should on be done by qualified Wildlife Control Expert Permits may be required	On bird feeders suspended by rope. Place rope through plastic conduit to reduce climbing

Species	Habitat Modification	Exclusion	Frightening	Repellents	Toxicants/ Fumigants	Trapping	Other
Voles	Eliminate ground cover such as grass and weeds Remove mulch from base of trees and plants Soil cultivation to destroy burrows, tunnels and ground cover	Recommended to protect trees, ornamentals and gardens Use ¼ inch mesh hardware cloth buried 1-2 feet deep	Not effective	None proven effective	Anticoagulants like rat poisons always use caution around pets and children	Very effective using standard rat or mouse traps baited with peanut butter	None
Moles	Reduce soil moisture and food sources by reducing watering and cautiously using lawn pesticides to treat for insects and grubs	May be cost effective in very small area like flower bed or garden ¼-inch hard ware cloth or sheet metal	Not effective	None are registered	Several products (poisons) are available for placing in the tunnel or hole	Difficult but can be effective in some situations	None
Deer	Difficult; habitat modification is not generally recommended Plant deer resistant plants Harvest crops early Lure crops may draw deer away from valuable crops	Fences – up to 8 feet tall; less if with dog Electric fences can be effective Individual tree protector; fence or pipe to prevent antler rubs	May provided some limited protection in certain situations	Many are available; some commercial; some 'home' remedies Effectiveness varies with ingredients and timing; start applying prior to damage; high density deer population will not likely be repelled Taste and odor repellents are available; beware of advertising Sound repellents are generally ineffective	None	Not available to landowners	Contraception is possible in lab situations and limited effectiveness in field; expensive Hunting is best in most situations but not allowable in some instances
Coyote	Destroy dens if possible Reduce habit at for mice and other food items	Fencing pastures and yards to reduce danger to livestock and pets Keep pets inside, especially at night	Guard dogs can be effective for livestock	None shown to be consistently effective	Available to livestock producers and Wildlife Control Experts; generally not available to homeowners/ gardeners	Can be very effective but requires considerable knowledge; best left to Wildlife Control Experts	Hunting if safe and legal
Hogs	Difficult	Fencing may be effective for small areas	May provide limited protection in some instances	None	None	Very effective but costly and time intensive	Shooting or hunting. Check all game regulations

REPELLENTS FOR DEER, RABBITS AND OTHER MAMMALS

These materials may give temporary protection. Repellents are most likely to produce satisfactory results if protection is needed for a week or two. If protection is required, fencing is often more effective treatment. Retreatment may be necessary, especially after rain. Repellents are most effective when applied before damage starts. Local density of animal may negate efficacy of any repellent treatment. Some repellents are contact and water soluble; other are systemic and therefore require less frequent application. Read and follow all label instructions. Some repellents are not labeled for use on food crops. Contact wildlife specialist for additional products.

PROBLEM OR LOCATION	CHEMICAL AND FORMULATION	METHOD AND RATE	TARGET SPECIES	REMARKS AND RESTRICTIONS
Browsing on conifer seedlings, ornamentals, hardwoods	Putrescent Whole Egg solids. Can be homemade.		Deer	A taste repellent. Not for use on edible plants. Brands or product names: Deer Away, BGR.
	Liquid 15% Powder 36%	Apply to vegetation—spray, dip, or shake as per label.		
Fruit trees, field crops, ornamentals, nursery stock, vegetables, non-crop areas	Ammonium Soaps of higher fatty acids	Dilute as per label. Spray on crops to be protected.	Deer Rabbit	Retreat after rain or an necessary.
	Liquid 15%	May work as border treatment. Label may include use as paint for stems and trunks,	Deer Rabbit	Brand or product names: Hinder
	Other taste repellents: – Mint Oil – Garlic Oil – Capsaicin – Bitrex®		Deer Rabbit	Retreat after rain or as necessary. Apply before damage is noticed. Follow label instructions—some products not labeled for edible crops. Brand or product names: Tree-Guard, Liquid Fence, Deer-Off, Phantskydd, This-1-Works®.
	Odor Repellents: – Milorganite®	Apply as per label	Deer Rabbit	Retreat as necessary. Most home odor repellents are not effective. Milorganite® is a mild organic fertilizer. Effective if used properly.
Gnawing on wood siding, decks, fence posts	Benzyidlethyl-methyl-Ammonium-Saccharide and Thymol sources.	Apply as per label. Do not apply indoors. Avoid contact with water or food sources. Do not mix with other chemicals.	Rats Squirrels Skunks Rabbits	Manufacturer claims of effectiveness may need further testing. May repel woodpeckers. Brand name: Ro-Pel®

REPTILES AND AMPHIBIANS

There are no toxicants or fumigants registered for reptiles and amphibians. Commercial snake repellents are available but none have been shown to be consistently effective. Snakes lack a sense of smell and do not hear sound so repellents are of questionable efficacy. Nearly all reptiles except venomous (poisonous) snakes are protected. Amphibians enjoy less legal protection. All native birds are protected and require state and federal permits. Harassment and repellents (non-lethal only) are generally allowed. Check with local wildlife law enforcement officials prior to working with birds.

ANIMAL	PROBLEM OR LOCATION	CHEMICAL AND FORMULATION	METHOD AND RATE	REMARKS AND RESTRICTIONS
Reptiles Snakes, lizards, turtles and alligators				No venomous lizards in Georgia. Six of 40 species of snakes are venomous. All harmless snakes protected. Send skins, frozen or preserved specimens to state specialist for identification. Call DNR. Do not kill. Fix in Formalin. Frozen is better. Do not damage head. Alligators are protected in Georgia. Contact Georgia Wildlife Resources biologists for alligator problems. Use traps to remove nuisance turtles.
Amphibians Frogs, toads, salamanders, and their tadpoles	Animals getting into swimming pools, houses	None		No chemical controls currently available. Hand removal with a dip net is recommended. Keeping sticks or rocks in small garden pools will allow animal to climb out.
Birds	Nesting in rafters of pole barns; pecking holes in siding; roosting; eating fruit.	No toxicants or fumigants registered.		Recommendations are for physical exclusion with fence, net or barrier. Brand name: Bird-X® netting, Nix-A-Lite®, sticky caulking.
Goose	Droppings on lawn, playground, drive way; eating grass; nesting	Methyl anthranilate	Follow label directions.	Goose repellent made from Concord grapes. Expensive. Must reapply after mowing, rain or irrigation.

PESTICIDE SAFETY AND OTHER PESTICIDE INFORMATION

USE PESTICIDES SAFELY

Paul Guillebeau, Extension Entomologist

Pesticides are poisonous chemicals that can injure or kill nontarget plants and animals, including man if they are handled improperly. Follow these guidelines to minimize the risk of pesticides to human health and the environment.

1. Use Integrated Pest Management (IPM) (http://ipm .ent.uga.edu). IPM reduces dependence on pesticides by integrating nonchemical methods to help control or prevent damaging pest populations. Ask your county agent about IPM techniques that can be used for your situation.
2. **Apply pesticides only when they are needed.** Properly identify the pest and evaluate whether it will cause enough damage to justify a pesticide application. Your local extension office can help you identify and evaluate your pest problems.
3. **Choose the correct pesticide.** Refer to the pesticide label to make sure it is registered for the site you need to treat. This handbook and your local Extension office can help you choose the right pesticide.
4. **FOLLOW THE LABEL DIRECTIONS!** Nearly all pesticide accidents are the result of not following all of the directions, restrictions, and precautions on the label. Avoid the temptation to use greater than the labeled rates; you increase your risk and you may injure or damage the site of application. Additionally, it is illegal to use any pesticide in a manner not prescribed on the label.
5. **Store pesticides safely.** Nearly 50% of U.S. households with a child under five years old have a pesticide stored within reach of children. Keep pesticides clearly labeled. The storage area should be clearly marked and locked if possible. Keep pesticides beyond the reach of children and animals. Do not store pesticides with food, feed, or clothing. 'NEVER store pesticides in any food or drink container!'
6. **Prevent pesticide drift and runoff**. Never apply pesticide when the wind is blowing more than 5 mph or when rain is imminent. Crops that receive regular pesticide applications should not be planted near bodies of water or near sensitive areas, such as schools or wildlife habitat.
7. **Wear the proper protective clothing.** If you wear the right protective equipment, your risk from pesticides is very small. The label will tell you what protective clothing you need.
8. **Measure pesticides carefully.** Do not mix more pesticide than you need. It is much easier to use pesticides than to dispose of them.
9. **Dispose of pesticide waste properly.** Empty containers that are properly rinsed can be recycled or placed in landfills. Excess pesticides and rinse water can be applied to labeled sites if you will not exceed labeled rates. Refer to the pesticide label for proper disposal.
10. **Wash your hands** before you eat, drink, use tobacco, or go to the restroom. Shower as soon as you can, washing your hair and fingernails. Wash your clothes before wearing them again.
11. **If you or someone else is exposed to a pesticide, take immediate action.** Remove any contaminated clothing. If pesticide is on the skin, wash immediately. If pesticide is in the eye, rinse with clean water for at least 15 minutes. If pesticide is swallowed, give large amounts of water or milk to drink. DO NOT induce vomiting unless the label directs you to. Never give liquids or induce vomiting if a person is unconscious or convulsive. If pesticide is inhaled, move victim to fresh air. Seek medical attention.

Selecting and Purchasing the Pesticide

1. When you choose a pesticide, consider 1) effectiveness, 2) hazard, 3) restrictions on use, 4) experience of the applicator, 5) required protective clothing, and 6) equipment needed to apply the product. You may want to choose a safer pesticide or formulation if the applicator is not well-trained.

Transporting the Pesticide

1. NEVER transport pesticides in the passenger section of a vehicle.
2. NEVER transport pesticides with food, feed, or other products that may come in contact with humans or animals.
3. NEVER leave pesticides unattended. You are responsible for any accidents that ma y occur while you are away.
4. Secure pesticide containers in the back of a truck to prevent breaks and spills. Protect paper/cardboard from moisture.
5. Transport pesticides in properly labeled packages.
6. Report spills on roadways immediately to the local authorities.

Storing the Pesticide

1. Store pesticides in a locked and posted place that is accessible only to qualified personnel. Keep pesticides out of reach of children, unqualified people, or animals.
2. Store pesticides in their original containers with intact labels. NEVER place a pesticide in a food or beverage container.
3. Do not store pesticides with food, feed, or seed. Store pesticides at least 100 feet from wells and other waterways.
4. Make sure the storage place is fire-resistant (including a concrete floor), well ventilated, well lighted, locked, dry, protected from direct sunlight, and insulated against temperature extremes.
5. Check containers frequently for leaks or breaks. Transfer the contents of a damaged container into a labeled container that held exactly the same pesticide.
6. Immediately clean up any spills using the correct methods.
7. Store empty pesticide containers securely until proper disposal is available.

Mixing and Loading Pesticides

1. READ THE LABEL! Make sure you understand all directions and precautions. Mix only the amount you need.
2. Keep an adequate supply of clean water and soap nearby.
3. Check your protective equipment for wear and leaks.
4. Know the early symptoms of pesticide poisoning.
5. Be sure that emergency equipment for spills and first-aid are readily available.
6. Keep unauthorized people and animals out of the mixing area.
7. Work in a well lighted and well ventilated area, preferably outdoors. Do not work alone.
8. Wear all of the protective equipment required by the pesticide label. Be sure you know how to use it properly.
9. Mix in an area where spills can be contained, at least 100 feet from wells and other waterways.
10. NEVER mix pesticides near a well or where other bodies of water may be contaminated. Keep the end of the hose above pesticide/water level.
11. NEVER eat, drink, or smoke while mixing pesticides.
12. NEVER mix or load pesticides at or above eye-level. Close containers that are not in use.
13. When you are mixing or loading, stand so that the wind does not blow pesticide on you.

Applying the Pesticide

1. Calibrate your equipment regularly. Check for leaks, clogged nozzles, and excessive wear.
2. Wear the protective clothing indicated on the label.
3. Clear the area of other people and animals.
4. Avoid drift and run off. Spray only when there is little or no wind. Do not spray when rain is imminent. Use the lowest spray pressure and largest nozzle orifices that are practical.
5. Be prepared for leaks, spills, or equipment failures.
6. Check the label to see what precautions are indicated. Post the area if required. Be sure that people entering the area during the re-entry interval are properly protected.

Cleaning Equipment

1. Thoroughly clean mixing, loading, and application equipment inside and out after each use.
2. Wear protective clothing while you are cleaning equipment or repairing it during use.
3. Clean equipment in an area where drainage will not endanger man or the environment.

Disposing of Excess Pesticides and Empty Containers*

1. Use excess pesticides according to label directions if possible. Otherwise follow label instructions for disposal.
2. Empty metal, plastic or glass containers should be pressure-rinsed or triple-rinsed. The rinse water should be directed into the spray tank. Properly rinsed containers can be placed in landfills or recycled. Contact your local extension office for recycling programs in your area.
3. Consult the label or your local extension office for other disposal information.

*See Waste Disposal under Pesticide Legislation and Regulations and telephone numbers under information numbers.

PROTECT HONEY BEES FROM PESTICIDES

Keith S. Delaplane, Extension Entomologist

Many crops cannot be economically produced unless there are large numbers of honey bees to pollinate them. In addition, honey bees produce more than $50 million of honey and beeswax annually, and honey bee pollination accounts for over $14 billion added value to American agriculture each year. Beekeeping in Georgia adds an estimated $ 70 million annually to our state's economy.

Many pesticides are extremely hazardous to honey bees. But damage can be minimized if the pesticide user and the beekeeper cooperate and take proper precautions.

The Pesticide User's Role

1. Use pesticides only when needed.
2. If possible, select one of the least hazardous pesticides from the following list, especially on flowering plants that attract bees.
3. Use the least hazardous method of application. Granules are usually harmless to honey bees. Sprays drift less than dusts and are less likely to kill bees in nearby areas. Whenever possible, minimize drift by applying pesticides with ground application equipment rather than with airplanes.
4. Do not apply pesticides when honey bees are active in the field. Applications in late evening or night are least likely to kill bees. Do not apply pesticides when plants are in flower unless it is absolutely necessary.
5. Avoid pesticide drift into apiaries or areas where crops or wild plants are flowering. With crops that require heavy pesticide applications, plant them in non-sensitive areas if possible.
6. Notify nearby beekeepers several days before you apply a pesticide.

The Beekeeper's Role

1. Whenever possible, locate colonies away from areas of heavy pesticide use.
2. Post your name, address, and phone number conspicuously at your apiary and tell nearby farmers where your hives are located.
3. Know which pesticides are commonly used in your area and be prepared to confine or remove your bees if you are notified that a pesticide will be applied. Commonly used pesticides are grouped according to hazard in the following list.

If you cannot move hives in time to avoid a pesticide application, you can cover each hive with a plastic sheet at night and in the early morning to confine the bees and protect them from short-residual pesticides. However, heat builds up rapidly once the plastic is exposed to the sun and it must be removed. An alternative — wet burlap, can be used for a day or more. This may be impractical for large numbers of hives. Colonies that are repeatedly exposed to pesticides in Groups I or II of the list below should be relocated.

Commonly Used Pesticides Grouped According To Their Relative Hazards To Honey Bees[1]

Group I
Hazardous

abamectin (Agri-Mek, Avid)
acephate (Orthene, Address)
aminocarb (Matacil)
azinphosmethyl (Guthion)
benzene hexachloride (BHC. lindane)
bifenthrin (Capture, Brigade)
carbaryl (Sevin, Sevin XLR-Plus)
carbofuran (Furadan)
chlorpyrifos (Dursban, Lorsban)

chlorethoxyfos (Fortress)
clofentezine (Apollo)
crotoxyphos (Cyodrin)
cypermethrin (Ammo))
cyfluthrin (Baythroid)
cyhalothrin (Warrior)
cypermethrin (Ammo)
deltamethrin (Decis)
diazinon (Diazinon, Spectracide)
dichlorvos (DDVP, Vapona)
dicrotophos (Bidrin)
dimethoate (Cygon, Dimethoate, Rebelate)

emamectin (Proclaim)
endosulfan (Thiodan)
EPN
esfenvalerate (Asana)
ethyl parathion (Parathion)
fenpropathrin (Danitol)
fenthion (Baytex)
fipronil
hexythiazox (Savey)
imidacloprid (Provado)
indoxacarb (Avaunt)
lambda-cyhalothrin (Warrior)
malathion (Cythion ULV)

methamidophos (Monitor)
methidathion (Supracide)
methiocarb (Mesurol)
methomyl (Lannate)
methyl parathion (Penncap-M)
mevinphos (Phosdrin)[2]
monocrotophos (Azodrin)
naled (Dibrom)[2]
oxamyl (Vydate >1 lb/A)
permethrin (Ambush, Pounce)
phorate (Thimet EC)
phosmet (Imidan)
phosphamidon (Dimecron)

---

[1] List derived in part from Johansen, C.A. and Mayer, D.F. Pollination Protection. 1990, Wicwas Press; Bulletin E-5 3-W, Hunt, G.J., Purdue University; Environmental Entomology 33(5):1151-1154.

[2] Not all *Bacillus thuringiensis* insecticides are safe for bees. The label for XenTari® (Valent BioSciences), with active ingredient *B. thuringiensis aizawai*, reads "This product is highly toxic to honey bees exposed to direct treatment. Do not apply this product while bees are actively visiting the treatment area."

Group I
Hazardous (cont.)
propoxur (Baygon)
pyridaben (Pyramite)
resmethrin (Synthrin)
tebufenozide (Confirm)
tralomethrin (Scout)
zeta-cypermethrin (Fury,
    Mustang)

Group II
Moderately Hazardous
aldicarb (Temik)
carbaryl (Sevin XLR formulation
    only)
carbophenothion (Trithion)
coumaphos (Co-Ral)
cyromazine (Trigard)
diatomaceous earth (Diatect)
disulfoton (Di-Syston)
DSMA
emamectin benzoate (Proclaim)
ethoprop (Mocap)
fonofos (Dyfonate)
malathion (Cythion, ULV <3 fl
    oz/A)
methyl demeton (Metasystox)
MSMA
neem (Azatin, Neemix)
oxamyl (Vydate <0.5 lb/A)
oxydemeton-methyl
    (Metasystox R)
paraquat
perthane
pymetrozine (Fulfill)
pyriproxyfen (Esteem, Knack)
ronnel (Co-Ral, Korlan)
spinosad (SpinTor)
temephos (Abate)
terbufos (Counter)
thiamethoxam (Actara, Platinum)
thiodicarb (Larvin)

Group III
Relatively Nonhazardous
acetamiprid (Assail)
allethrin (Pynamin)
amitraz (Mitac)
amitrole
azadirachtin (Align)
azoxystrobin (Abound)
Bacillus thuringiensis (Biobit,
    DiPel, Full-Bac, Javelin,
    MVP)[3]

Beauveria (Mycotrol)
benomyl (Benlate)
binapacryl (Morocide)
bordeaux mixture
bromoxynil
capsaicin (Hot Pepper Wax)
captan
carbaryl (Sevin G, Bait G)
carbofuran (Furadan G)
chloramben
chlorbenzide (Mitox)
chlorobenzilate (Acaraben)
chlorothalonil (Bravo)
copper compounds (Kocide)
copper oxychloride sulphate
copper 8-quinolinolate
copper sulfate (Monohydrated)
cryolite (Cryolite, Kryocide)
cyromazine (Trigard)
dalapon
dazomet (Mylone)
demeton (Systox)
dexon
diazinon (Diazinon G)
dicamba (Banvel D)
dichlone (Phygon)
dicofol (Kelthane)
diflubenzuron (Dimilin)
dinocap (Karathane)
disulfoton (Di-Syston G)
dodine (Cyprex)
dyrene endothall
EPTC (Eptam)
ethion (Ethion)
ethoprop (Mocap G)
fenbutatin-oxide (Vendex)
fenhexamid (Elevate)
ferbam
fluvalinate (Spur)
folpet (Phaltan)
Garlic Barrier
genite 923
glyodin (Glyoxide)
kaolin (Surround)
malathion (Malathion G)
mancozeb (Dithane M-45)
maneb (Dithane M-22)
MCPA
metaldehyde (Metaldehyde Bait)
methoxychlor (Marlate)
metiram (Polyram)
monuron (Telvar)
myclobutanil (Rally)
nabam (Parzate)
nemagon

nicotine sulfate
oxythioquinox (Morestan)
pentac
propargite (Omite)
pyrethrum
pyrimidinamine (Vangard)
rotenone (rotenone)
ryania
silvex
imazine (Princep)
soap (M -Pede)
sulfurtebufenozide (Confirm)
TDE (Rhothane)
tetradifon (Tedion)
thioquinox (Eradex)
thiram (Arasan)
toxaphenetrichlorfon (Dylox)
trifloxystrobin (Flint)
zineb (Dithane)
ziram
2,4-D
2,4-DB
2,4,5-T

---

[1] List derived in part from Johansen, C.A. and Mayer, D.F. Pollination Protection. 1990, Wicwas Press; Bulletin E-5 3-W, Hunt, G.J., Purdue University; Environmental Entomology 33(5):1151-1154.

[2] Mevinphos (Phosdrin*), naled (Dibrom*), and TEPP have short residual activity and kill only the bees contacted at time of treatment or shortly thereafter. They are usually safe to use when bees are not in flight; they are not safe to use around colonies.

[3] Not all *Bacillus thuringiensis* insecticides are safe for bees. The label for XenTari® (Valent BioSciences), with active ingredient *B. thuringiensis aizawai*, reads "This product is highly toxic to honey bees exposed to direct treatment. Do not apply this product while bees are actively visiting the treatment area."

COMMON PESTICIDE PRODUCTS AVAILABLE FOR HOMEOWNERS

Dan Horton and John All, Entomologists

Always refer to the actual product label, which is the definitive guide for safe, legal pesticide use.

PRODUCTS	ACTIVE INGREDIENT	INDOORS, PATIOS, DECKS, EXTERIOR HARDSCAPES & PATHS	FLOWERS, SHRUBS, TREES, LAWNS	VEGE-TABLES	FRUIT
INSECTICIDES					
Bayer Advanced 12 Month Tree & Shrub Protect & Feed	imidacloprid	--	X	--	--
Bayer Advanced Carpenter Ant & Termite Killer Plus	b-cyfluthrin	X	X	--	--
Bayer Advanced Complete Insect Dust for Gardens	permethrin	X	--	X	X
Bayer Advanced Complete Insect Killer for Garden R-T-U	carbaryl	--	X	X	X
Bayer Advanced Complete Insect Killer for Soil & Turf	imidacloprid + beta-cyfluthrin	--	X	--	--
Bayer Advanced Dual Action Rose & Flower Insect Killer R-T-U	imidacloprid + beta cyfluthrin	--	X	--	--
Bayer Advanced Fire Ant Killer	beta-cyfluthrin	--	X	--	--
Bayer Advanced Home Carpenter Ant and Termite Killer Plus	deltamethrin	X	X	--	--
Bayer Advanced Home Pest Control Indoor & Outdoor Insect	beta-cyfluthrin	X	X	--	--
Bayer Advanced Home Pest Plus Germ Killer	sodium o-phenylphenate + b-cyfluthrin	X	--	--	--
Bayer Advanced Power Force Carpenter Ant & Termite Killer Plus	deltamethrin	X	X	--	--
Bayer Advanced Rose & Flower Care 2 in 1 systemic	disulfoton	--	X	--	--
Bayer Advanced Season - Long Grub Control Ready- to-Spread Granules	imidacloprid	--	X	--	--
Bayer Advanced Termite Killer Ready-to-Spread Granules	imidacloprid	--	X	--	--
Bengal Fire Ant Killer Ultra Dust 2X	deltamethrin	X	X		
Bengal Roach Spray Aerosol	permethrin	X	--	--	--
Black Flag Fogging Insecticide	resmethrin	X	X	--	--
Bonide Borer-Miner Killer	permethrin	X	X	X	X
Bonide Citrus, Fruit & Nut Orchard Spray	sulfur + pyrethrins	X	X	X	X
Bonide Eight Vegetable, Fruit & Flower	permethrin	X	X	X	X
Bonide Eight Yard & Garden	permethrin	X	X	--	--
Bonide Systemic Granules	disulfoton	--	X	--	--
Bonide Systemic Rose and Flower Care	disulfoton (Disyston)	X	X	--	--
Combat Quick Kill Formula 1	fipronil	X	--	--	--
Cutter Backyard Bug Control	lambda-cyhalothrin	outdoor	X		
Cutter Backyard Bug Control Outdoor Fogger	terramethrin + phenothrin	X	X		
Cutter Bug Free Backyard One-Step Fogger	tetramethrin , piperonyl butoxide, permethrin	X	--	--	--
Cutter Bug Free Backyard Outdoor Fogger Aerosol	permethrin	--	X	--	--
Cutter Bug Free Backyard Spray Concentrate	permethrin	--	X	--	--

PRODUCTS	ACTIVE INGREDIENT	INDOORS, PATIOS, DECKS, EXTERIOR HARDSCAPES & PATHS	FLOWERS, SHRUBS, TREES, LAWNS	VEGE-TABLES	FRUIT
Enforcer Flea Spray for homes	nylar + permethrin	X	--	--	--
Ferti-Lome Rose Food Cont Systemic Insecticide	disulfoton	--	X	--	--
Ferti-Lome Systemic Insecticide Granules	disulfoton	--	X	X	--
Garden Safe House Plant & Garden Insect Spray	pyrethrins + canola oil	X	X	X	X
Garden Safe Insect Killer Fruit & Vegetable	pyrethrin	X	X	X	X
Garden Safe Insect Killer Rose & Flower	pyrethrin	X	X	--	--
GardenTech Sevin Bug Killer	carbaryl	--	X	X	X
GardenTech Sevin-5 Dust	carbaryl	X	X	X	X
Green Light Borer Killer	permethrin	X	X	X	X
Green Light Conquest Insecticide Concentrate	permethrin	X	X	X	X
Green Light Fire Ant Dust	deltamethrin	X	X	--	--
Green Light Fruit Tree Spray	pyrethrins + piperonyl butoxide + hydrophdoic extract of neem oil	--	--	--	X
Green Light Roach, Ant & Spider Control	deltamethrin	X	X	--	--
Hot Shot Bedbug & Flea Fogger	pyrethrins + piperonyl butoxide + benzeneacetate	X			
Hot Shot Bedbug & Flea Killer	pyrethrins + piperonyl butoxide	X			
Hot Shot Flying Insect Aerosol	permethrin + d-trans allethrin	X	--	--	--
Hot Shot Fogger with Odor Neutralizer	tetramethrin + permethrin	X	--	--	--
Hot Shot Home Insect Control Clear Formula	lambda cyhalothrin	X	--	--	--
Hot Shot Kitchen Bug Killer Botanic al (aerosol)	pyrethrins + piperonyl butoxide	X	--	--	--
Hot Shot MaxAttrax Roach Killing Powder with Boric Acid	orthoboric acid	X	--	--	--
Hot Shot No-Mess Fogger	tetramethrin + permethrin + piperonyl butoxide	X	--	--	--
Hot Shot No-Pest Strip Kills Flying & Crawling Insects	dichlorvos	X	--	--	--
Hot Shot Pest Control Concentrate	cypermethrin	X	--	--	--
Hot Shot Roach & Ant Killer (aerosol)	prallethrin + lambda-cyhalothrin	X	--	--	--
Hot Shot Spider Killer Water-based Non-staining	prallethrin + lambda-cyhalothrin	X	X	--	--
Hot Shot Ultra Ant & Roach Killer Aerosol	imiprothrin + lambda-cyhalothrin	X	--	--	--
No-Pest Ant & Roach Killer Aerosol	d-trans allethrin + lambda-cyhalothrin	X	--	--	--
No-Pest Home Insect Control	lambda-cyhalothrin	X	X	--	--
No-Pest Wasp & Hornet Killer aerosol	prallethrin + lambda cyhalothrin	X	X	--	--
Ortho Ant-B-Gon Dust	permethrin	X	X	X	X

PRODUCTS	ACTIVE INGREDIENT	INDOORS, PATIOS, DECKS, EXTERIOR HARDSCAPES & PATHS	FLOWERS, SHRUBS, TREES, LAWNS	VEGE-TABLES	FRUIT
Ortho Bug-B-Gon MAX Garden & Landscape Insect Killer	esfenvalerate	X	X	X	X
Ortho Bug-B-Gon MAX Garden Insect Dust	permethrin	X	--	X	X
Ortho Bug-B-Gon MAX Insect Killer For Lawns Granules	bifenthrin	X	X	X	--
Ortho Bug-B-Gon MAX Lawn & Garden Insect Killer 1	bifenthrin	X	X	X	X
Ortho Bug-B-Gon Multi-Purpose Garden Dust 1	permethrin	X	X	X	X
Ortho Bug-B-Gon Multi-Purpose Insect Killer Ready-To-Use	esfenvalerate	X	X	X	X
Ortho Ecosense Brand Indoor Insect Killer	soybean oil	X			
Ortho Ecosense Brand Insecticidal Soap	potassium salts of fatty acids	X	X	X	X
Ortho Ecosense Brand Outdoor Insect Killer	pyrethrins + canola oil	X	X	X	
Ortho Home Defense Max	bifenthrin	exterior barrier	X	--	--
Ortho Home Defense MAX Indoor & Outdoor Insect Killer 5	bifenthrin	X	X	--	--
Ortho Malathion Plus Insect Spray Concentrate	malathion	--	X	X	X
Ortho MAX Ant & Roach Killer Aerosol	dicarboxamide	X	--	--	--
Ortho MAX Fire Ant Killer Broadcast Granules	bifenthrin	--	X	--	--
Ortho MAX Flower, Fruit, & Vegetable Killer	acetamiprid		X	X	X
Ortho MAX Flying Insect Killer Aerosol	tetramethrin + phenothrin	X	--	--	--
Ortho MAX Garden & Landscape Insect Killer	esfenvalerate	--	X	X	X
Ortho MAX Hornet & Wasp (aerosol) Killer	tetramethrin, sumithrin, cyclopropanecarboxylate	--	X	--	--
Ortho MAX Indoor Insect Fogger	pyrethrins + permethrin	X	--	--	--
Ortho MAX Lawn & Garden Insect Killer 1	bifenthrin	exterior	X	X	X
Ortho MAX Tree & Shrub Insect Control	imidacloprid		X		X
Ortho Orthene Fire Ant Killer	acephate	--	X	--	--
Ortho Ortho-Klor Termite and Carpenter Ant Killer	bifenthrin	X	X	--	--
Ortho Rose & Flower Insect Killer 1	bifenthrin	--	X	--	--
Ortho Rose Pride Insect Killer	acetamiprid		X		
Ortho RTU Houseplant & Garden Insect Killer	bifenthrin	--	X	--	--
Ortho Volck Oil Spray	horticultural oil	--	X	--	X
Pointer Insecticide	imidacloprid	--	X	--	--
Pre-Strike Mosquito Torpedo	methoprene	exterior	X	--	--
Raid Ant & Roach Aerosol	imiprothrin + cypermethrin	X	--	--	--
Raid Concentrated Deep Roach Fogger	cypermethrin	X	--	--	--
Raid Flying Insect Aerosol	permethrin + tetramethrin _ d-trans allethrin	X	--	--	--
Raid Fumigator	permethrin	X	--	--	--

PRODUCTS	ACTIVE INGREDIENT	INDOORS, PATIOS, DECKS, EXTERIOR HARDSCAPES & PATHS	FLOWERS, SHRUBS, TREES, LAWNS	VEGE-TABLES	FRUIT
Raid Max 2-Way Roach Spray (aerosol)	imiprothrin + deltamethrin	X	--	--	--
Raid Max Concentrated Deep Roach Fogger	cypermethrin	X	--	--	--
Raid Wasp & Hornet (aerosol)	tetramethrin + permethrin	X	X	--	--
Raid Yard-Guard Mosquito Fogger	permethrin + d-cis/trans allethrin	--	X	--	--
Real Kill Ant & Roach Killer (aerosol)	d-trans allethrin + lambda-cyhalothrin	X	--	--	--
Real Kill Ant Killer Aerosol[2]	d-trans allethrin + lambda-cyhalothrin	X	--	--	--
Real Kill Flea Fogger Indoor	pyrethrins, piperonyl butoxide	X	--	--	--
Real Kill Home Insect Control Indoor & Outdoor	lambda-cyhalothrin	X	X	--	--
Real Kill Home Insect Control Indoor & Outdoor Insect Killer	cyfluthrin	X	--	--	--
Real Kill Indoor Fogger	cypermethrin	X	--	--	--
Schultz Houseplant & Garden Insect Spray	pyrethrin	X	X	X	X
Scotts Outdoor Defense Insect Killer	permethrin	--	X	--	--
Spectracide Ant Shield Home Barrier Granules	lambda-cyhalothrin	exterior barrier	X	--	--
Spectracide Ant Shield Home Barrier Insect Killer	permethrin	--	X	--	--
Spectracide Ant Shield Outdoor Killing Stakes	indoxacarb	--	X	--	--
Spectracide Bug Stop for Gardens	permethrin	--	X	X	X
Spectracide Bug Stop Indoor/Outdoor Home Insect Control	tralomethrin	X	X	--	--
Spectracide Commercial Wasp & Hornet Killer aerosol	tetramethrin + permethrin + piperonyl butoxide	X	--	--	--
Spectracide Fire Ant Killer Granules Mound Destroyer	lambda-cyhalothrin	--	X	--	--
Spectracide Fire Ant Killer Ready-to-Use Dust	permethrin	--	X	--	--
Spectracide Garden Insect Killer R-T-U	pyrethrins + piperonyl butoxide	--	X	X	X
Spectracide Malathion Insect Spray	malathion	X	X	X	X
Spectracide Pro Wasp & Hornet Killer	tetramethrin + permethrin + piperonyl butoxide	X	--	--	--
Spectracide Terminate Termite & Carpenter Ant Killer Concentrate	lambda cyhalothrin	X	X	--	--
Spectracide Terminate Termite & Carpenter Ant Killing Dust	disodium octaborate tetrahydrate	X	--	--	--
Spectracide Terminate Termite Detection & Killing Stakes	sulfluramid	--	X	--	--
Spectracide Terminate Termite Killing Foam aerosol	tralomethrin + d-trans allethrin	X	X	--	--
Spectracide Triazicide Brand Lawn & Garden Insect Killer	lambda-cyhalothrin	X	X	X	--
Spectracide Triazicide Once & Done! Insect Killer 2 Conc. for Lawn	gamma-cyhalothrin	X	X	X	X
Spectracide Triazicide Once & Done! Insect Killer for Lawn & Landscape	lambda cyhalothrin	--	X	X	--

PRODUCTS	ACTIVE INGREDIENT	INDOORS, PATIOS, DECKS, EXTERIOR HARDSCAPES & PATHS	FLOWERS, SHRUBS, TREES, LAWNS	VEGE-TABLES	FRUIT
Spectracide Triazicide Once & Done! Insect Killer Granules	lambda-cyhalothrin	X	X	--	--
Spectracide Wasp & Hornet Killers aerosol	prallethrin + lambda cyhalothrin	X	X	--	--
SunSpray Ultra-Fine Pest Oil	refined horticultural oil	--	X	X	X
Terro Ant Killer Outdoor	permethrin	X	X	--	--
Terro Ant Killer Plus Outdoor Shaker Bag	lambda-cyhalothrin	--	X	--	--
Terro Spider Killer Aerosol	pyrethrins + permethrin + piperonyl butoxide	X	--	--	--
Total Kill Lawn & Garden Insect Killer Concentrate	permethrin	X	X	X	X
Total Kill Lawn & Garden Insect Killer Granules	bifenthrin	X	X	X	
Total Kill Wasp & Hornet Killer (aerosol)	tetramethrin & /trans phenothrin	X	--	--	--
Ultra-Kill Wasp & Hornet Killer	prollethrin + lambda-cyhalothrin	X	X		
Ultra-Kill Ant & Roach Killer (aerosol)	d-trans allethrin + lambda-cyhalothrin	X	X	--	--
Ultra-Kill Home Insect Killer	lambda-cyhalothrin	X	--	--	--
COMBINATION INSECTICIDE AND FUNGICIDE PRODUCTS					
Bayer Advanced All-in-One Rose and Flower Care Concentrate	tebuconazole + imidacloprid	--	X	--	--
Bonide Fruit Tree Spray	captan + malathion + carbaryl	--	X	--	X
Bonide Insecticide-Miticide Fungicide	captan + malathion + carbaryl	--	X		X
Green Light Rose Defense II	neem + pyrethrin	--	X	X	X
Ortho Econsense Brand 3-in-1 Rose & Flower Care	sulfer + pyrethrin		X	X	X
Ortho Orthenex Garden Insect & Disease Control Concentrate	resmethrin + funginex + orthene		X	--	--
Spectracide Immunox Plus	permethrin + myclobutanil	--	X	--	--
COMBINATION INSECTICIDE, FUNGICIDE, AND MITICIDE PRODUCTS					
Bayer Advanced 3-in-1 Insect, Disease, & Mite Control	imidachloprid, tau -fluvalinate, tebuconazole	X	X	--	--
CONTACT MITICIDES					
Ortho Isotox Insect Killer Formula IV Concentrate	acephate + fenbutatin-oxide	--	X	--	--
SunSpray Ultra-Fine Pest Oil	refined horticultural oil	X	X	X	X
BAIT INSECTICIDES					
Amdro Ant Bait Stations	hydramethylnon	X	X		
Amdro Ant Block Home Perimeter Ant Bait	hydramethylnon	--	X	--	--
Amdro Fire Ant Bait	hydramethylnon	--	X	--	--
Amdro Firestrike Fire Ant Bait	hydramethylnon	--	X	--	--
Amdro Kills Ants & Roaches Gel Bait	hydramethylnon	X	X		

PRODUCTS	ACTIVE INGREDIENT	INDOORS, PATIOS, DECKS, EXTERIOR HARDSCAPES & PATHS	FLOWERS, SHRUBS, TREES, LAWNS	VEGE-TABLES	FRUIT
Combat Ant-Killing Gel	fipronil	X	--	--	--
Combat Platinum Brand Roach Killing Gel	fipronil	X	--	--	--
GardenTech Over'n Out Fire Ant Killer Granules	fipronil	--	X	--	--
GardenTech Over'n Out! Fire Ant Killer Mound Treatment	indoxacarb	--	X	--	--
Grant's Kills Ants Ant Stakes	arsenic trioxide	X	X	--	--
Hot Shot MaxAttrax Roach Bait	chlorpyrifos	X			
Hot Shot MaxAttrax Ant Bait Station	indoxacarb	X	--	--	--
Hot Shot MaxAttrax Ultra Brand Nest Destroyer Roach Bait Station	indoxacarb	X	--	--	--
Hot Shot Nest Destroyer Roach Bait Station	indoxacarb	X	--	--	--
Hot Shot Ultra Clear Roach Gel Bait	dinotefuran	X	--	--	--
Hot Shot Ultra Liquid Ant Bait Station	dinotefuran	X	--	--	--
Hot Shot Ultra Liquid Roach Bait	dinotefuran	X	--	--	--
Logic	fenoxycarb	X	--	--	--
Ortho Ant-B-Gon Bait	propoxur	X	X	--	--
Ortho Ecosense Fire Ant Bait Granules	spinosad	X	X	X	X
Raid Ant Baits III	avermectin B1	X	--	--	--
Raid Double Control Roach Baits	abamectin	X	--	--	--
Raid Max Double Control Large Roach Baits	avermectin B1	X	--	--	--
Raid Outdoor Ant Spikes	avermectin	X	X	X	X
Real-kill Ant Bait Stations	indoxacarb	X	X		
Real-kill Ant Bait	indoxacarb	X	--	--	--
Spectracide Fire Ant Killer Plus Preventer	pyriproxyfen	X	X	--	--
Spectracide Fire Ant Killer Plus Preventer Bait Once & Done!	indoxacarb	--	X	--	--
Terro Ant Killer Liquid Ant Baits	sodium tetraborate decahydrate (borax)	X	--	--	--
Terro Liquid Ant Baits Outdoor	borax	X	--	--	--
BAIT RODENTICIDES					
d-Con Mini Blocks Rodent Control Bait	difethialone	X	--	--	--
d-Con Mouse-Prufe II	brodifacoum 3	X	--	--	--
d-Con Ready Mixed Baitbits	brodifacoum	X	--	--	--
Enforcer Rat Bait	indandione	X	X	--	--
Farnam Just One Bite II Bait Chunks	bromadiolone	X	X		
No-Pest Rat & Mouse All Weather Bait Bars	bromethalin	X	--	--	--
Ortho Max-Home Defense No Touch Bait Blocks – mice, rats	difethialone	X			
Ortho Max-Home Defense No Touch Bait Paste Packs	difethialone	X			

PRODUCTS	ACTIVE INGREDIENT	INDOORS, PATIOS, DECKS, EXTERIOR HARDSCAPES & PATHS	FLOWERS, SHRUBS, TREES, LAWNS	VEGE-TABLES	FRUIT
Real-kill Rat & Mouse Killer Weather Bars Bait	bromethalin	X	--	--	--
Real-kill Rat & Mouse Killer Pellets (also Place Packs)	bromethalin	X	X		
Sweeney's Kill Moles & Gophers Poison Peanuts Pellets	zinc phosphide	--	X	--	--
Sweeney's No Mess Mouse Paste Bait	difethialone	X	--	--	--
Tom Cat Vitamin D3 Mouse Poison Bait Trays	cholecalciferol	X	--	--	--
Tomcat Mole & Gopher Bait	zinc phosphide	--	X	--	--
Tomcat Mole Killer Worm Shaped Baits	bromethalin	--	X	--	--
Tomcat Ultra All-Weather Block Bait	brodadiolone	X	--	--	--
Tomcat Ultra Pelleted Bait (kills mice & rats)	brodadiolone	X	--	--	--
Victor Kills Mice! Mouse Bait Packs (pellets)	bromadiolone	X	--	--	--
VARMINT TRAPS					
d-Con Ultra Set Mouse Trap	trap	X	--	--	--
d-Con, No View, No Touch Mouse Trap	no toxin	X	--	--	--
Havahart Live Animal Cage Trap	non toxic	X	X	X	X
Ortho Home Defense Max Press 'N Set Mouse Trap	--	X			
Real Kill Large Glue Traps for Rats & Mice	non toxin	X	--	--	--
Sweeney's Mole Trap	mechanical trap	--	X	--	--
Tomcat Glue Traps for Mice	adhesive trap	X	--	--	--
Tomcat Live Mouse Traps	live trap	X	--	--	--
Tomcat Mouse Attractant Gel for Traps	non toxic	X	--	--	--
Tomcat Rat & Mouse Snap Traps	trap	X	--	--	--
Tomcat Wooden Mouse Traps	kill trap	X	--	--	--
Victor Electronic Mouse Trap	no toxin	X	--	--	--
Victor Mice Trap	no toxin	X	--	--	--
Victor Power Kill Rat Trap	no toxin	X	--	--	--
Victor Snap Mouse Trap	non toxic	X	--	--	--
INSECT TRAPS AND ATTRACTANTS					
Mosquito Magnet Trap Octenol Biting Insect Attractant	1-octen-3-ol, octenol	outdoor	X	--	--
Mosquito Octenol Lure	1-octen-3-ol	X	X	--	--
Mosquito 2 in 1 Power Bait	1-octen-3-ol + lactic acid	X	X	--	--
Raid Disposable Yellow Jacket Trap	plant-based attractant	X	X	--	--
Rescue Disposable Fly Trap	no toxin	X	X	--	--
Rescue Yellow Jacket Trap	attractant, no pesticide	X	X	X	X
Rescue Yellow Jacket Trap attractant & Trap	non-toxic	X	X	--	--
Safer The Pantry Pest	lure	X			

COMMON PESTICIDE PRODUCTS AVAILABLE FOR HOMEOWNERS (continued)

PRODUCTS	ACTIVE INGREDIENT	INDOORS, PATIOS, DECKS, EXTERIOR HARDSCAPES & PATHS	FLOWERS, SHRUBS, TREES, LAWNS	VEGE-TABLES	FRUIT
Stinger Bug Zapper Bulbs	UVB4S + UV40	X	X	--	--
Stinger Insect Killer	bug zapper	--	X	--	--
Stinger Mosquito Power Bait	octenol + lactic acid	X	X		
Tomcat Pest Glue Boards	adhesive trap	X	--	--	--
Victor Fly Catcher Sticky Roll	no toxin	X	--		
INSECT REPELLENTS					
Cutter Backwoods Insect Repellent	deet	X	--	--	--
Cutter Backwoods Mosquito Wipes	deet	X			
Cutter Citro Guard Candle	oil of citronella	X			
Cutter Lemon Eucalyptus Insect Repellent	oil of lemon + eucalyptus	X	--	--	--
Cutter Skinsations Insect Repellent	deet	X	--	--	--
Enoz Old Fashioned Moth Balls	naphthalene	X	--		
Green Light Yard Safe Insect Repellent Granules	cedar oil	--	X	X	
Off Clip On	metofluthrin	X			
Off Deep Woods Spray	deet	X	--	--	--
Off Power Pad Lamp/Lantern	d-cis-trans allethrin	X	X	--	--
Scotts Insect Repellent Granules	cedar oil		X	X	X
VARMINT REPELLENTS					
Black & Decker Electronic Pest Repellers	no toxin	X	--	--	--
Bonide Shot-Gun Repels-All Animal Repellent R-T-U	dried blood + putrescent whole egg solids + garlic oil	--	X	--	--
Cutter Advanced Light & Clean	picaridin	X	--		
Dr. T's Nature Products Mole Out Mole Repelling Granules	castor oil	--	X	--	--
Dr. T's Nature Products Snake-A-Way snake Repelling Granules	naphthalene sulfur	X	X	--	--
Exhart Gopher & Mole Mover	electronic deterrent	--	X	--	--
Havahart – Caring Control for Pets & Wildlife Get Away Granules	methyl nonyl ketone	--	X	--	--
Havahart Critter Ridder Granular	oil of black pepper + piperine + capsaicinoids	X	X	--	--
Havahart Critter Ridder Ready to Use Liquid	oil of black pepper + piperine + capsaicinoids	--	X	--	--
Havahart Deer Off	putrescent whole egg solids + capsaicinoids + garlic	--	X	X	X
Pestocator 2000 Plus Ultrasonic Rodent Repellent	no toxins	X	--	--	--
Spectracide Mole Stop Spray Concentrate	castor oil + soybean oil	--	X	X	X
Sweeney's All Out Deer & Rabbit Repellent	capsaicin + garlic oil + butyl mercaptan		X	X	X
Sweeney's All Season Deer & Rabbit Repellent	dried blood		X	X	X

148

COMMON PESTICIDE PRODUCTS AVAILABLE FOR HOMEOWNERS (continued)

PRODUCTS	ACTIVE INGREDIENT	INDOORS, PATIOS, DECKS, EXTERIOR HARDSCAPES & PATHS	FLOWERS, SHRUBS, TREES, LAWNS	VEGE-TABLES	FRUIT
Sweeney's Mole & Gopher Repellent Lawn Protection	castor oil	--	X	--	--
Sweeney's Solar Powered Sonic Spike (for moles, gophers)	sonic pulse	--	X	--	--
Terracycle Natural Ingredient Deer Repellent Spray	whole egg solids, peppermint oil, clove oil, cinnamon oil, white pepper	--	X	X	X
Victor Pest Chaser High Frequency Sound	non-toxic	X	--	--	--
Worryfree Outdoor Dog, Cat, & Bird Repellent Granules (organic)	white pepper, peppermint oil, thyme oil	--	X	X	X
FUNGICIDES					
Armicarb 100®	potassium bicarbonate	--	X	X	X
Banner Maxx	propiconazole	--	X	--	--
Bayer Advanced Fungus Control for Lawns	triadimefon	--	X	--	--
Bayer Advanced Garden Rose, Flowers & Shrubs Disease Concentrate	tebuconazole	--	X	--	--
Bonide Captan	captan		X	--	X
Ferti-Lome Halt Systemic Rose, Flower, Lawn, Ornamental Fungicide	thiophanate-methyl	--	X		X
Garden Tech Daconil Fungicide Ready-To-Use	chlorothalonil	--	X	X	X
Green Light Fung-Away Systemic Fungicide	bayleton	--	X	--	nuts
Green Light Fung-Away Systemic Lawn Fungicide	myclobutanil	--	X	--	--
Green Light Fung-Away Systemic Lawn Spray	bayleton	--	X	--	nuts
Green Light Powdery Mildew Killer	neem oil	--	X	X	--
Hi-Yield American Brand Copper Fungicide	copper hydroxide	--	X	X	X
Kaligreen Potassium Bicarbonate Soluble Powder	potassium bicarbonate	X	X	X	X
Monterey Aliette	aluminum tris (O-ethyl phosphonate)	--	X	--	--
Monterey E-rase RTU	jojoba oil	--	X	X	X
Ortho Garden Disease Control	chlorothalonil	--	X	X	X
Ortho Rose Pride Disease Control	triforine		X		
Ortho Rose Pride Rose & Shrub Disease Control Concentrate	funginex	--	X	--	--
Remedy	potassium bicarbonate	--	X	X	X
Safer Flower, Fruit And Vegetable Garden Fung. RTU	sulfur	--	X	X	X
Scott's Lawn Fungus Control	thiophanate-methyl	--	X	--	--
Southern Ag Liquid Copper Fungicide	copper ammonium complex	--	X	--	--
Spectracide Immunox Lawn Disease Control	myclobutanil	--	X	--	--

PRODUCTS	ACTIVE INGREDIENT	INDOORS, PATIOS, DECKS, EXTERIOR HARDSCAPES & PATHS	FLOWERS, SHRUBS, TREES, LAWNS	VEGE-TABLES	FRUIT
BACTERICIDES					
Agri-mycin	streptomycin sulfate	--	X	X	X
Bonide Fire Blight Spray	streptomycin sulfate	--	X	--	X
Bonide Mancozeb Flowable with Zinc	mancozeb		X	X	X
Lime-sulfur	lime-sulfur	--	X	--	X
MOLLUSCICIDES (slugs and snails)					
Bayer Advanced Dual Action Snail & Slug Killer Bait	iron phosphate	--	X	X	X
Deadline Bug Bait	metaldehyde	--	X	X	--
Green Light Bug and Snail Bait	carbaryl + metaldehyde	X	X	X	X
Ortho Bug-Geta Snail & Slug Killer	metaldehyde	--	X	X	X
Ortho Ecosense Brand Slug & Snail Killer Granule	iron phosphate	X	X	X	X
Sluggo	iron phosphate	X	X	X	X
HERBICIDES					
Balan	benefin		X	--	--
BASF Vantage	sethoxydim		X	X	X
Bayer Advanced All-in-One Lawn Weed & Crabgrass Killer 1	2,4-D + quincloroc + dicamba + dimethalamine salt		X		
Bayer Advanced All-in-One Weed Killer	MSMA + 2,4-D + MCPP + dicamba	--	X	--	--
Bayer Advanced Bermudagrass Control for Lawns R-T-U	fenoxyaprop-p-ethyl	--	X	--	--
Bayer Advanced Power Force Brush Killer Plus	triclopyr	--	X	--	--
Bayer Advanced Southern Weed Killer for Lawn	2,4-D + MCPP + dicamba	--	X	--	--
Bonide Kleen Up Grass & Weed Killer	glyphosate + acifluorfen		X	--	--
Bonide Kleen Up Plus	glyphosate + oxyfluorfen	X	X	--	--
Bonide Total Vegetation Killer	prometon	X	--	--	--
Enforcer Brush Killer	triclopyr	X	--	--	--
Enforcer Next Day Grass & Weed Killer	diquat (or cacodylic acid, read label)		X	--	--
Enforcer Weed Shot Lawn Weed Killer	2,4-D + MCPP + dicamba		X		
Gallery	isoxaben		X	--	--
Garden Place Grass & Weed Killer	diquat + fluazifop		X	--	--
Goal	oxyfluorfen	.	X	X	--
Green Light Amaze Grass & Weed Preventer	benefin + oryzalin	--	X	--	--
Green Light Bermudagrass Killer	fluazifop		X	--	--
Green Light Betasan 3.6 Granules	betasan	--	X	--	--
Green Light Com-Pleet	prometon	X	X	X	--
Green Light Com-Pleet Systemic Grass and Weed Killer	glyphosate		X	--	--

PRODUCTS	ACTIVE INGREDIENT	INDOORS, PATIOS, DECKS, EXTERIOR HARDSCAPES & PATHS	FLOWERS, SHRUBS, TREES, LAWNS	VEGE-TABLES	FRUIT
Green Light MSMA Crabgrass Killer 2	monosodium methanearsonate		X	--	--
Green Light Portrait Broadleaf Weed Preventer	isoxaben	--	X	--	--
Green Light Wipe-Out Broadleaf Weed Killer	2,4-D + MCPP + dicamba		X	--	--
Halts	pendimethalin		X	--	--
Hi-Yield Killzall	glyphosate		X	--	--
Image for St. Augustine & Centipede Grass – Kills Weeds	atrazine		X		
Image Kills Crabgrass with MSMA	MSMA	--	X	--	--
Image Kills Nutsedge	ammonium salt of imazaquin	--	X	--	--
Image Year-Long Vegetation Killer – Kills Grass & Weeds	dichlobenil	exterior	--	--	--
LESCO Pre-M Plus	pendimethalin		X	--	--
Monsanto Manage	halosulfuron		X	--	nuts
Monsanto Roundup	glyphosate		X	X	X
Ortho Brush-B -Gon Poison Ivy Killer RTU	triclopyr	X	--	--	--
Ortho Gras s-B-Gon Garden Grass Killer	fluazifop -p-butyl	--	X	--	--
Ortho Gras s-B-Gon Grass Killer for Landscapes RTU	fluazifop	--	X	--	--
Ortho Ground Clear Vegetation Killer	glyphosate, imazapyr	exterior	X	--	--
Ortho Max Poison Ivy & Tough Brush Killer	triclopyr	--	X	--	--
Ortho Max Season-Long Weed & Grass Killer + Preventer	glyphosate + oxyfluorfen	exterior	X	X	X
Ortho Total Kill Lawn Weed Killer	dimethylamine salt of 2,4-D, dimethylamine salt of meco-prop-p, dimethylamine salt of dichlorprop-p	--	X	--	--
Ortho Weed-B-Gon Chickweed, Clover & Oxalis Killer	triclopyr		X	--	--
Ortho Weed-B-Gon Lawn Weed Killer 2 Concentrate	2,4-D + MCPP + dicamba		X	--	--
Ortho Weed-B-Gon Max Plus Crabgrass Control	quinclorac, mecoprop-p, 2,4-D, dicamba	--	X	--	--
Preen	trifluralin		X	X	X
Round Up Extended Control Weed & Grass Killer + Weed Preventer	glyphosate, imazapic, diquat dibromide	exterior	X	--	--
Round Up Poison Ivy & Tough Brush Killer Plus	glyphosate + triclopyr	exterior	X	--	--
Scotts Liquid Turf Builder with Plus 2 Weed Control	2,4-D	--	X	--	--
Shoot Out Weed & Grass Killer	glyphosate + isopropylamine salt	--	X	--	--
Snapshot	treflan + isoxaben		X	--	--
Spectracide Brush Killer	2,4-D + MCPP + dicamba		X	--	--
Spectracide Systemic Grass & Weed Killer 2	diquat + fluazifop		X	--	--
Spectracide Total Vegetation Killer	prometon	X	--	--	--

COMMON PESTICIDE PRODUCTS AVAILABLE FOR HOMEOWNERS (continued)

PRODUCTS	ACTIVE INGREDIENT	INDOORS, PATIOS, DECKS, EXTERIOR HARDSCAPES & PATHS	FLOWERS, SHRUBS, TREES, LAWNS	VEGE-TABLES	FRUIT
Spectracide Triple Strike Grass, Weed, Root Killer	diquat dibromide, fluazifop-p-butyl, dicamba	exterior	X	--	--
Spectracide Weed & Grass Killer	diquat dibromide, fluazifop-p-butyl, dicamba, dimethylamine salt	exterior	X	--	--
Spectracide Weed Stop Weed Killer for Lawns	2,4-D + MCPP + dicamba		X	--	--
Sta-Green Phos-Free Crab-Ex Plus Crabgrass Preventer Plus Fert 30-0-5	dithiopyr		X	--	--
Sta-Green Weed & Feed R-T-U	2,4-D	--	X	--	--
Team	benefin + trifluralin		X	--	--
Total Kill by Ortho Weed & Grass Killer Ready To Use	glyphosate	paths	X	X	X
Ultra Kill Weed & Grass Killer	glyphosate	exterior	X	X	X
Vigoro Ultra Turf Lawn Weed Control	2,4-D + MCPP + dicamba		X	--	--
Vigoro Weed Stop Crab grass & Weed Preventer	dithiopyr		X	--	--
XL2G	benefin + oryzalin		X	--	--
HERBICIDES (MOSS AND ALGAE CONTROL)					
Bayer Advanced 2-in-1 Moss & Algae Killer R-T-U	potassium soap of fatty acids	X	X		
Image Brush & Vine Killer	triclopyr + triethylamine salt		X		
Lilly Miller Moss Out	ferrous sulfate	--	X	--	--
ORGANIC PESTICIDE PRODUCTS, ACTIVE INGREDIENT, AND USES					
ORGANIC INSECTICIDES					
Azadirachtin	leaf extracts from the neem tree	X	X	X	X
Bonide All Seasons Spray Oil – Horticultural & Dormant	petroleum Oil	X	X	X	X
Bonide Garden Dust	copper, rotenone	--	X	X	X
Diatomaceous earth	fossilized bodies of diatoms	X	X	X	X
Doom, Milky Spore Disease	*Bacillus popillae*	--	X	--	--
Ferti-Lome 'Come and Get It' Fire Ant Killer	spinosad	X	X	X	X
Ferti-Lome Borer, Bagworm, Leafminer & Tent Caterpillar Spray	spinosad	--	X	X	X
Garden Safe Insect Killer Insecticidal Soap	potassium salts	X	X	X	X
Garden Safe Multi -Purpose Garden Insect Killer	pyrethrin + pyperonyl butoxide	X	X	X	--
Gardens Alive Bulls Eye Bioinsecticide	spinosad	--	X	X	X
Gardens Alive Surround at Home Crop Protectant	kaolin clay	--	--	X	X
Green Light BT Worm Killer	*Bacillus thuringiensis* subspecies kurstaki	--	X	X	X
Green Light Roach Powder	boric acid	X	--	--	--
Green Light Rose Defense	neem oil	--	X	X	X

PRODUCTS	ACTIVE INGREDIENT	INDOORS, PATIOS, DECKS, EXTERIOR HARDSCAPES & PATHS	FLOWERS, SHRUBS, TREES, LAWNS	VEGE-TABLES	FRUIT
Greenlight Home & Garden Insect Spray	thyme oil, clove oil, sesame oil	X	X	X	X
Mosquito Dunks, Mosquito Bits	*Bacillus thuringiensis* subspecies israelensis	X	--	--	--
Neem	oil extracted from neem tree nuts	--	X	X	X
Nematodes	nematodes that attack insects	--	X	X	X
Organocide Organic Insecticide & Fungicide	sesame oil	X	X	X	X
Pyrethrin products	chemical from chrysanthemum flowers	X	X	X	X
Safer Ant & Crawling Insect Killer	diatomaceous earth	X	X	X	X
Safer Ant & Roach Killer	D-limonene + pyrethrins + potassium salts of fatty acids	X	--	--	--
Safer Caterpillar Killer	Bacillus thuringiensis subspecies kurstaki	--	X	X	--
Safer Fire Ant Bait R-T-U	spinosad	--	X	X	--
Safer Flying Insect Killer	d-limonene + pyrethrins + salts of fatty acids	X	--	--	--
Safer Insect Killing Soap	potassium salts of fatty acids	X	X	X	X
Safer Roach & ant Killing Powder	boric acid + German cockroach pheromone	X	--	--	--
Safer Tomato & Vegetable Insect Killer II	insecticidal soap + pyrethrin	--	X	X	X
Safer Wasp & Hornet Killer	D-limonene + pyrethrins + potassium salts of fatty acids	X	--	--	--
SunSpray Ultra-Fine Pest Oil	refined petroleum oil	X	X	X	X
ORGANIC COMBINATION INSECTICIDES, FUNGICIDES AND MITICIDES					
Greenlight Neem Concentrate Insecticide, Fungicide, Miticide	clarified hydrophobic extract of neem oil	X	X	X	X
Safer 3-in-1 Garden Spray II - kills: fungus, mites, insects	potassium salts of fatty acids + sulfur	--	X	X	X
ORGANIC FUNGICIDES					
Bordeaux mixture	copper sulfate + lime + water	--	X	X	X
Concern Copper Soap Fungicide	copper octanoate	X	X	X	X
Copper	copper salts	--	X	X	X
Garden Safe Fungicide	neem oil	X	X	X	X
Garden sulfur	sulfur	--	--	X	X
Gardens Alive Serenade	*Bacillus subtilis* strain QST 713	X	X	X	X
Greenlight Blossom-End Rot Spray	calcium + chlorine	--	--	X	--
Lime-sulfur	calcium polysulfide	X	X	--	X
Odo Ban Germ Control Earth Choice Fungicide Virucide	silver + citric acid	X	--	--	--
Organocide Organic Insecticide & Fungicide	sesame oil		X	X	X

PRODUCTS	ACTIVE INGREDIENT	INDOORS, PATIOS, DECKS, EXTERIOR HARDSCAPES & PATHS	FLOWERS, SHRUBS, TREES, LAWNS	VEGE-TABLES	FRUIT
Ortho Ecosense Garden Disease Control	copper octanoate		X	X	X
ORGANIC MOLLUSCICIDES					
Garden Safe Slug & Snail Bait	iron phosphate	--	X	X	X
Monterey Sluggo	iron phosphate	--	--		--
Worryfree Slug & Snail Bait	iron phosphate	--	X	X	X
ORGANIC HERBICIDES					
Concem Weed Prevention Plus	corn gluten meal	--	X	X	--
Garden Safe Weed & Grass Killer	ammoniated soap of fatty acids	exterior	X	--	--
Nature's Glory Weed & Grass Killer	acetic acid	X	--	--	--
St. Gabriel Laboratories Burnout	clove oil	X	X	--	--
St. Gabriel Laboratories Premerge	corn gluten meal	--	X	--	--

NAMES, CLASSIFICATION AND TOXICITY OF PESTICIDES

Paul Guillebeau, Extension Entomologist

The tables on the following pages of this section will help you to identify specific pesticide active ingredients and give you an indication of their toxicities.

NAMES. The chemical names of pesticide active ingredients are usually so long and complex that they are generally used only in the active ingredient statement on the pesticide label and in scientific or technical publications. The common name of a pesticide active ingredient is one that is commonly used and has usually been approved by an appropriate scientific group. The trade name of a pesticide active ingredient is a copyrighted name used by its producer. A pesticide active ingredient will usually have only one common name but it may have several trade names. For example, glyphosphate is the common name for the chemical name isopropylamine salt of N-(phosphonomethyl) glycine, the active ingredient in Roundup. The trade names listed in the tables are capitalized and bear an asterisk(*). These trade names should not be confused with the brand names used by formulators and distributors of pesticide products.

CLASSIFICATION. Insecticides, herbicides, fungicides and other pesticides are primarily classified on the basis of their chemical structure or origin. The inorganic pesticides are those which contain no carbon in their chemical structure. The organic pesticides, those that contain carbon, are usually synthetic but some are obtained from natural sources such as plants or microorganisms. Some synthetic organic pesticides such as the pyrethroids, or synthetic pyrethrins, are based on naturally occurring chemicals.

TOXICITY. The Environmental Protection Agency uses the results of acute toxicity studies on test animals, usually rats and rabbits, to place pesticides in toxicity categories (I-IV) which determine what signal word must appear on the label. Although inhalation toxicity, eye corrosiveness and skin corrosiveness studies are also used, results of acute dermal and acute oral toxicity studies are more publicized and usually more important.

The below table shows the signal words that must appear on the pesticide label for each toxicity category and the range of the oral and dermal medianlethal doses (LD_{50}) for each category. A pesticide that falls into category I only because of eye or skin corrosiveness must bear "Danger" but not "Poison" nor the skull and crossbones symbol on its label.

The LD_{50} is the dose of a substance at which one-half of the exposed test animals are killed . It is based on the body weight of the animal and is expressed in milligrams of the substance per kilogram of animal (mg/kg). One mg./kg. is equivalent to 1 ppm. The lower the LD_{50}, the greater the toxicity. Although most LD_{50} values that are readily available in publications are for the pesticide active ingredient or actual toxicant, the signal word on each pesticide product is determined by the toxicity of that particular formulation. Formulated pesticides are usually, but not necessarily, less toxic than the active ingredient. The toxicity categories given in the following tables are based solely on the accompanying LD_{50} values which, unless stated otherwise, are for the active ingredient. EPA would not necessarily assign the same category shown in the tables.

TOXICITY CATEGORY	SIGNAL WORDS REQUIRED ON LABEL BY EPA	ORAL LD_{50} (M.G./K.G.)	DERMAL LD_{50} (MG./KG.) 24 HR. EXPOSURE	ORAL DOSAGE TO KILL AN ADULT*
I. Highly Toxic	DANGER, POISON, Plus Skull & Crossbones symbol	0 to 50	0 to 200	A few drops to 1 tsp
II. Moderately Toxic	WARNING	50 to 500	200 to 2,000	1 tsp. to 2 Tbsp.
III. Slightly Toxic	CAUTION	500 to 5,000	2,000 to 20,000	1 oz. to 1 pt. (1 lb.)
IV. Low Toxicity	CAUTION	>5,000	>20,000	1 pt. (1 lb.) or more

Toxicity categories and signal words on the pesticide label are based on acute toxicity studies, but sub-acute and chronic toxicity studies are also conducted. Acute toxicity involves the short-term response of the test animal to a single large exposure to the pesticide. Sub-acute toxicity refers to the response of the animal to repeated or continuous exposure to smaller doses over less than one-half of its normal life span. In chronic toxicity studies exposures are repeated or continued for longer than one-half of the animal's life span.

*Less for child/pet

You should not keep or use pesticides with the words DANGER-POISON on the label. Contact Paul Guillebeau 706-542-2816 (bugman@uga.edu) for information about disposal.

PESTICIDE RATE AND DOSAGE CALCULATIONS

Paul Guillebeau, Extension Entomologist

How to Calculate Pesticide Dilutions and Dosages For Large Areas

Pesticides for use in sprays are generally available as wettable or soluble powders and as liquid concentrates. These must be diluted, usually with water, before use. Other diluents, such as deodorized kerosene, may be used for special applications.

The precise amount of water applied to an acre (or other given area) is immaterial as long as it falls within a recommended range, delivers the recommended amount of pesticide, provides adequate coverage, and does not result in excessive runoff or drift. If you know the area (acres, sq. ft., etc.) or units (trees, cows, etc.) covered by a given amount of spray you can determine the dosage or rate of active ingredient each receives by adding the proper quantity of pesticide to that amount of water. Dusts and granules are applied without dilution by the user. Therefore the amount applied per acre or unit is much more critical because you have no other way of controlling the dosage or rate of active ingredient.

The amount of active ingredient in liquid concentrates is expressed in pounds per gallon. In granules, dusts, wettable or soluble powders, and other solids it is n early always expressed as percent by weight. Application rates are usually expressed as amount of pesticide product but sometimes they may be expressed as pounds of active ingredient or actual toxicant. Actual toxicant and active ingredient are practically synonymous.

1. To find the pounds of wettable powder (WP), dust (D) or granules (G) per acre to obtain the desired pounds of active ingredient (a.i.) per acre:

$$lbs.\ of\ WP,\ D\ or\ G\ per\ acre = \frac{lbs.\ a.i.\ desired\ x\ 100}{\%\ a.i.\ in\ WP,\ D\ or\ G}$$

2. To find the pints of liquid concentrate per acre to obtain the desired pounds of active ingredient (a.i.) per acre: pints of liq.

$$conc.\ per\ acre = \frac{lbs.\ a.i.\ desired\ x\ 8*}{lbs.\ a.i.\ per\ gallon\ of\ liq.\ conc.}$$

*If you want the answer in gallons, quarts, or fluid ounces substitute 1, 4, or 128 respectively for 8.

3. To find the amount of wettable powder (WP) or liquid con cent rate to use in a given amount of spray:

   amt. of WP or liq conc. = no. of acres treated with amount of spray X desired amount of WP or liq. conc. per acre*

   *Trees, animal, etc. can be substituted for acres.

4. To find the pounds of wettable powder needed to obtain a desired percentage of active ingredient in water:

$$lbs.\ of\ WP = \frac{gals.\ of\ spray\ desired\ x\ \%\ a.i.\ desired\ X\ 8.3**}{\%\ of\ a.i.\ in\ WP}$$

5. To find the gallons of liquid concentrate needed to obtain a desired percentage of active ingredient in water:

$$gal.\ of\ liq.\ conc. = \frac{gals.\ of\ spray\ desired\ x\ \%\ a.i.\ desired\ X\ 8.3**}{lbs.\ a.i.\ per\ gal.\ of\ liq.\ conc.\ x\ 100}$$

**One gallon of water weighs approximately 8.3 pounds. If another diluent is used the weight per gallon of the other diluent should be substituted for 8.3.

Pesticide Conversion Table for Large Areas

LIQUID FORMULATIONS
Amount of Commercial Product to Add to Spray Tank for Each Acre Treated

FORMULATION LBS./GAL. ACTIVE INGREDIENT	Desired Rate Per Acre if Active Ingredient, Lbs.															
	0.1	0.2	0.3	0.4	0.5	0.6	0.8	1	1.1	1.5	2	2.5	3	4	6	9
1.5	10 oz	17 oz	26 oz	34 oz	43 oz	51 oz	64 oz	85 oz	96 oz	128 oz	171 oz	213 oz	256 oz	341 oz	512 oz	768 oz
2	8 oz	13 oz	19 oz	26 oz	32 oz	38 oz	48 oz	64 oz	72 oz	96 oz	128 oz	160 oz	192 oz	256 oz	384 oz	576 oz
3	5 oz	9 oz	13 oz	17 oz	21 oz	26 oz	32 oz	43 oz	48 oz	64 oz	85 oz	107 oz	128 oz	171 oz	256 oz	384 oz
4	4 oz	6 oz	10 oz	13 oz	16 oz	19 oz	24 oz	32 oz	36 oz	48 oz	64 oz	80 oz	96 oz	128 oz	192 oz	288 oz
6	2.6 oz	4.3 oz	6.4 oz	9 oz	11 oz	13 oz	16 oz	21 oz	24 oz	32 oz	43 oz	53 oz	64 oz	85 oz	128 oz	192 oz
6.7	2.3 oz	3.8 oz	5.7 oz	7.6 oz	9.6 oz	11.5 oz	14.3 oz	19.1 oz	21 oz	29 oz	38 oz	48 oz	57 oz	76 oz	115 oz	172 oz
7	2.2 oz	3.7 oz	5.5 oz	7.3 oz	9.1 oz	11 oz	13.7 oz	18 oz	20 oz	27 oz	37 oz	46 oz	55 oz	73 oz	110 oz	165 oz
8	2 oz	3.2 oz	4.8 oz	6.4 oz	8 oz	9.6 oz	12 oz	16 oz	18 oz	24 oz	32 oz	40 oz	48 oz	64 oz	96 oz	144 oz

WETTABLE POWDER FORMULATIONS
Pounds of Commercial Product to Add to Spray Tank for Each Acre Treated

FORMULATION LBS./GAL. ACTIVE INGREDIENT	Desired Rate Per Acre if Active Ingredient, Lbs.															
	0.2	0.3	0.4	0.5	0.6	0.8	0.8	1	1	2	2	3	3	4	5	8	10
50	0.4	0.6	0.8	1	1.2	1.5	1.6	2	2	3	4	5	6	8	10	16	20
75	0.3	0.4	0.5	0.7	0.8	1	1.1	1.3	2	2	3	3	4	5.3	6.6	10.7	13.33
80	0.3	0.4	0.5	0.6	0.8	0.9	1	1.2	2	2	3	3	4	5	6.2	10	12.5

GRANULES AND DUSTS
Pounds of Commercial Product to Apply Per Acre

FORMULATION LBS./GAL. ACTIVE INGREDIENT	Desired Rate Per Acre if Active Ingredient, Lbs.					
	1	2	3	4	5	10
2.5	40	80	120	160	200	400
5	20	40	60	80	100	200
10	10	20	30	40	50	100
15	6.6	13.3	20	26.6	33.3	66.6
20	5	10	15	20	25	50

PESTICIDE RATE AND DOSAGE CALCULATIONS (continued)

Converting Large Volume Recommendations to Small Volumes or Areas

Frequently, pesticide recommendations are given only for large volume applications, i.e., amount per 100 gallons or per acre, but only a small amount is needed. Conversion of liquids to smaller quantities is relatively easy and precise because suitable equipment such as measuring spoons are readily available. Scales sensitive enough to handle small quantities of solid materials are not widely available and it is often more practical to use volumetric measures. Various conversion tables have been prepared on the premise that there are 200 to 300 teaspoons (roughly 2 to 3 pints) per pound of solid pesticide product. These tables are grossly inaccurate because of the wide variation in bulk density among solid pesticide formulations. For instance, a pint of almost any insecticide wettable powder will weigh much less than a pint of fungicide that has a high metal content. Greater accuracy can be obtained if one first determines the weight of a given volume of the solid material and then calculates the volumetric measure. This will usually provide acceptable accuracy but it is still not as accurate as actually weighing a solid formulation. When coupled with a little simple and obvious arithmetic the following formulas will enable you to convert large volume recommendations to smaller quantities.

1. To find the amount of liquid concentrate per gallon when label recommendations are given in pints per 100 gallons:

    teaspoons/gallon = recommended pints per 100 gallons

    OR

    milliliters/gallon = recommended pints per 100 gallons x 4.73*

2. To find the amount of wettable powder (WP) or other solid formulation per gallon when label recommendations are given as pounds per 100 gallons:

    teaspoons/gallon = recommended lbs./ 100 gals. x cupful in 1 lb. of formulation x 0.0 53*

    OR

    teaspoons/gallon = recommended lbs./100 gals. x Tbs. in 1 ounce of formulation x 0.53*

    OR

    grams/gallon = recommended lbs./100 gals x 4.54*

3. To find the amount of liquid concentrate to apply per 1,000 square feet when label recommendations are given as pints per ac re:

    teaspoons/1,000 sq. ft. = recommended pints/acre x 2.20*

    OR

    milliliters/1,000 sq. ft. = recommended pints/acre x 10.9*

4. To find the amount of dust (D), granules (G) or wettable powder (WP) to apply per 1,000 square feet when label recommendations are given as pounds per acre:

    lbs./1,000 sq. ft. = recommended lbs./acre x 0.023*

    OR

    Tbs/1,000 sq. ft. = recommended lbs./acre x cupful in 1 lb. of formulation x 0.37*

    or

    Tbs/1,000 sq . ft. = recommended lbs./ac re x Tbs. in 1 lb. of formulation x 0.0 23*

    or

    grams/1,000 sq. ft. = recommended lbs./acre x 10.4*

*These values have been rounded off to facilitate calculations.

Conversion Tables for Small Areas

LIQUID FORMULATIONS[1]
Amount of Commercial Product to Add to Spray Tank to Treat 1000 Sq. Ft

FORMULATION LBS./GAL. ACTIVE INGREDIENT	Desired Rate Per Acre if Active Ingredient, Lbs.							
	0.25	0.5	1	2	4	8	10	12
0.5	3 Tbs[1] (43.4)[3]	3 oz[2] (86.8)	6 oz (173.7)	11 oz 1 Tbs (347.4)				
1	1 Tbs 1 tsp (21.7)	3 Tbs (43.4)	3 oz (86.8)	5 oz 1 Tbs (173.7)				
2	2 tsp (10.8)	1 Tbs 1 tsp (21.7)	3 Tbs (43.4)	3 oz (86.8)	5 oz 1 Tbs (173.7)	11 oz 1 Tbs (342.4)		
4	1 tsp (5.4)	2 tsp (10.8)	1 Tbs 1 tsp (21.7)	3 Tbs (43.4)	3 oz (86.8)	6 oz (173.7)	7 oz 2 tsp (217.1)	8 oz 4 tsp (260.6)

[1] approximate values
[2] refers to level measure
[3] figure in parentheses refers to milliliters

AIRBLAST SPRAYER CALIBRATION FOR ORCHARD AND VINEYARD

Paul E. Sumner, Extension Engineer

Calibrations is the process of measuring and adjusting the gallons per acre of spray actually applied. Sprayers need to be calibrated to meet the coverage needs of the orchards to be sprayed and to facilitate precise dosing of each material. A sprayer should be set up to apply a gallon per acre rate at a desired speed and pressure. In-orchard calibration frequently indicates a need for adjustments to achieve the target gallons per acre.

Speed of travel of a sprayer is a vital factor in obtaining the number of gallons of spray per acre desired. Change in gallons per acre (GPA) applied is inversely proportional to the change in speed. If speed is doubled, the gallons per acre will be halved. Thus, if nozzles have been installed and pressure set to provide a gallon per acre rate at a certain speed, the sprayer should apply the GPA rate at the speed.

To determine the travel speed, measure a known distance. Use fence posts or flags to identify this distance. A distance over 100 feet and a tank at least half full are recommended. Travel the distance determined at your normal spraying speed and record the elapsed time in seconds. Repeat this step and take the average of the two measurements. Use the following equation to determine the travel speed in miles per hour.

$$Travel\ Speed\ (MPH) = \frac{Distance\ (feet)\ x\ 0.68}{Time\ (seconds)}$$

(0.68 is a constant to convert feet/second to miles/hour)

Calculating Gallons per Minute (GPM) Output

The gallons per minute output required for a sprayer traveling along both sides of each row spraying from one side for a desired gallon per acre rate can be calculated with the following equation:

$$GPM\ (required) = \frac{GPA\ (required)\ x\ MPH\ (determined)\ x\ Row\ Spacing\ (feet)}{990\ (spraying\ one\ side)}$$

(If one pass is made between rows spaying from both sides of the sprayer, use 495 as contant.)
GPA = Gallons per Acre
MPH = Miles per Hour

To check actual GPM output:

1. Fill sprayer with water. Note the level of fill. If a material with considerably different flow characteristics than water is to be sprayed fill the sprayer with this material.

2. Operate the sprayer at the pressure that will be used during application for a measured length of time. A time period of several minutes will increase accuracy over a time period of 1 minute. A suggested time is 5 - 10 minutes.

3. Measure the gallons of liquid required to refill sprayer to the same level it was prior to the timed spray trial with the sprayer in the same position as when it was filled initially. The actual GPM can be calculated as follows:

$$GPM\ (actual) = \frac{Gallons\ to\ refill\ sprayer\ tank}{minutes\ of\ spray\ time}$$

4. Calculate the GPA being applied spraying from one side on both sides of row by the sprayer.

$$GPA\ (actual) = \frac{GPM\ (actual)\ x\ 990\ (spraying\ one\ side)}{MPH\ x\ Row\ Spacing\ (feet)}$$

If the actual GPA is slightly different from the required GPA, the actual GPA can be increased or decreased in increasing or decreasing spray pressure on sprayer models that have provisions for adjusting pressure. Only small output changes should be made by adjusting pressure. Major changes in output should be done by changing nozzles or ground speed.

Nozzle Setup

Nozzle arrangement and air guide or director vane settings should place most of the spray in the top half of the plants, where most of the foliage and fruit are located. Airblast sprayers are typically set up to apply 2/3 to 3/4 to the spray to the top half, and 1/4 to 1/3 to the bottom half (Figure 3). This targeted spraying is accomplished by placing more or larger nozzles on manifolds in the area that supplies spray to the upper half of the trees and setting the air directors on the fan outlet to direct the air stream accordingly. Plant growth and target pest habits should be considered in determining the setup for specific applications.

CALIBRATION METHOD FOR HYDRAULIC BOOM AND BAND SPRAYERS, AND OTHER LIQUID APPLICATORS

Paul E. Sumner, Extension Engineer

The procedure below is based on spraying 1/128 of an acre per nozzle or row spacing and collecting the spray that would be released during the time it takes to spray the area. Because there are 128 ounces of liquid in 1 gallon, this convenient relationship result in ounces of liquid caught being directly equal to the application rate in gallons per acre.

Calibrate with clean water when applying toxic pesticides mixed with large volumes of water. Check uniformity of nozzle output across the boom. Collect from each for a known time period. Each nozzle should be within 10 percent of the average output. Replace with new nozzles if necessary. When applying materials that are appreciably different from water in weight or flow characteristics, such as fertilizer solutions, etc., calibrate with the material to be applied. Exercise extreme care and use protective equipment when active ingredient is involved.

Step 1. Determine type of application to be made and select appropriate procedure from Table 1. Example – Herbicide Broadcast - Procedure A.

Table 1. Corresponding procedures for different spray applications.

Type of Application	Procedure	Coverage Basis
	Herbicide, Insecticide, Nematicide, Fungicide, or Liquid Fertilizer	
Broadcast	A	Broadcast (gal/ acre)
Band	B	Broadcast (gal/acre of band)
Row (See note)	C (Use this procedure when rates are given for row treatment)	Row (gal/acre of row)

Note: Determine and use average row spacing for modified row patterns. Use width of area covered per row as row spacing in skip row patterns.

Step 2. Using procedure A, B, or C below as selected in Step 1, determine appropriate calibration distance from Table 2.

   (A) Broadcast Application: Outlets or nozzles must be evenly spaced. Measure outlet (nozzle, etc.) spacing. Find this spacing in left column of Table 2 and read the corresponding calibration distance. Example – for a 19" spacing the distance would be 214.9 feet.

   (B) Band Application: Measure band width. Find this band width in the left column of Table 2 and read the corresponding calibration distance. Example – for a 12" band, the distance would be 340.3.

   (C) Row Application: Measure row spacing for evenly spaced rows. Find this row spacing in the left column of Table 2 and read the corresponding calibration distance from the column on the right. Example – for a 38" row spacing, the distance would be 107.5 feet. (See note above for modified and skip rows.)

CAUTION: AGRICULTURAL CHEMICALS CAN BE DANGEROUS. IMPROPER SELECTION OR USE CAN SERIOUSLY INJURE PERSONS, ANIMALS, PLANTS, SOIL, OR OTHER PROPERTY. BE SAFE: SELECT THE RIGHT CHEMICAL FOR THE JOB. HANDLE IT WITH CARE. FOLLOW THE INSTRUCTIONS ON THE CONTAINER LABEL AND INSTRUCTIONS FROM THE EQUIPMENT MANUFACTURER.

Step 3. Measure and mark calibration distance in a _typical_ portion of the field to be sprayed.

Step 4. With all attachments in operation (harrows, planters, etc.) and traveling at the desired operating speed, determine the number of seconds it takes to travel calibration distance. Be sure machinery is traveling at full operating speed the full length of the calibration distance. Mark or make note of engine RPM and gear. Machine must be operated at same speed for calibration.

Step 5. With sprayer sitting still and operating at same throttle setting or engine R.P.M. as used in Step 4, adjust pressure to the desired setting. Machine must be operated at same pressure used for calibration.

Step 6. For procedure (A) Step 2, broadcast application, collect spray from one nozzle or outlet for the number of seconds required to travel the calibration distance.

   For procedure (B) Step 2, band application, collect spray from all nozzles or out lets used on one band width for the number of seconds required to travel the calibration distance.

   For procedure (C) Step 2, row application, collect spray from all outlets (nozzles, etc.) used for one row for the number of seconds required to travel the calibration distance.

Table 2. Calibration distances with corresponding widths.

Row Spacing, Outlet Spacing or Band Width (Whichever Applies) (Inches)	Calibration Distance (feet)
48**	85.1
46	88.8
44	92.8
42	97.2
40	102.1
38	107.5
36	113.4
32	127.6
30	136.1
24	170.2
20	204.2
19	214.9
18	226.9
14	291.7
12	340.3
10	408.4
8	510.5

To determine distance for spacing or band width not listed, divide the spacing or band width expressed in feet into 340.3. *Example:* **for a 13" band the calibration distance would be 340 divided by 13/12 = 314.1.**

** To increase calibration accuracy for a wide nozzle spacing, multiply calibration distance by a factor (for example, 2); then, divide the fluid amount collected by the same factor for GPA. For narrow nozzle spacings with long calibration distances, divide calibration distance by a factor (for example, 4); then, multiply the fluid amount collected by the same factor for GPA.

Step 7. Measure the amount of liquid collected in fluid ounces. The number of ounces collected is the gallons per acre rate on the coverage bas is indicated in Table 1. For example, if you collect 18 ounces, the sprayer will apply 18 gallons per acre. Adjust applicator speed, pressure, nozzle size, etc. to obtain recommended rate. If speed is adjusted, start at Step 4 and recalibrate. If pressure or nozzles are changed, start at Step 5 and recalibrate.

Step 8. To determine amount of pesticide to put into a sprayer or applicator tank, divide the total number of gallons of mixture to be made (tank capacity for a full tank) by the gallons per acre rate from Step 7 and use recommended amount of pesticide for this number of acres.

Band Application

Use the recommended **broadcast** pesticide rates to make tank mixtures for band applications when calibrating with procedure (B) of this method. The number of gallons/acre determined in Step 7 is the gallons that will be applied to each acre of actually treated band.

To determine the gallons of spray mixture required to make a band application on a field, the number of acres that will be in the actually treated band must be determined. When all treated bands are the same width and all untreated bands are the same width, which is usually the case, the acres in the actually treated band can be calculated by placing the width of the treated band over the sum of the widths of the treated band and the untreated band, and multiplying this fraction times the number of acres in the field. Example – How many acres will actually be treated in a 30 acre field if a 12" band of chemical is applied over the drill of rows spaced 36" apart. The treated band width is 12". The untreated band width is (36" - 12") = 24". Acres actually treated will be 12" divided by (12" + 24") times 30 acres equals 10 acres. The amount of mixture required will be 10 times the number of gallons per acre from Step 7. The amount of chemical required will be 10 times the recommended broadcast rate for one acre.

Check rate recommendations carefully as to type of application, broadcast, band or row, and type of material specified, formulated product, active ingredient, etc.

Calculating Formulation Requirements For Active Ingredient Rates.

To determine amount of liquid pesticide required for a rate given in pounds of active ingredient per acre, divide recommended rate by pounds active ingredient per gallon stated on label. Example – Pesticide label states 4 lbs. active ingredient per gallon and recommends 1/2 pound active ingredient per acre. Amount of pesticide required: 1/2 lb./A divided by 4 lb./gal. = 1/8 gal./ A.

To determine amount of wettable powder required for a rate given in pounds active ingredient per acre, divide recommended rate by percent active ingredient stated on label. Example – Pesticide label states powder is 50% active ingredient. Two pounds of active ingredient is recommended per acre. Amount of pesticide powder required: 2 lbs. AI/A divided b y 0.5 AI/lb. = 4 lbs./A.

CALIBRATION METHOD FOR BOOMLESS BROADCAST SPRAYERS

Paul E. Sumner, Extension Engineer

All sprayers should be calibrated often to ensure that pesticide is being applied at the correct rate. Most broadcast applications are made with a boom arrangement where the nozzle tips are spaced evenly along the boom. However, in some situations this may be impossible or undesirable, so a cluster nozzle or a single nozzle with a wide spray pattern may be used.

Calibrate with clean water when applying toxic pesticides mixed with large volumes of water. When applying materials that are appreciably different from water in weight or flow characteristics, such as fertilizer solutions, etc., calibrate with the material to be applied. Exercise extreme care and use protective equipment when active ingredient is involved.

The following instructions outline a simple method to calibrate a boomless broadcast sprayer.

Step 1. Determine spray width. The spray width is the distance between successive passes through a field. This is usually given in the manufacturers' literature for a specific nozzle. If you are unable to find this in the catalogs, use 80 to 85 percent of the wetted spray width.

Step 2. Using the spray width in Step 1, determine the calibration distance from Table 1.

Step 3. Measure and mark calibration distance on <u>typical</u> terrain to be sprayed.

Step 4. With all attachments in operation and traveling at the desired operating speed, determine the number of seconds it takes to travel the calibration distance. Be sure machinery is traveling at full operating speed the full length of the calibration distance. Mark or make note of engine RPM and gear. <u>Machine must be operated at same speed for calibration.</u>

Step 5. With sprayer sitting still and operating at same throttle setting or <u>engine R.P.M.</u> as used in Step 4, adjust pressure to the desired setting. <u>Machine must be operated at same pressure used for calibration.</u>

Step 6. Collect spray from all nozzles or outlets for the n umber of seconds required to travel the calibration distance.

Table 1. Calibration distances with corresponding widths.

Swath Width (feet)	Calibration Distance (feet)
40	85.1
38	89.5
36	89.5
32	106.3
30	113.4
28	121.5
24	141.8
20	170.2
18	189
16	212.7
12	283.6
10	340.3
8	425

To determine distance for swath width not listed, divide the swath width expressed in feet into 340.3 and multiply by 10. Example – for 13 feet swath the calibration distance would be 340.3 divided by 13 multiplied by 10 = 261.8.

Step 7. Measure the amount of liquid collected in fluid ounces.

Step 8. <u>Divide the total number of fluid ounces by 10 to obtain gallons per acre applied.</u> For example, if you collect 180 ounces, the sprayer will apply 18 gallons per acre. Adjust applicator speed, pressure, nozzle size, etc. to obtain recommended rate. If speed is adjusted, start at Step 3 and recalibrate. If pressure or nozzles are changed, start at Step 5 and recalibrate.

Step 9. To determine amount of pesticide to put into a sprayer or applicator tank, divide the total number of gallons of mixture to be made (tank capacity for a full tank) by the gallons per acre rate from Step 8 and use recommended amount of pesticide for this number of acres.

CAUTION: AGRICULTURAL CHEMICALS CAN BE DANGEROUS. IMPROPER SELECTION OR USE CAN SERIOUSLY INJURE PERSONS, ANIMALS, PLANTS, SOIL, OR OTHER PROPERTY. BE SAFE: SELECT THE RIGHT CHEMICAL FOR THE JOB. HANDLE IT WITH CARE. FOLLOW THE INSTRUCTIONS ON THE CONTAINER LABEL AND INSTRUCTIONS FROM THE EQUIPMENT MANUFACTURER.

CALIBRATION METHOD FOR GRANULAR APPLICATIONS

Paul E. Sumner, Extension Engineer

Several factors influence the amount of granular material applied to a given area. Granular material is usually metered with an adjustable orifice. The amount of material that flows through the orifice per revolution relies on orifice opening size and may rely on rotor speed. A wide variation in product characteristics, such as size, density, and shape, requires that a calibration be made for every chemical applied. Also changes in climatic conditions, such as temperature and humidity, can result in a different flow rate.

CAUTION: Calibration is done using the chemical to be applied. Protective equipment, such as rubber gloves, etc. should be used to avoid contact with the chemicals to be applied.

Granular application is usually done in combination with another operation, such as planting or cultivating. The applicator may be ground driven or driven with a small electric motor. The following procedure will give the pounds (total weight) of material applied per acre broadcast or row basis as indicated. A weight scale incremented in ounces is required for this procedure.

Step 1. Determine type of application to be made and select appropriate procedure from Table 1. Example – Broadcast – Procedure A.

Table 1. Corresponding procedures for different spray applications.

Type of Application	Procedure	Coverage Basis (Volume of Application)
Broadcast	A	Broadcast (lbs /acre)
Band	B	Broadcast (lbs/acre of band)
Row (See note)	C (Use this procedure when rates are given for row treatment)	Row (lbs/acre of row)

Note: Determine and use average row spacing for modified row patterns. Use width of area covered per row as row spacing in skip row patterns for broadcast rates.

Step 2. Using procedure A, B, or C below as selected in Step 1, determine appropriate calibration distance from Table 2.

    (A) Broadcast Application: Outlets must be evenly spaced. Measure outlet spacing. Find this spacing in left column of Table 2 and read the corresponding calibration distance. Example – for a 19" spacing the distance would be 214.9 feet.

    (B) Band Application: Measure band width. Find this band width in the left column of Table 2 and read the corresponding calibration distance. Example – for a 12" band, the distance would be 340.3.

    (C) Row Application: Measure row spacing for evenly spaced rows. Find this row spacing in the left column of Table 2 and read the corresponding calibration distance from the column on the right. Example – for a 38" row spacing, the distance would be 107.5 feet.

CAUTION: AGRICULTURAL CHEMICALS CAN BE DANGEROUS. IMPROPER SELECTION OR USE CAN SERIOUSLY INJURE PERSONS, ANIMALS, PLANTS, SOIL, OR OTHER PROPERTY. BE SAFE: SELECT THE RIGHT CHEMICAL FOR THE JOB. HANDLE IT WITH CARE. FOLLOW THE INSTRUCTIONS ON THE CONTAINER LABEL AND INSTRUCTIONS FROM THE EQUIPMENT MANUFACTURER.

Step 3. Measure and mark calibration distance in a <u>typical</u> portion of the field to be applied.

Step 4. With all attachments in operation (harrows, planters, etc.) and traveling at the desired operating speed, determine the number of seconds it takes to travel calibration distance. Be sure machinery is traveling at full operating speed the full length of the calibration distance. Mark or make note of engine RPM and gear. <u>Machine must be operated at same speed for calibration</u>.

Step 5. Multiply the number seconds required to travel calibration distance by 8. This is the number of seconds to collect.

Step 6. With applicator sitting still and operating at same speed as used in Step 4, adjust gate openings to desired setting. Check uniformity of outlets across the swath or rows. Collect from each outlet for a known time period. Each outlet should be within 5 percent of the average outlet output.

Table 2. Calibration distances with corresponding widths.

Row Spacing, Outlet Spacing or Band Width (Whichever Applies) (Inches)	Calibration Distance (feet)
48*	85.1
46	88.8
44	92.8
42	97.2
40	102.1
38	107.5
36	113.4
32	127.6
30	136.1
24	170.2
20	204.2
19	214.9
18	226.9
14	291.7
12	340.3
10	408.4
8	510.5

To determine distance for spacing or band width not listed, divide the spacing or band width expressed in feet into 340.3. Example: for a 13" band the calibration distance would be 340 divided by 13/12 = 314.1.

* To increase calibration accuracy for a wide outlet spacing, multiply calibration distance by a factor (for example, 2); then, divide Step 8 material collected by the same factor for pounds per acre. For narrow spacings with long calibration distances, divide calibration distance by a factor (for example, 4); then, multiply Step 8 by the same factor for pounds per acre. Keep in mind that application accuracy will decrease when factoring narrow outlet or band spacings.

Step 7.** For procedure (A), Step 2, broadcast application, collect from <u>one</u> outlet for the number of seconds indicated in Step 5. For procedure (B), Step 2, band application, collect from <u>all</u> outlets used on one band width for the number of seconds indicated in Step 5. For procedure (C), Step 2, row application, collect from all <u>outlets</u> used for one row for the number of seconds indicated in Step 5.

**For ground driven equipment, multiply the calibration distance by 8 and collect from each outlet while traveling the calibration distance.

Step 8. Weigh the amount of material collected in ounces. <u>The number of ounces collected is the pounds per acre rate</u> on the coverage basis indicated in Table 1. For example, if you collect 18 ounces using procedure (A) or (B), the applicator will apply 18 pounds per acre on a broadcast coverage basis. Adjust applicator speed, gate opening, etc. to obtain recommended rate.

Step 9. Applicators should be checked for proper calibration every 4-8 hours of use. Simply repeat steps 7 and 8. If there is a difference of more than 5 percent of original calibration, check the system.

Band Application

To determine the pounds of material required to make a band application on a field, the number of acres that will be in the actual treated band must be determined. When all treated bands are the same width and all untreated bands are the same width, which is usually the case, the acres in the actual treated band can be calculated by placing the width of the treated band over the sum of the widths of the treated band and the untreated band, and multiplying this fraction times the number of acres in the field. Example – How many acres will actually be treated in a 30 acre field if a 12" band of chemical is applied over the drill of rows spaced 36" a part. The treated band width is 12 inches. The untreated band width is (36" - 12") = 24". Acres actually treated will be 12 inches divided by (12" + 24 ") times 30 acres equals 10 acres. The amount of material required for the 30 acre field will be 10 times the number of pounds per acre from Step 8.

Check rate recommendations carefully as to type of application, broadcast, band or row, and type of material specified, formulated product, active ingredient, etc.

CALIBRATION OF BACKPACK SPRAYERS 1000 FT^2 METHOD

Paul E. Sumner, Extension Engineer

Backpack sprayers are often used to treat ornamental or small areas of turf. Herbicide recommendations are based amount per acre and amount per 1000 ft^2 Regardless of the type of sprayer used to apply herbicides, the speed, pressure and nozzle height must be kept constant for accurate application. The backpack sprayer may require some modification so that it is better suited for application. A pressure gauge mounted on the tank side of the shutoff valve will allow continuous monitoring of the tank pressure, which must remain uniform. Optimum pressure control can be achieved by inserting a pressure regulator between the pressure gauge and nozzle. To prevent dripping after the shutoff valve is closed, use a quick, positive pressure shutoff valve or a strainer with a check valve. Nozzle clogging, a problem associated with the use of wettable powders (as well as DF and WDG formulations) can be reduced by inserting a 50 mesh in-line strainer and keeping the solution constantly agitated. The following is a procedure of 1000 ft^2.

Step 1. Measure the length and width of the test area to be sprayed. Then calculate the area to be covered.

Test Area is: length _____ ft   X   width _____ ft = _____ ft^2

Step 2. Fill sprayer with water and spray the test area. Record the amount of water to refill the sprayer.

Volume (ounces) per test area _____

Step 3. Find the label rate of material to be applied per 1000 ft^2.

Rate _____ per 1000 ft^2

Step 4.
$$\frac{1000\ ft^2\ x\ ounces\ per\ test\ area}{Test\ Area\ (ft^2)} = Volume\ (ounces)\ per\ 1000\ ft^2$$

Step 5. Calculate the area covered per tank as follows:

$$\frac{Tank\ volume\ (ounces)\ x\ 1000\ ft^2}{Volume\ (ounces)\ per\ 1000\ ft^2} = Area\ covered\ per\ tank\ (ft^2)$$

Step 6. Calculate amount of material to add to tank.

$$\frac{Area\ per\ tank\ (ft^2)\ x\ rate\ per\ 1000\ ft^2}{1000} = Amount\ to\ add\ (rate\ units)$$

Solutions derived from the above may need to be converted to a smaller unit in order to accurately measure the pesticide accurately. The following conversion will help simplify this problem.

Conversions:

Volume

gallon x 128	= fluid ounces (fl oz)
pints x 16	= fluid ounces (fl oz)
fl oz x 29.57	= milliliters (ml)
gallon x 4	= quarts (qts)
quarts x 2	= pints (pts)
fl oz x 2	= Tablespoons (Tbs)
tsp x 3	= Tablespoons (Tbs)
tsp x 5	= milliliters (ml)

Weight

pounds x 16	= weight ounces (wt. oz)
wt. ounces x 28.35	= grams (g)
grams x 1000	= milligrams (mg)

CALIBRATING TURFGRASS SPRAYERS (GALLONS PER 1000 SQ FT)

Paul E. Sumner, Extension Engineer

Low-pressure boom sprayers are used frequently for applying chemicals on large areas such as golf courses and recreational areas. Application rates for turf are normally given in gallons per 1000 sq. ft. Calibrating a boom sprayer is not as difficult as it sounds. Calibrate your sprayer often to compensate for nozzle wear, pump wear and speed changes.

Calibrate with clean water. Check uniformity of nozzle output across the boom. Collect from each for a known time period. Each nozzle should be within 10 percent of the average output. Replace with new nozzles if necessary. When applying materials that are appreciably different from water in weight or flow characteristics, such as fertilizer solutions, etc., calibrate with the material to be applied. Exercise extreme care and use protective equipment when active ingredient is involved..

Step 1. Determine the Effective Swath Width (W) per Nozzle
For boom spraying, the effective spray width of each nozzle (W) is equal to the distance in inches between two nozzles.

Step 2: Determine Travel Speed (MPH)
To determine the travel speed, measure a known distance. Use fence posts or flags to identify this distance. A distance over 200 feet and a tank at least half full are recommended. Travel the distance determined at your normal spraying speed and record the elapsed time in seconds. Repeat this step and take the average of the two measurements. Use the following equation to determine the travel speed in miles per hour:

$$Travel\ speed\ (MPH) = \frac{Distance\ (feet)\ x\ 0.68}{Time\ (seconds)}$$

(0.68 is a constant to convert feet/second to miles/hour)

Step 3. Determine Nozzle Flow Rate (GPM)
With the sprayer parked, operate the sprayer at the same pressure level and catch the output from each nozzle in a measuring jar for one minute (or collect output for half a minute and then double the ounces collected) to determine the nozzle flow rate in ounces per minute (OPM) Then, convert the final average output in OPM to gallons per minute (GPM) using the following equation:

GPM = OPM/128 (1 Gallon = 128 ounces)

Step 4. Determine the Actual Application Rate in Gallons per Gal/1000 sq ft
Use the following equation to determine the gallons per acre application rate:

$$Gallons\ per\ 1000\ ft^2 = \frac{136\ x\ gpm\ (per\ nozzle)}{MPH\ x\ W}$$

GPM: average nozzle flow rate in gallons per minute
MPH: travel speed in miles per hour
W: distance between two nozzles in inches
136 a constant to convert units to gallons/1000^2

Step 5. Calculate the area covered per tank as follows:

$$\frac{Tank\ Volume\ (gallons)\ x\ 1000}{Application\ Rate\ (gallons\ per\ 1000\ ft^2)} = Area\ covered\ per\ tank\ (ft^2)$$

Step 6. Calculate amount of material to add to tank.

$$\frac{Area\ covered\ per\ tank\ (ft^2)\ x\ Material\ rate\ per\ 1000\ ft^2}{1000} = Amount\ to\ add\ (rate\ units)$$

HAND SPRAYER CALIBRATION FOR ORNAMENTAL AND TURF

Paul E. Sumner, Extension Engineer

Hand sprayers are often used to treat ornamental or small areas of turf. The directions on many ornament al pesticide product labels say to "spray until foliage is wet" or perhaps "spray until runoff." Unfortunately, these directions are subject to each applicator's interpretation of what "wet" or "runoff" is.

Recommendations are based on amount per 100 gallons. This is the dilution ratio for the chemical applied. Use the following to convert 100 gallon rate to bed area rate.

1. Measure the length and width of the area to be sprayed. Then calculated the area to be covered.

    Bed Area is: length _____ X width _____ = _____ ft²

2. Fill sprayer with water and spray the area. Record the amount of water to refill the sprayer.

    Gallons per bed area _____

3. Obtain the rate of material to be applied per 100 gallons.

    Rate _____

4. $$\frac{Rate \times Gallons\ per\ bed\ area}{100} = Amount\ per\ bed\ area$$

5. Calculate the total amount of material to be used for the application (total bed area) as follows

$$\frac{Amount\ of\ bed\ area \times Area\ to\ be\ sprayed}{Bed\ area\ (ft^2)} = Amount\ of\ material$$

6. Total solution to prepare is:

$$\frac{Gallons\ per\ bed\ area \times Area\ to\ be\ sprayed\ (ft^2)}{Bed\ area\ (ft^2)} = Total\ Solution$$

Solutions derived from the above may need to be converted to a smaller unit in order to accurately measure the pesticide. Refer to the conversion section to help simplify this problem.

Conversions:

Volume

pints x 16	= fluid ounces (fl oz)
fl oz x 29.57	= milliliters (ml)
gallon x 4	= quarts (qts)
quarts x 2	= pints (pts)
fl oz x 2	= Tablespoons (Tbs)
tsp x 3	= Tablespoons (Tbs)
tsp x 5	= milliliters (ml)

Weight

pounds x 16	= weight ounces (wt oz)
wt. ounces x 28.35	= grams (g)
grams x 1000	= milligrams (mg)

ATTENTION!
PESTICIDE PRECAUTIONS

1. Observe all directions, restrictions and precautions on pesticide labels. It is dangerous, wasteful and illegal to do otherwise.

2. Store all pesticides in original containers with labels intact and behind locked doors. "KEEP PESTICIDES OUT OF THE REACH OF CHILDREN."

3. Use pesticides correct label dosages and intervals to avoid illegal residues or injury to plants and animals.

4. Apply pesticides carefully to avoid drift or contamination of non-target areas.

5. Surplus pesticides and containers should be disposed of in accordance with label instructions so that contamination of water and other hazards will not result.

6. Follow directions on the pesticide label regarding restrictions as required by State and Federal Laws and Regulations.

7. Avoid any action that may threaten an Endangered Species or its habitat. Your county extension agent can inform you of Endangered Species in your area, help you identify them, and through the Fish and Wildlife Service Field Office identify actions that may threaten Endangered Species or their habit.

INDEX

Specific insects, diseases, and weeds are found by the plants or crop with which they are associated. For example. aphids on peanuts are found by looking under "peanut insect control" and turning to the page indicated. Pest of animals are found by looking under the animal with which they are associated. Household, structural, public health, recreational pests and vertebrate pests are found by looking up the specific pest.

A

abbreviations 10
alligators 136
ants 86
apple
    home orchard disease control 39, 40
    home orchard insect control 38–40
    organic strategies 81–85
aquatic environment
    calculating pesticide concentrations 132
    fishery chemicals 125
    herbicide use restrictions 130
    weed control 126–128
    weed response to herbicides 129
asparagus
    disease control 21
    home insect control 12

B

bats 133
bean
    home insect control 12, 13
bean (lima)
    disease control 21, 22
bean (snap) 21, 22
beaver 133
bedbugs 116
beet
    disease control 22
    home insect control 13
bird mites 120
birds
    pets 99, 100
biting flies 122
blackberry
    home orchard disease control 42, 43
    home orchard insect control 42
blueberry
    home orchard disease control 41
    home orchard insect control 41
    organic strategies 81–85
bramble
    home orchard disease control 42
    home orchard insect control 42
broccoli
    disease control 22
    home insect control 13

Brussels sprout
    disease control 22
    home insect control 13, 14
building perimeter treatments 122

C

cabbage
    disease control 22, 23
    home insect control 13, 14
calibration
    airblast sprayer 159
    backpack sprayer 165
    boomless broadcast sprayers 162
    for calibrating liquid applications 158–161
    for granular applications 163, 164
    for pesticides in aquatic situations 132
    hand sprayer 167
    household pesticide dilution table 114
    hydraulic boom and band sprayers & other liquid applicators 160, 161
    pesticide rate and dose 156–158
    turfgrass sprayer 166
cantaloupe
    disease control 23
    home insect control 14
carrot
    disease control 24
cauliflower
    home insect control 13
chiggers 122
chipmunk 133
clover mites 120
cockroaches 109
collard
    disease control 24, 30
    home insect control 15
corn (sweet)
    disease control 24
coyote 134
cucumber
    disease control 24, 25
    home insect control 14, 15

D

deer 134
drain flies 122

E

earwigs 86

eggplant

    disease control 25

    home insect control 16

eye gnats 117

F

fire ants

    homeowner control 115, 116

    in homeowner turf 86

fish

    fish chemicals 125

    parasite control 125

    pesticide toxicity 130, 131

    piscicides 125

    pond weed control 130, 131

flea control products

    pets 99, 101

fleas 122

flower

    disease control 65–72

    homeowner fungicide guide 77–80

flower (homeowner indoor)

    insect control 57

flower (homeowner outdoor)

    insect control 53–55

    weed control 56

frogs 136

G

garlic

    disease control 25

gnats 122

grape

    home orchard disease control (bunch) 44

    home orchard disease control (muscadine) 45

    home orchard insect control (bunch) 44

    home orchard insect control (muscadine) 45

    organic strategies 81–83

H

herbaceous ornamentals

    organic strategies 81–85

home orchard

    insect control 38–40

homeowner fungicide guide

    flower 77–80

    ornamentals 77–80

    woody ornamentals 77–80

honey bee

    disease and pest control 102–104

    protecting from pesticides 139

household and structural pests

    insect control 105–113

    pesticide dilution table 114

I

important telephone numbers 5

K

kale

    disease control 26

L

lettuce

    disease control 26

    home insect control 16

lice

    bird 100

lizard 136

M

mite

    bird 120

    honey bee 103, 104

    rodent 120

    straw itch 120

mole 134

mosquito 121

mustard

    disease control 30

    home insect control 17

N

nectarine

    home orchard disease control 46, 47

    home orchard insect control 46, 47

    organic strategies 81–85

O

okra

    disease control 26

    home insect control 17

onion

    home insect control 18

onion (dry)

    disease control 26

onion (green)

    disease control 26

organic strategies 81–85

    fruits 84, 85

    ornamentals 84, 85

    vegetables 84, 85

ornamentals
    disease control 65–75
    homeowner fungicide guide 77–80
    weed response to herbicides 62–64

P

pea
    home insect control 12, 13
peach
    home orchard disease control 46, 47
    home orchard insect control 46, 47
    organic strategies 81–85
pea (English)
    disease control 27
pear
    home orchard disease control 48
    home orchard insect control 48
    organic strategies 81–85
pea (southern or blackeye)
    disease control 27
pepper
    disease control 27
    home insect control 18
pesticide products
    household use 141–153
pesticides
    airblast sprayer 159
    calibrating granular applications 163, 165
    calibrating hand sprayer 167
    calibrating liquid applications 160–162
    fruit insecticide effectiveness 50–52
    important phone numbers 4, 5
    names, classifications, and toxicity 155
    rate calculations 156–158
    safe use 137, 138
    spills 3, 4
    symptoms of poisoning 2
    turfgrass sprayer 166
pets
    external parasite control 99, 100
    flea control products 101
piscicides (see also fish) 125
plum
    home orchard disease control 46, 47
    home orchard insect control 46, 47
potato (Irish)
    disease control 26
    home insect control 18, 19
potato (sweet)
    home insect control 19
public health insect control 115–124

pumpkin
    disease control 27, 28
    home insect control 14, 15

R

radish
    disease control 28
    home insect control 19
raspberry
    home orchard disease control 42, 43
    home orchard insect control 42, 43
repellents
    biting insects 122
    deer and rabbit 135

S

salamander 136
scabies 120
snake 136
specimen
    collecting, preparing, and shipping 11
    fish 11
    insect 11
    nematode 11
    plant disease 11
    vertebrate 11
    virus diagnosis 11
    weed 11
spinach
    disease control 28
    insect control 16, 17
squash
    disease control 29
    home insect control 14, 15
squirrel 133
strawberry
    home orchard disease control 49
    home orchard insect control 49
    organic strategies 81–85

T

tick 122
    area treatment 124
    outside 123
    pet 99
toad 136
tomato
    disease control 29
    home insect control 19, 20
turf
    disease control 87–89
    home insect control 86

    home weed control 91–93

    weed response to herbicides 97, 98

turnip

    disease control 29

    home insect control 20

turtle 136

V

vegetable

    disease control 21–30

    foliar boron sprays 36

    foliar calcium sprays 33–35

    home insect control 12–20

    home weed control 31, 32

    organic strategies 81–85

vertebrate pest control 133, 134, 135

    mammal 133–135

vole 134

W

watermelon

    disease control 30

    home insect control 14, 15

weed response to herbicides

    aquatic weeds 129

    ornamentals 62–64

    turf 97, 98

woody ornamentals

    disease control 65–76

    home insect control 58, 59

    homeowner fungicide guide 77–80

    home weed control 60, 61

    organic strategies 81–85

    weed response to herbicides 62–64

THE UNIVERSITY OF GEORGIA
COLLEGE OF AGRICULTURAL & ENVIRONMENTAL SCIENCES

2010 Georgia Pest Management Handbook
Homeowner Edition

Copies are available at $15.00 each. Please make check or money order payable to the UNIVERSITY OF GEORGIA and send to:

> Office of Communications
> 117 – Hoke Smith Annex
> The University of Georgia
> Athens, GA 30602

Name: _____

Address: _____
(Need a street address—UPS will not deliver to Post Office Box)

City: _____ State: _____ Zip: _____

Credit card orders can be made by calling 706-542-2657 or fax 706-542-0817.